WEIRDWORLD

THE MULTIVERSE WAS DESTROYED!

•

THE HEROES OF EARTH-616 AND EARTH-1610 WERE POWERLESS TO SAVE IT!

•

NOW, ALL THAT REMAINS...IS **BATTLEWORLD:**

A MASSIVE, PATCHWORK PLANET COMPOSED OF THE FRAGMENTS OF WORLDS THAT NO LONGER EXIST, MAINTAINED BY THE IRON WILL OF ITS GOD AND MASTER, VICTOR VON DOOM!

EACH REGION IS A DOMAIN UNTO ITSELF!

• WARZONES! •

WRITER
JASON AARON

ARTIST
MIKE DEL MUNDO

COLORS
MIKE DEL MUNDO & MARCO D'ALFONSO

LETTERER:
VC'S CORY PETIT

COVER ART
MIKE DEL MUNDO

ASSISTANT EDITORS
JON MOISAN & ALANNA SMITH

EDITORS
TOM BREVOORT WITH WIL MOSS

COLLECTION EDITOR: JENNIFER GRÜNWALD
ASSISTANT EDITOR: SARAH BRUNSTAD
ASSOCIATE MANAGING EDITOR: ALEX STARBUCK
EDITOR, SPECIAL PROJECTS: MARK D. BEAZLEY
SENIOR EDITOR, SPECIAL PROJECTS: JEFF YOUNGQUIST
SVP PRINT, SALES & MARKETING: DAVID GABRIEL
BOOK DESIGNER: RODOLFO MURAGUCHI

EDITOR IN CHIEF: AXEL ALONSO
CHIEF CREATIVE OFFICER: JOE QUESADA
PUBLISHER: DAN BUCKLEY
EXECUTIVE PRODUCER: ALAN FINE

WEIRDWORLD VOL. 0: WARZONES! Contains material originally published in magazine form as WEIRDWORLD #1-5. First printing 2015. ISBN# 978-0-7851-9891-8. Published by MARVEL WORLDWIDE, INC., a subsidiary of MARVEL ENTERTAINMENT, LLC. OFFICE OF PUBLICATION: 135 West 50th Street, New York, NY 10020. Copyright © 2015 MARVEL No similarity between any of the names, characters, persons, and/or institutions in this magazine with those of any living or dead person or institution is intended, and any such similarity which may exist is purely coincidental. **Printed in Canada.** ALAN FINE, President, Marvel Entertainment; DAN BUCKLEY, President, TV, Publishing and Brand Management; JOE QUESADA, Chief Creative Officer; TOM BREVOORT, SVP of Publishing; DAVID BOGART, SVP of Operations & Procurement, Publishing; C.B. CEBULSKI, VP of International Development & Brand Management; DAVID GABRIEL, SVP Print, Sales & Marketing; JIM O'KEEFE, VP of Operations & Logistics; DAN CARR, Executive Director of Publishing Technology; SUSAN CRESPI, Editorial Operations Manager; ALEX MORALES, Publishing Operations Manager; STAN LEE, Chairman Emeritus. For information regarding advertising in Marvel Comics or on Marvel.com, please contact Jonathan Rheingold, VP of Custom Solutions & Ad Sales, at jrheingold@marvel.com. For Marvel subscription inquiries, please call 800-217-9158. **Manufactured between 10/23/2015 and 11/30/2015 by SOLISCO PRINTERS, SCOTT, QC, CANADA.**

10 9 8 7 6 5 4 3 2 1

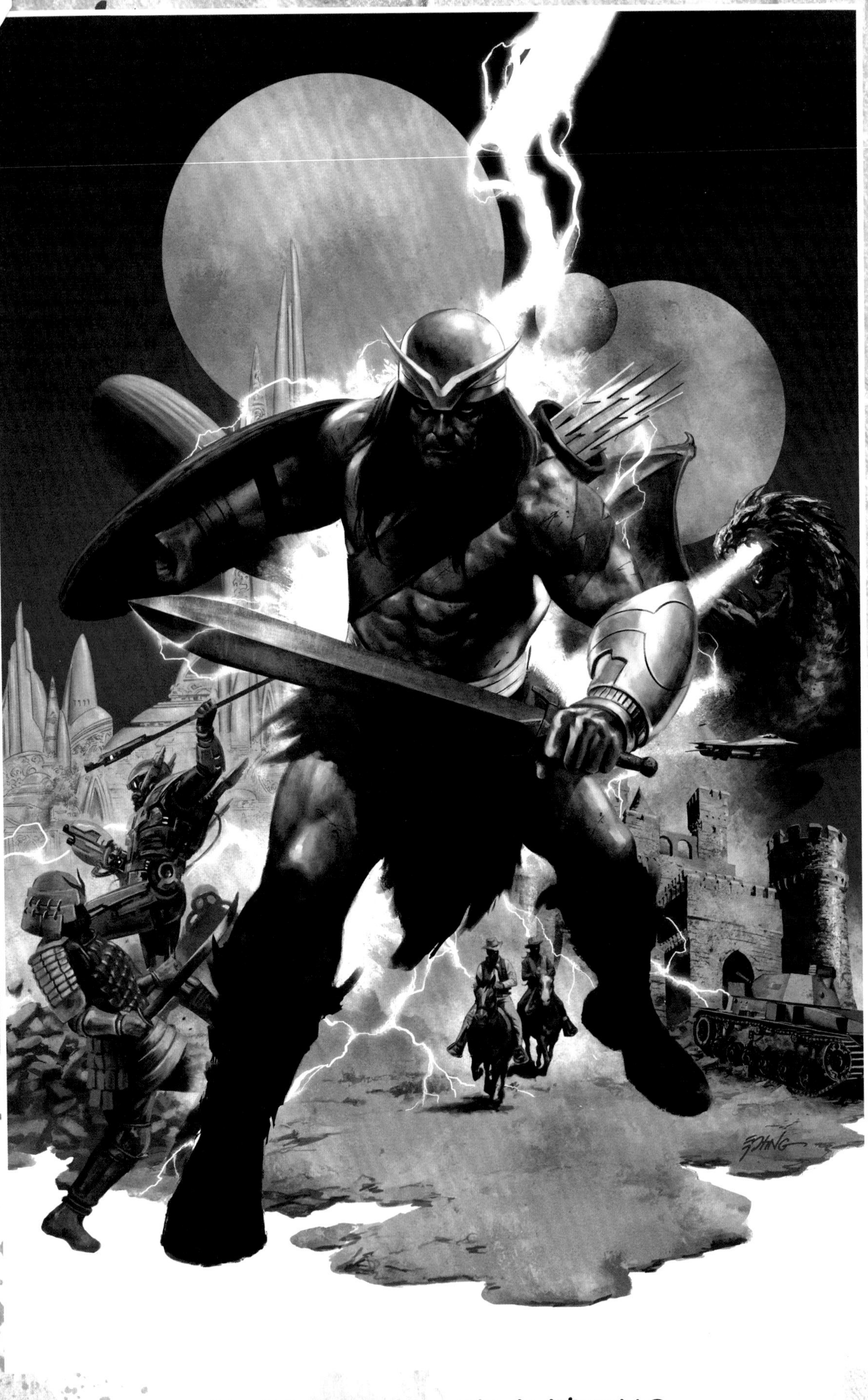

#1 VARIANT BY STEVE EPTING

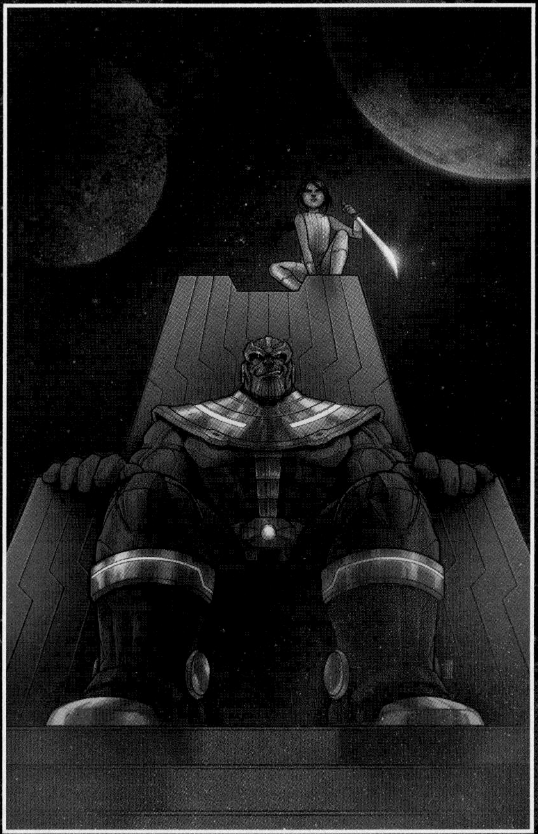

THANOS #2 VARIANT BY
JEN BARTEL

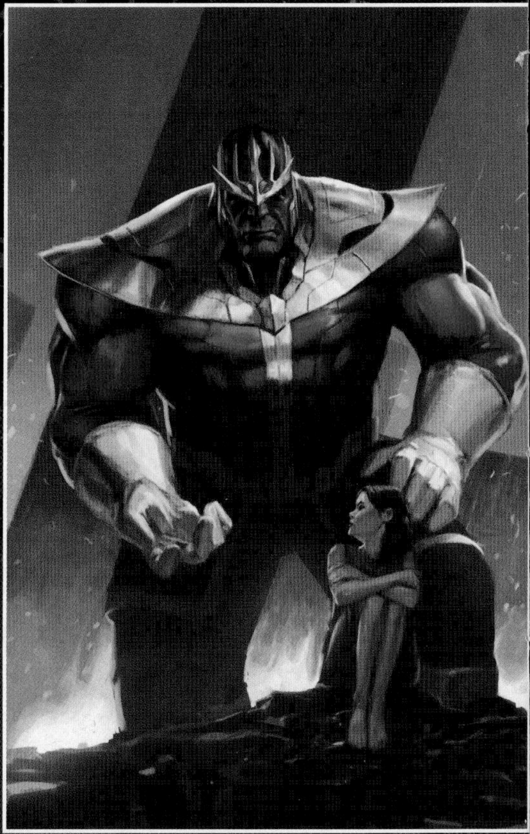

THANOS #3 VARIANT BY
PYEONG-JUN PARK

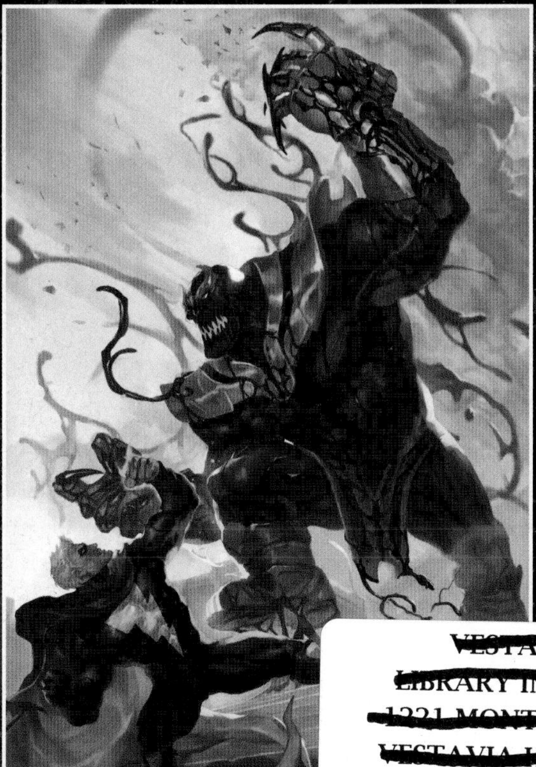

THANOS #4 CARNAGE-IZED VARIANT BY
SUNGHAN YUNE

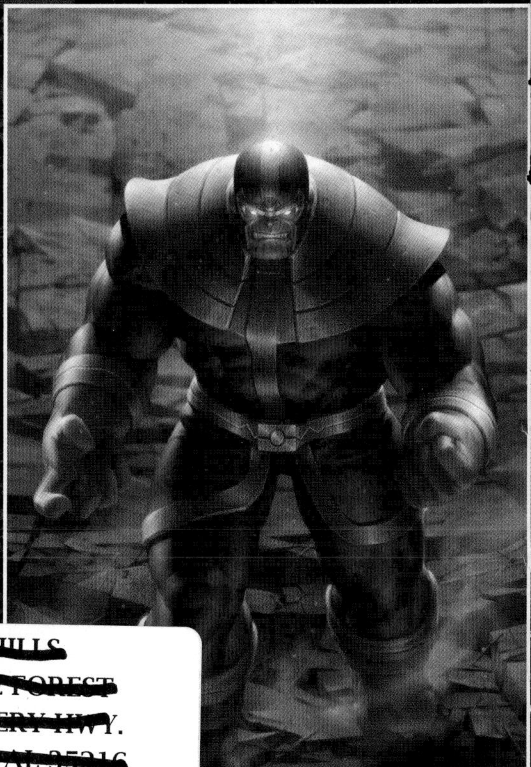

THANOS #5 BRING ON THE BAD GUYS
VARIANT BY **JUNGGEUN YOON**

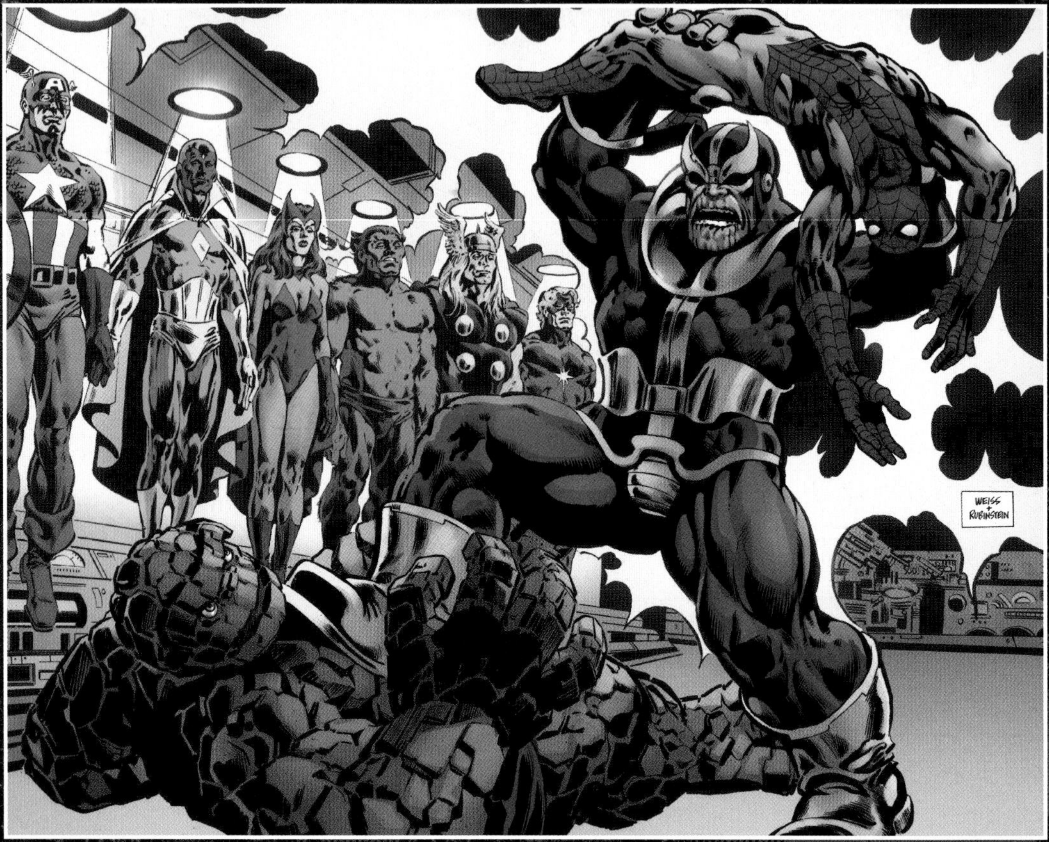
WEISS
+
RUBINSTEIN

THANOS #1 HIDDEN GEM VARIANT BY
ALAN WEISS, JOE RUBENSTEIN & JASON KEITH

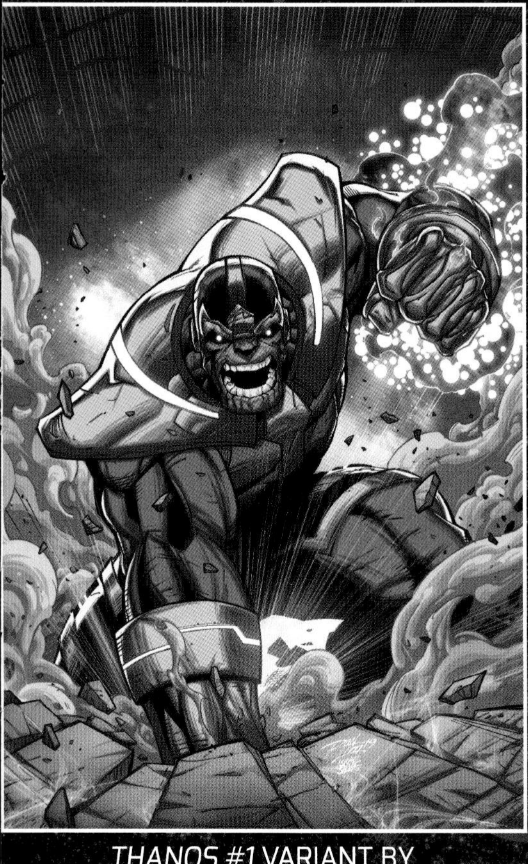

THANOS #1 VARIANT BY
RON LIM & **ISRAEL SILVA**

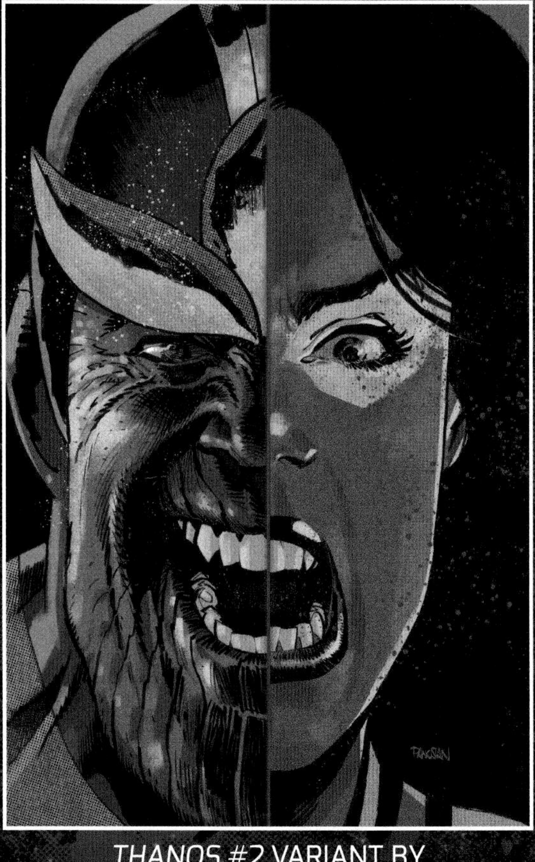
PANOSIAN

THANOS #2 VARIANT BY
DAN PANOSIAN

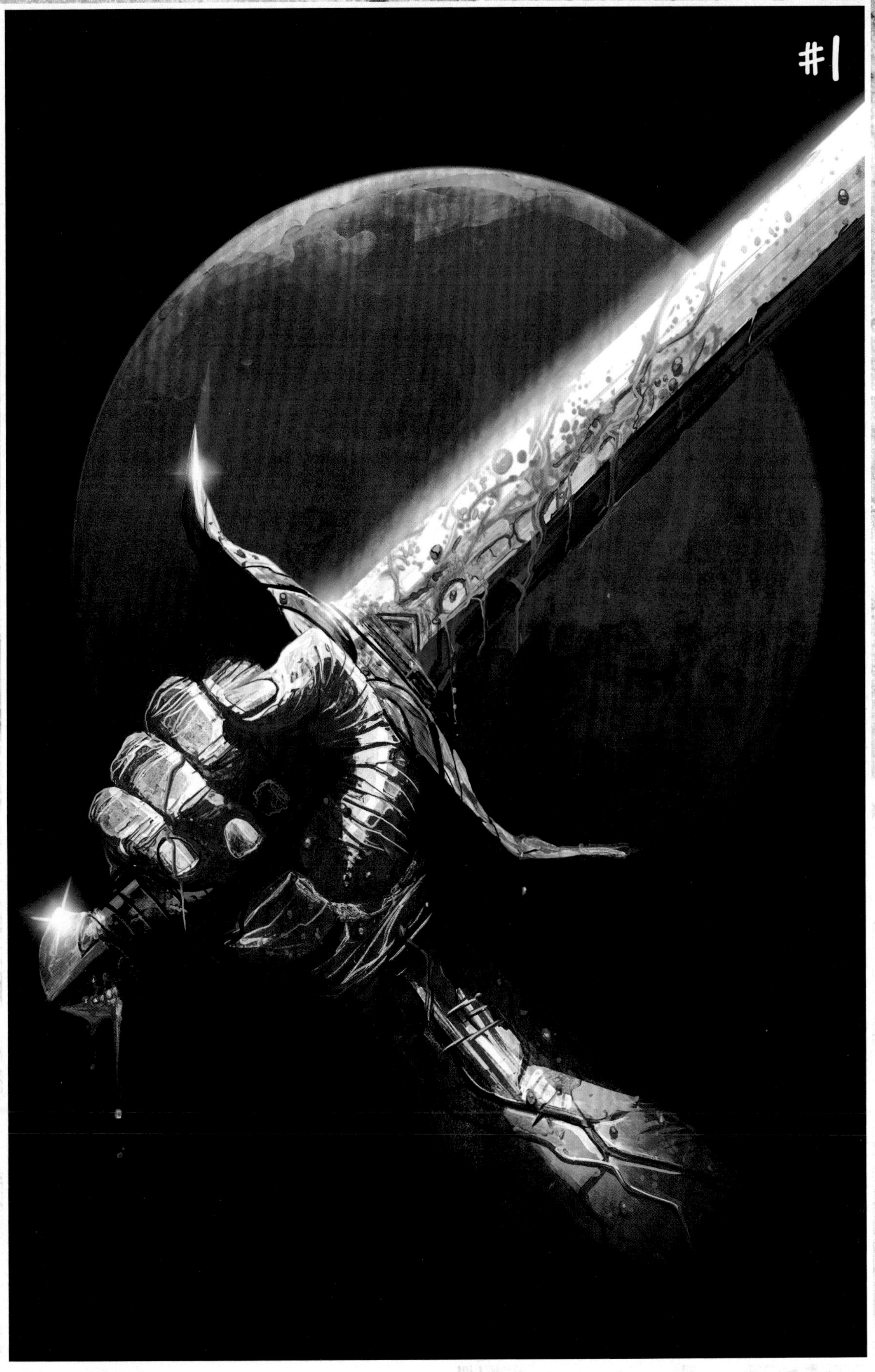
#1

• WHERE LOST THINGS GO •

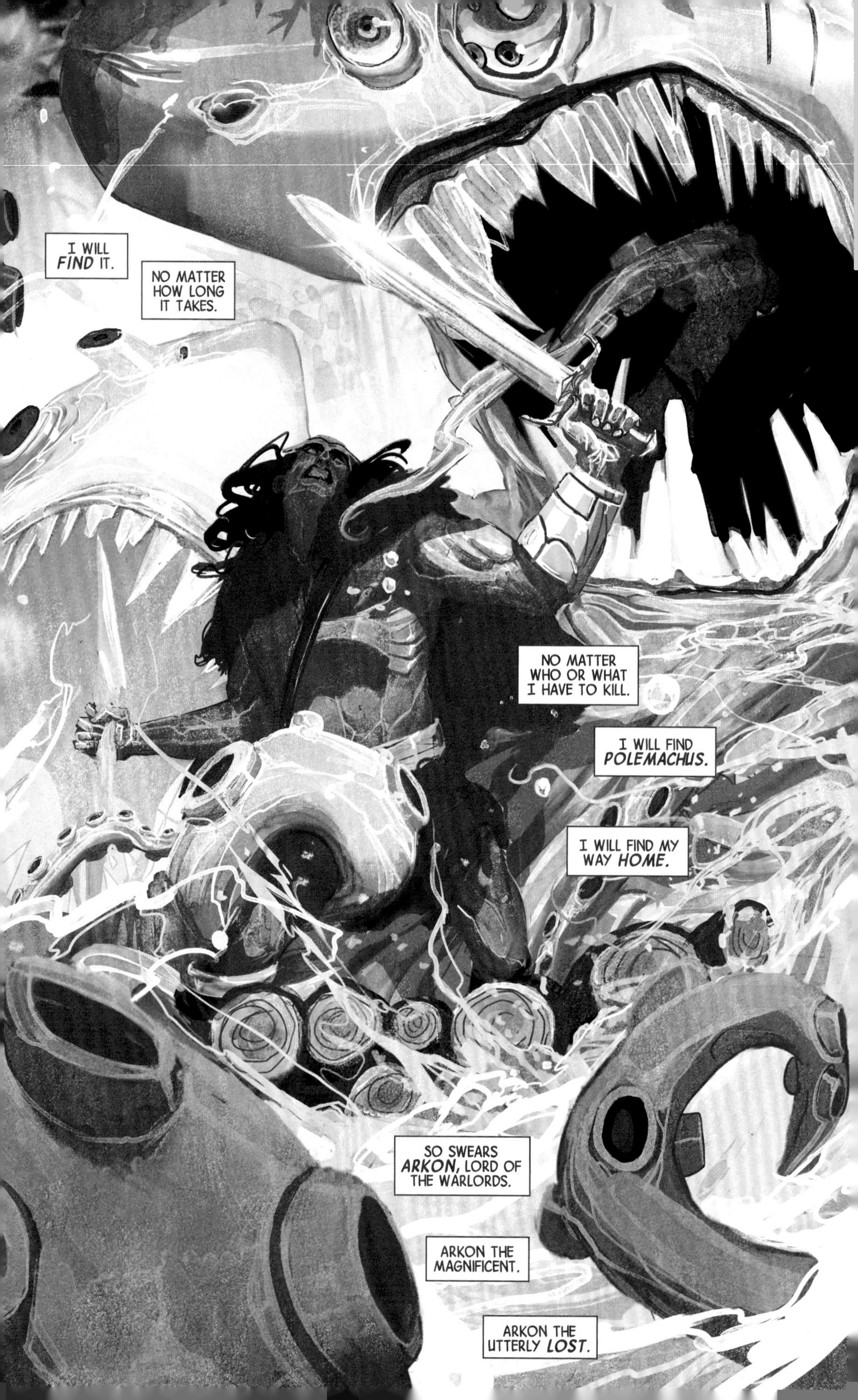
I WILL FIND IT.
NO MATTER HOW LONG IT TAKES.
NO MATTER WHO OR WHAT I HAVE TO KILL.
I WILL FIND POLEMACHUS.
I WILL FIND MY WAY HOME.
SO SWEARS ARKON, LORD OF THE WARLORDS.
ARKON THE MAGNIFICENT.
ARKON THE UTTERLY LOST.

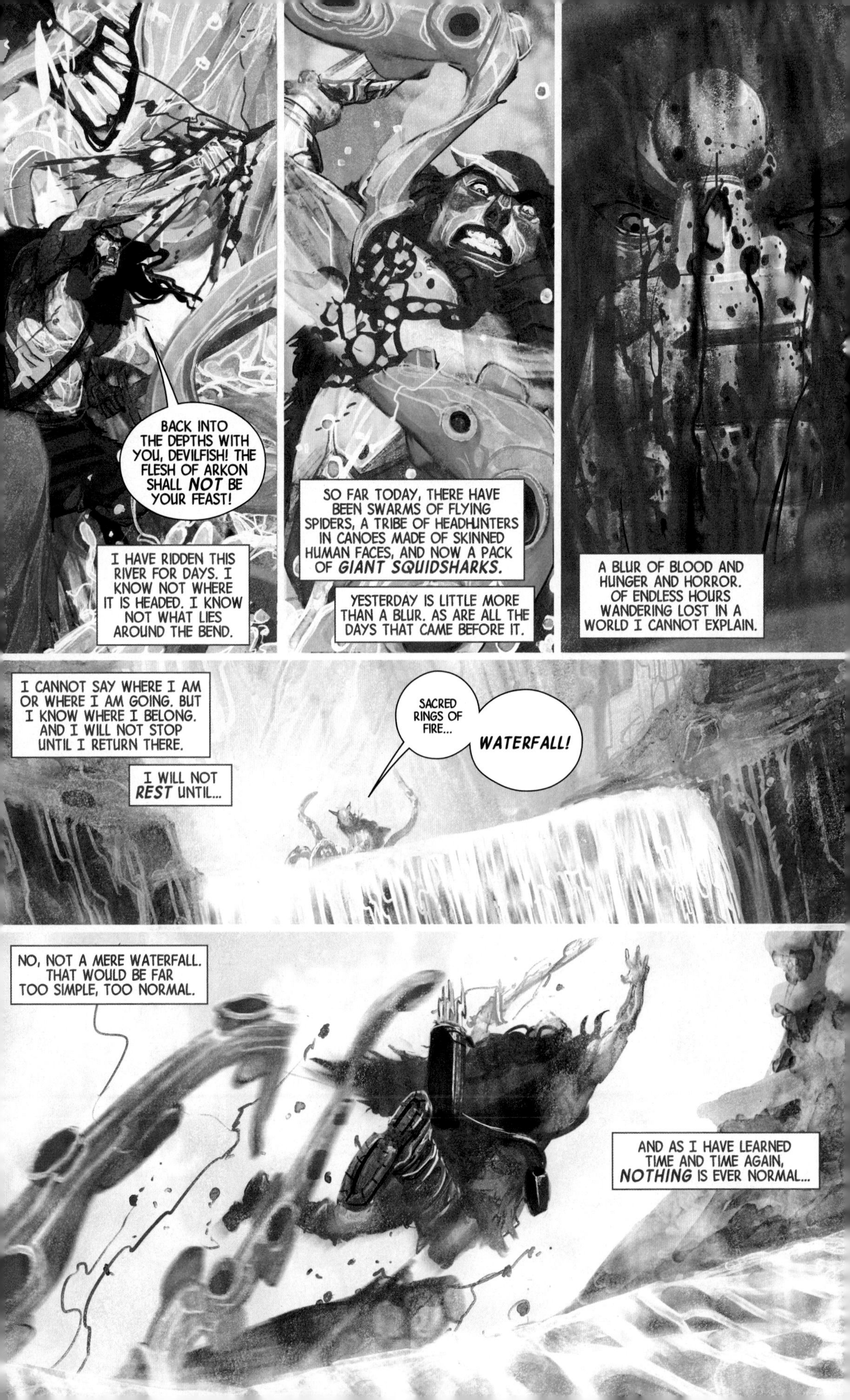
BACK INTO THE DEPTHS WITH YOU, DEVILFISH! THE FLESH OF ARKON SHALL NOT BE YOUR FEAST!
I HAVE RIDDEN THIS RIVER FOR DAYS. I KNOW NOT WHERE IT IS HEADED. I KNOW NOT WHAT LIES AROUND THE BEND.
SO FAR TODAY, THERE HAVE BEEN SWARMS OF FLYING SPIDERS, A TRIBE OF HEADHUNTERS IN CANOES MADE OF SKINNED HUMAN FACES, AND NOW A PACK OF GIANT SQUIDSHARKS.
YESTERDAY IS LITTLE MORE THAN A BLUR. AS ARE ALL THE DAYS THAT CAME BEFORE IT.
A BLUR OF BLOOD AND HUNGER AND HORROR. OF ENDLESS HOURS WANDERING LOST IN A WORLD I CANNOT EXPLAIN.
I CANNOT SAY WHERE I AM OR WHERE I AM GOING. BUT I KNOW WHERE I BELONG. AND I WILL NOT STOP UNTIL I RETURN THERE.
I WILL NOT REST UNTIL...
SACRED RINGS OF FIRE...
WATERFALL!
NO, NOT A MERE WATERFALL. THAT WOULD BE FAR TOO SIMPLE, TOO NORMAL.
AND AS I HAVE LEARNED TIME AND TIME AGAIN, NOTHING IS EVER NORMAL...

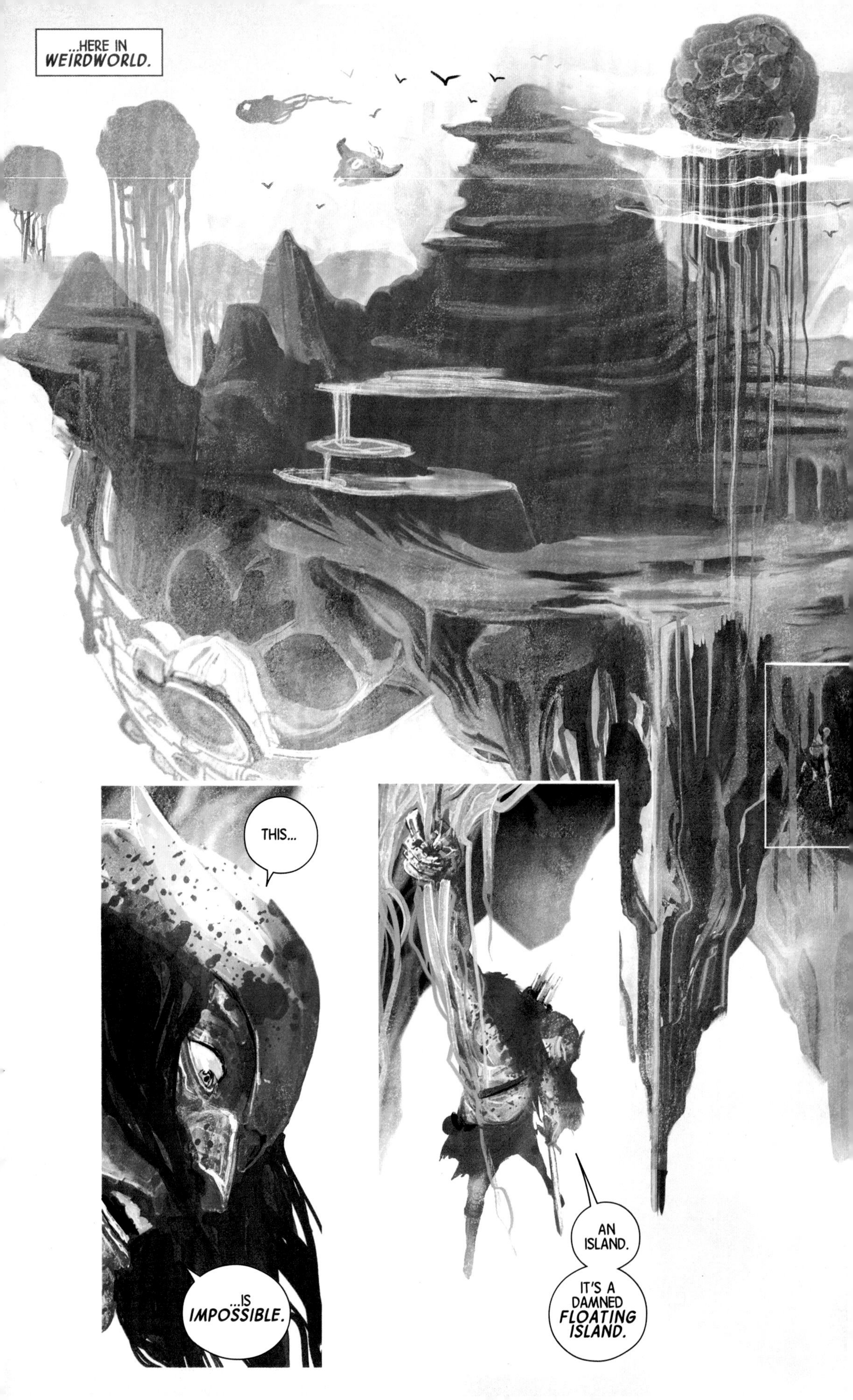
...HERE IN WEIRDWORLD.
THIS...
...IS IMPOSSIBLE.
AN ISLAND.
IT'S A DAMNED FLOATING ISLAND.

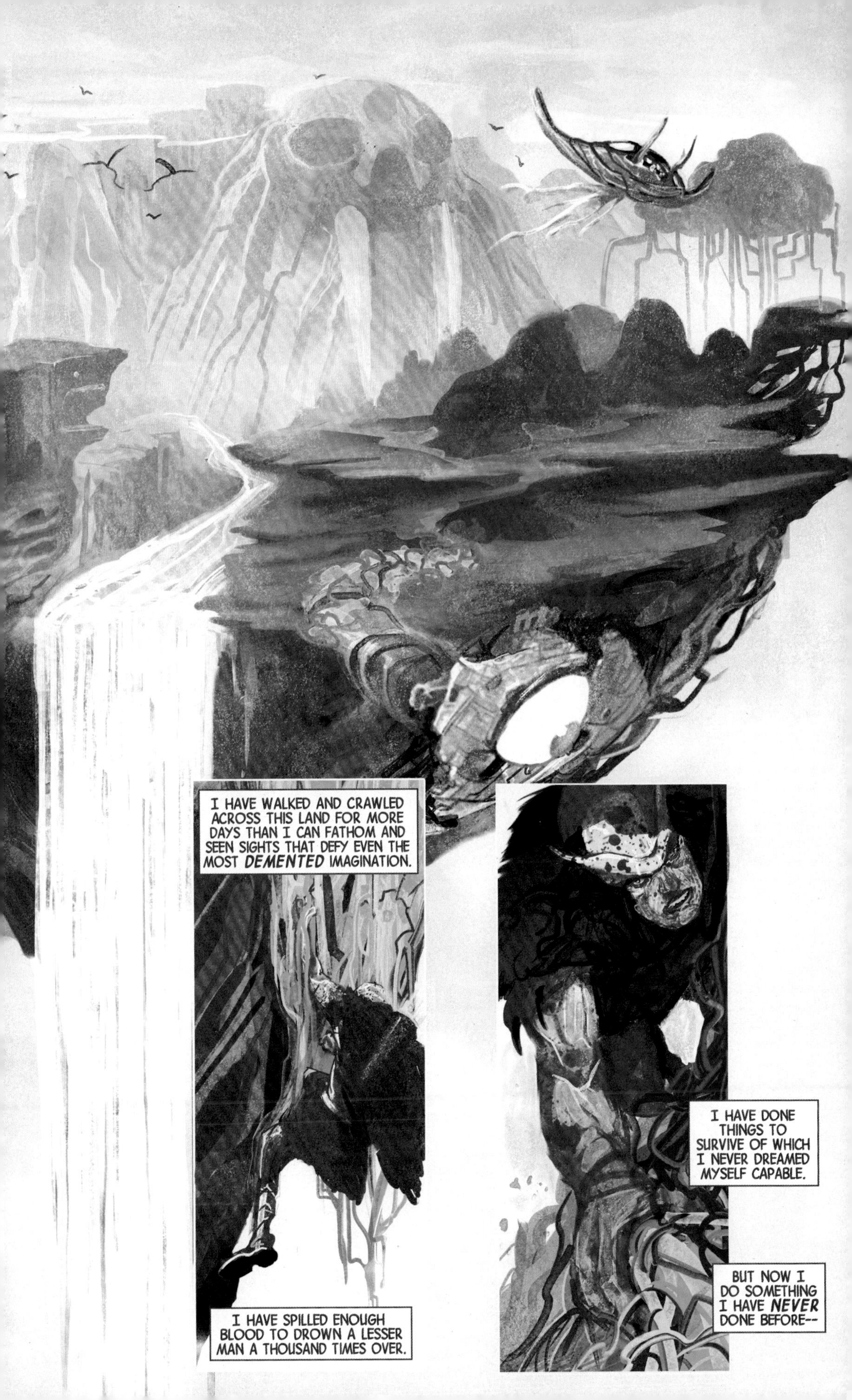
I HAVE WALKED AND CRAWLED ACROSS THIS LAND FOR MORE DAYS THAN I CAN FATHOM AND SEEN SIGHTS THAT DEFY EVEN THE MOST *DEMENTED* IMAGINATION.
I HAVE SPILLED ENOUGH BLOOD TO DROWN A LESSER MAN A THOUSAND TIMES OVER.
I HAVE DONE THINGS TO SURVIVE OF WHICH I NEVER DREAMED MYSELF CAPABLE.
BUT NOW I DO SOMETHING I HAVE *NEVER* DONE BEFORE--

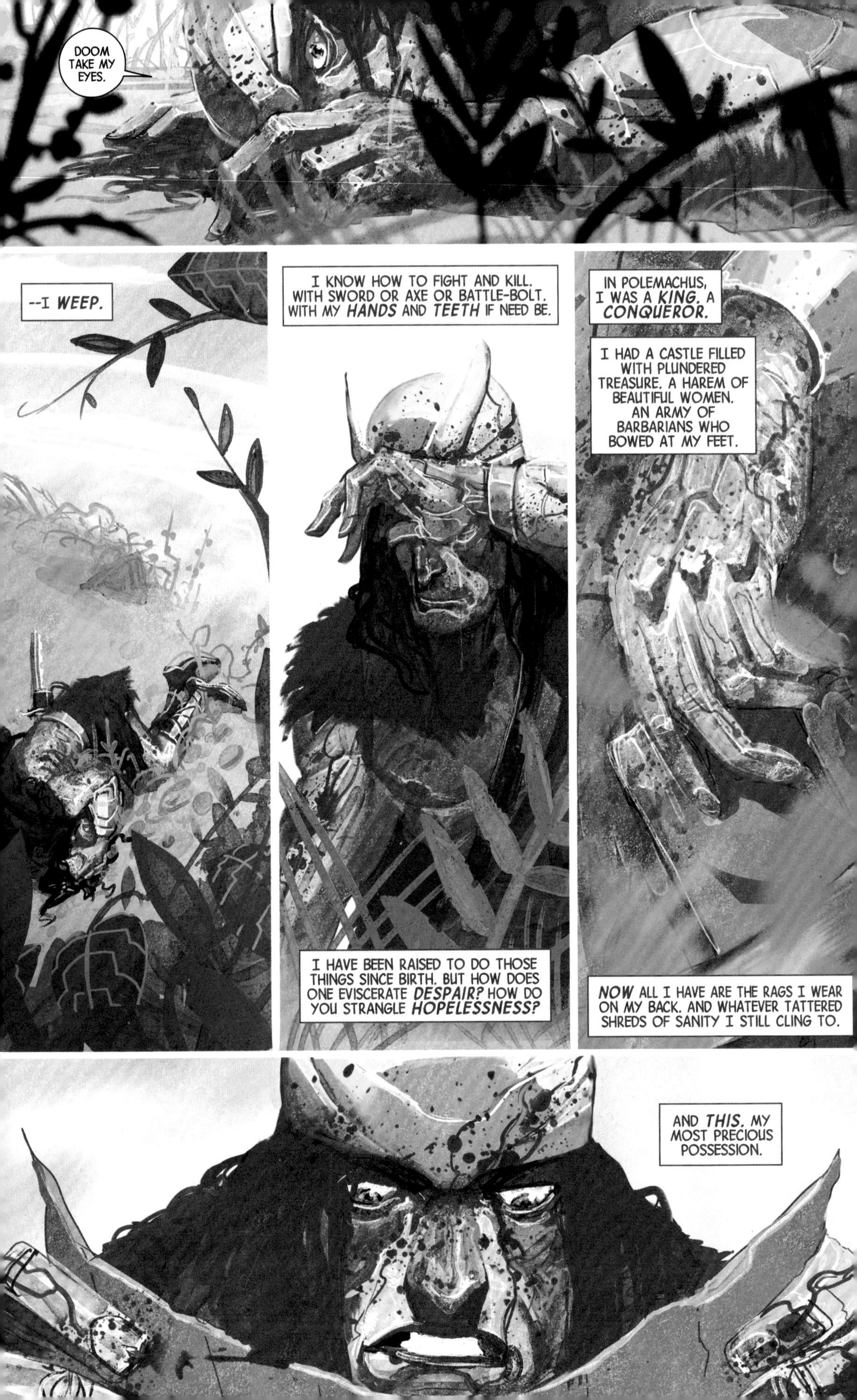
DOOM TAKE MY EYES.
--I WEEP.
I KNOW HOW TO FIGHT AND KILL. WITH SWORD OR AXE OR BATTLE-BOLT. WITH MY HANDS AND TEETH IF NEED BE.
I HAVE BEEN RAISED TO DO THOSE THINGS SINCE BIRTH. BUT HOW DOES ONE EVISCERATE DESPAIR? HOW DO YOU STRANGLE HOPELESSNESS?
IN POLEMACHUS, I WAS A KING. A CONQUEROR.
I HAD A CASTLE FILLED WITH PLUNDERED TREASURE. A HAREM OF BEAUTIFUL WOMEN. AN ARMY OF BARBARIANS WHO BOWED AT MY FEET.
NOW ALL I HAVE ARE THE RAGS I WEAR ON MY BACK. AND WHATEVER TATTERED SHREDS OF SANITY I STILL CLING TO.
AND THIS. MY MOST PRECIOUS POSSESSION.

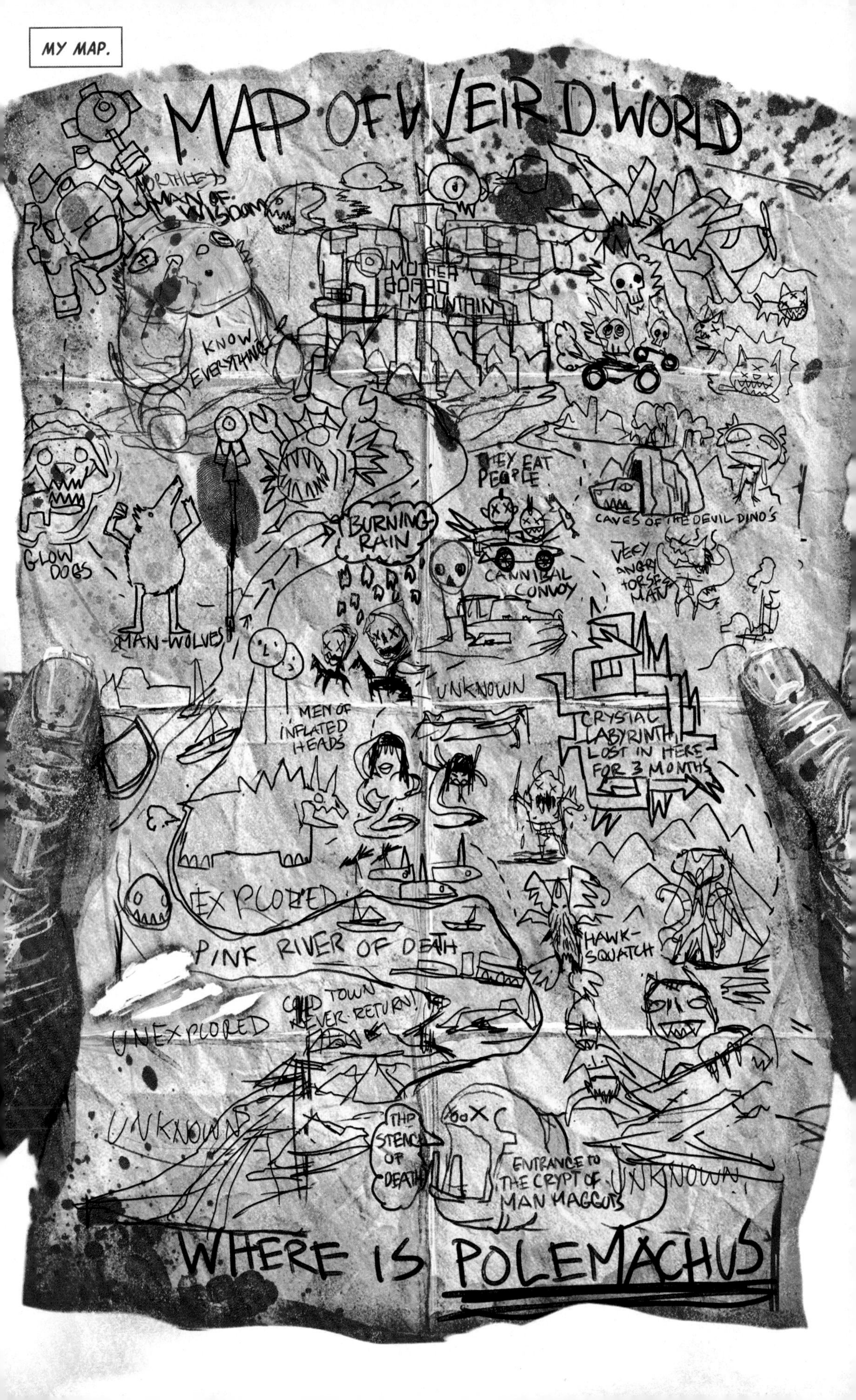
MY MAP.
MAP OF WEIRD WORLD
WORTHLESS MAN OF WISDOM
MOTHER BOARD MOUNTAIN
I KNOW EVERYTHING
THEY EAT PEOPLE
GLOW DOGS
BURNING RAIN
CAVES OF THE DEVIL DINO'S
CANNIBAL CONVOY
VERY ANGRY TORSE MAN
MAN-WOLVES
UNKNOWN
MEN OF INFLATED HEADS
CRYSTAL LABYRINTH LOST IN HERE FOR 3 MONTHS
EXPLORED
HAWK-SQUATCH
PINK RIVER OF DEATH
COLD TOWN NEVER RETURN!
UNEXPLORED
UNKNOWN
THE STENCH OF DEATH
ENTRANCE TO THE CRYPT OF MAN MAGGOTS
UNKNOWN
WHERE IS POLEMACHUS

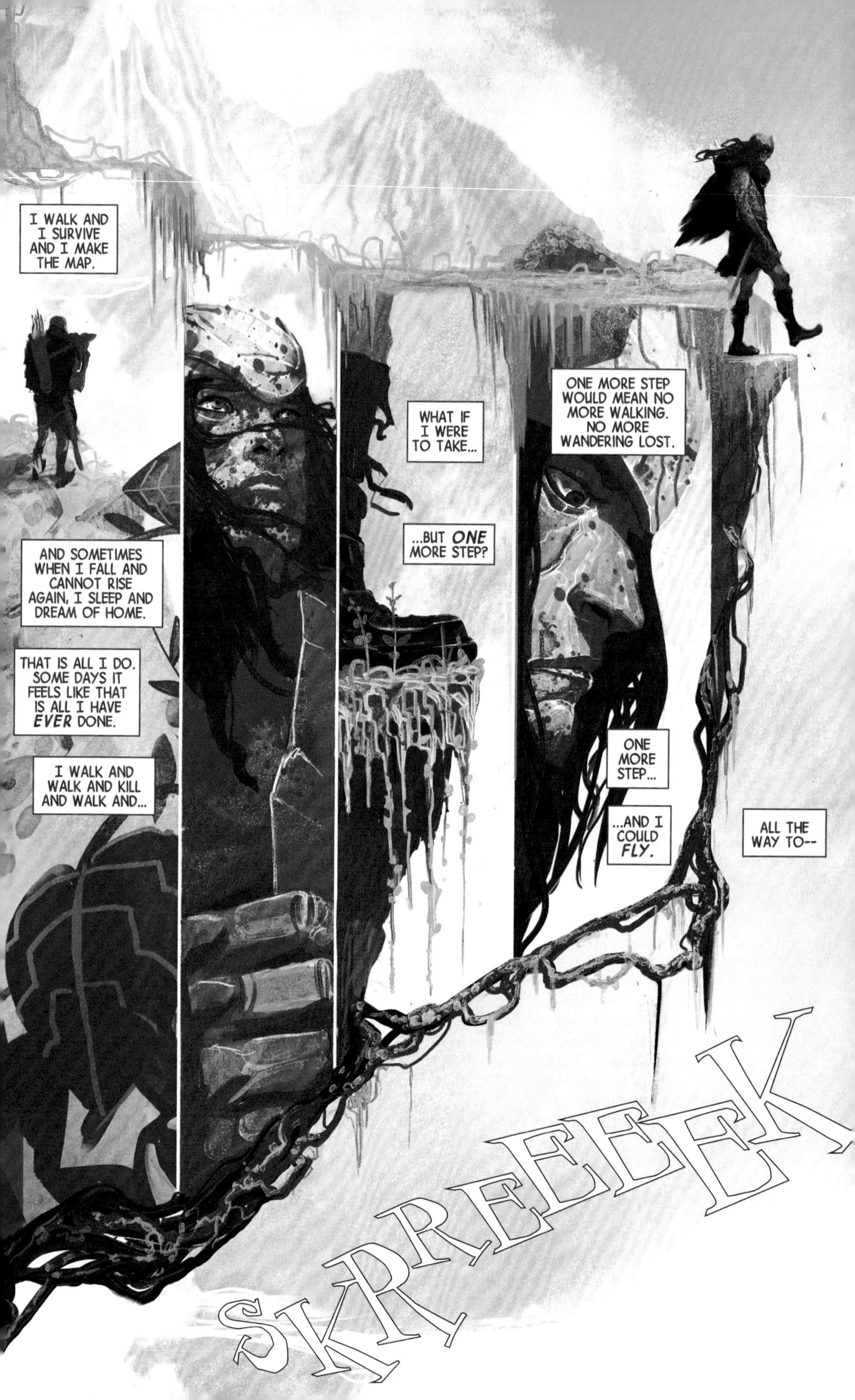
I WALK AND I SURVIVE AND I MAKE THE MAP.
AND SOMETIMES WHEN I FALL AND CANNOT RISE AGAIN, I SLEEP AND DREAM OF HOME.
THAT IS ALL I DO. SOME DAYS IT FEELS LIKE THAT IS ALL I HAVE *EVER* DONE.
I WALK AND WALK AND KILL AND WALK AND...
WHAT IF I WERE TO TAKE...
...BUT *ONE* MORE STEP?
ONE MORE STEP WOULD MEAN NO MORE WALKING. NO MORE WANDERING LOST.
ONE MORE STEP...
...AND I COULD *FLY*.
ALL THE WAY TO--
SKREEEEK

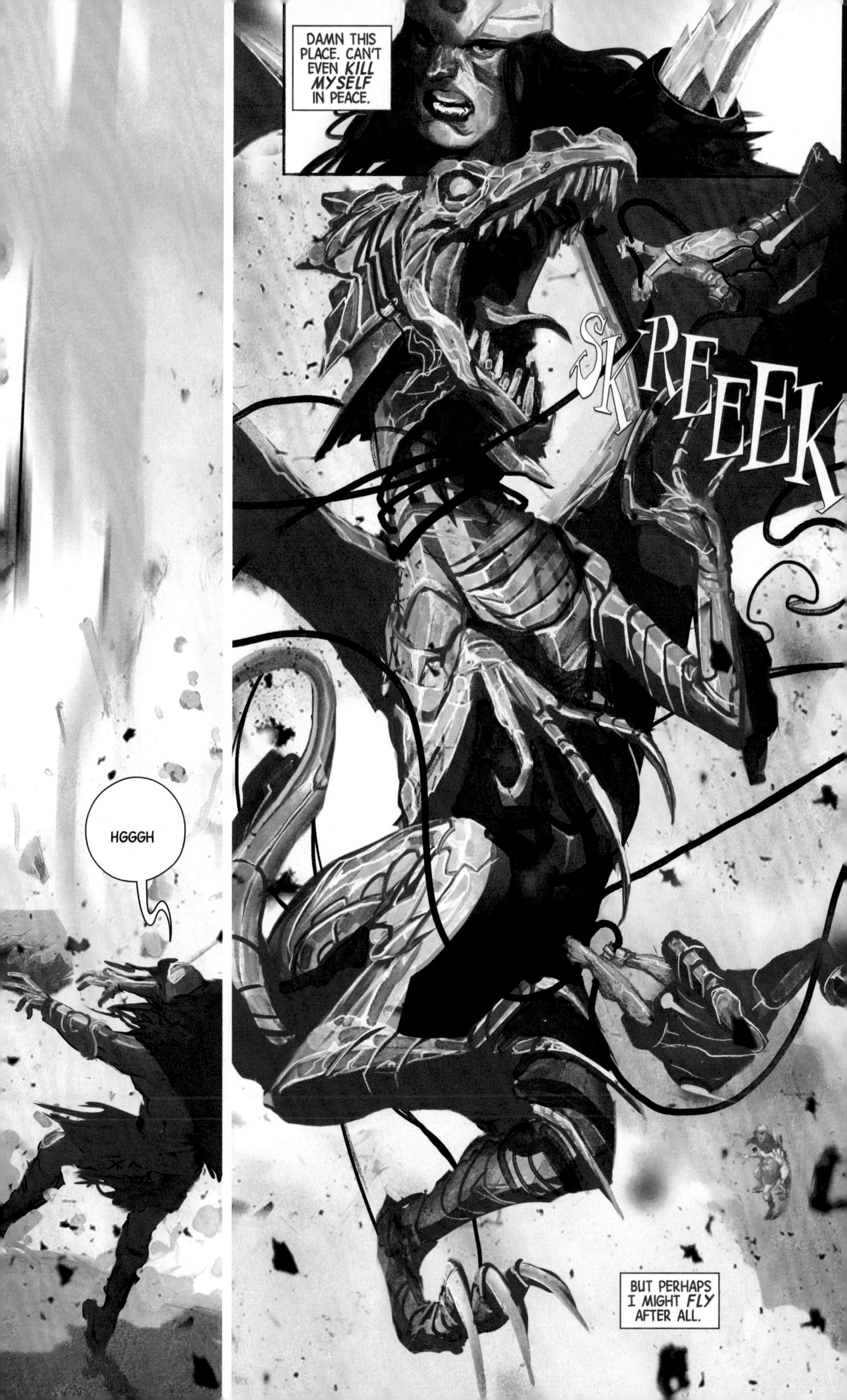
DAMN THIS PLACE. CAN'T EVEN KILL MYSELF IN PEACE.
SKREEEK
HGGGH
BUT PERHAPS I MIGHT FLY AFTER ALL.

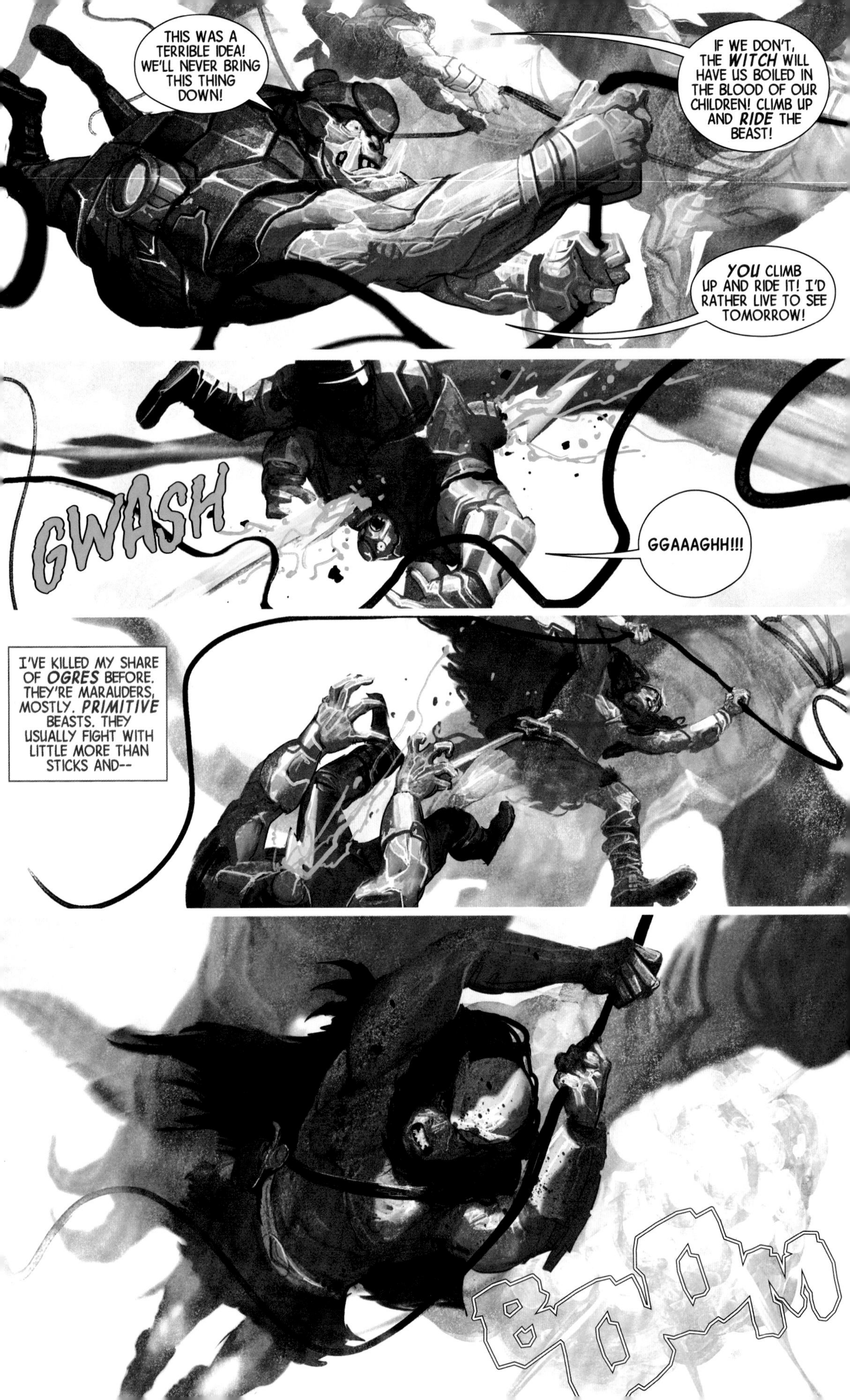
THIS WAS A TERRIBLE IDEA! WE'LL NEVER BRING THIS THING DOWN!
IF WE DON'T, THE WITCH WILL HAVE US BOILED IN THE BLOOD OF OUR CHILDREN! CLIMB UP AND RIDE THE BEAST!
YOU CLIMB UP AND RIDE IT! I'D RATHER LIVE TO SEE TOMORROW!
GWASH
GGAAAGHH!!!
I'VE KILLED MY SHARE OF OGRES BEFORE. THEY'RE MARAUDERS, MOSTLY. PRIMITIVE BEASTS. THEY USUALLY FIGHT WITH LITTLE MORE THAN STICKS AND--
BOOOM

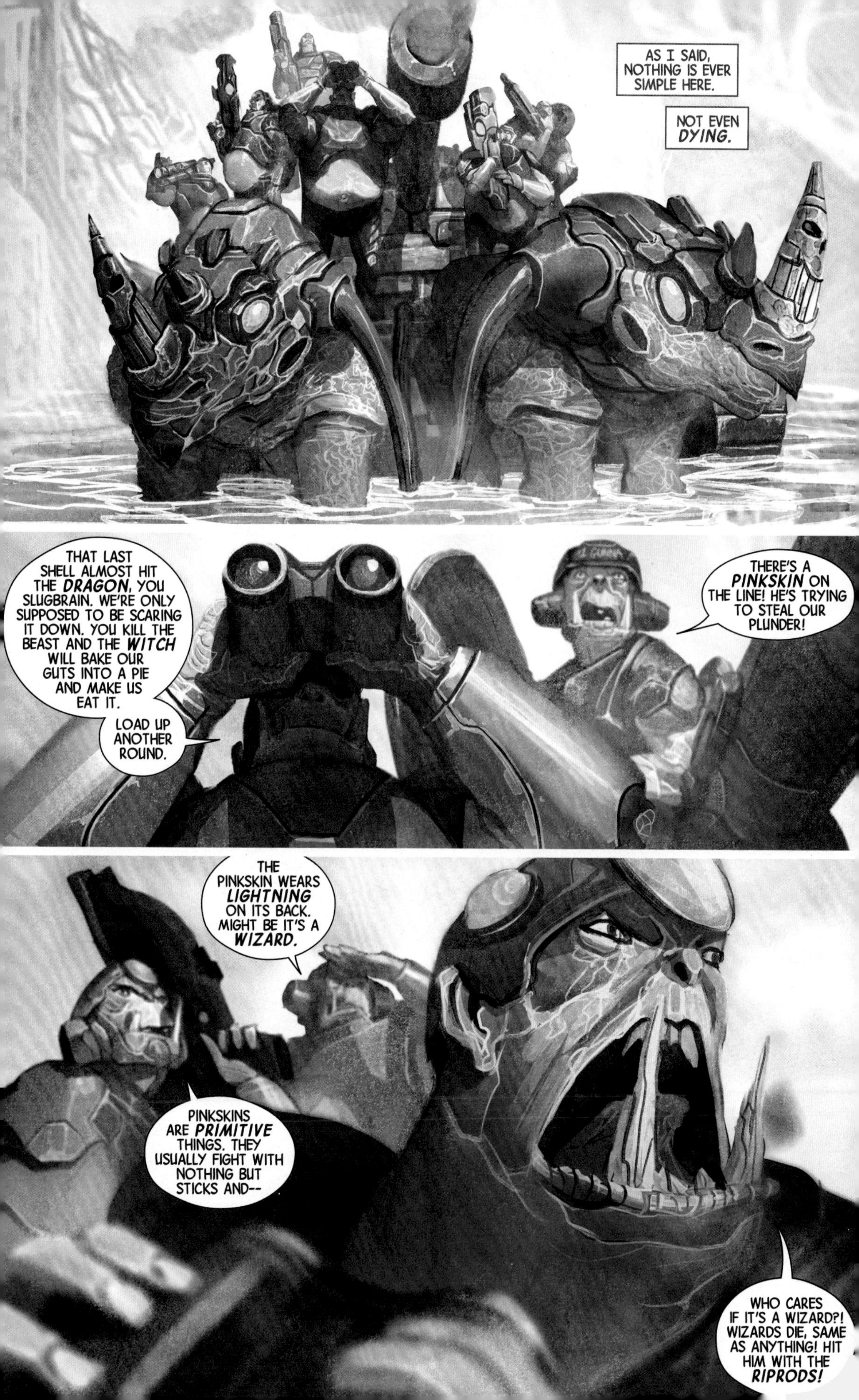
AS I SAID, NOTHING IS EVER SIMPLE HERE.
NOT EVEN *DYING.*
THAT LAST SHELL ALMOST HIT THE *DRAGON*, YOU SLUGBRAIN. WE'RE ONLY SUPPOSED TO BE SCARING IT DOWN. YOU KILL THE BEAST AND THE *WITCH* WILL BAKE OUR GUTS INTO A PIE AND MAKE US EAT IT.
LOAD UP ANOTHER ROUND.
THERE'S A *PINKSKIN* ON THE LINE! HE'S TRYING TO STEAL OUR PLUNDER!
THE PINKSKIN WEARS *LIGHTNING* ON ITS BACK. MIGHT BE IT'S A *WIZARD.*
PINKSKINS ARE *PRIMITIVE* THINGS. THEY USUALLY FIGHT WITH NOTHING BUT STICKS AND--
WHO CARES IF IT'S A WIZARD?! WIZARDS DIE, SAME AS ANYTHING! HIT HIM WITH THE *RIPRODS!*

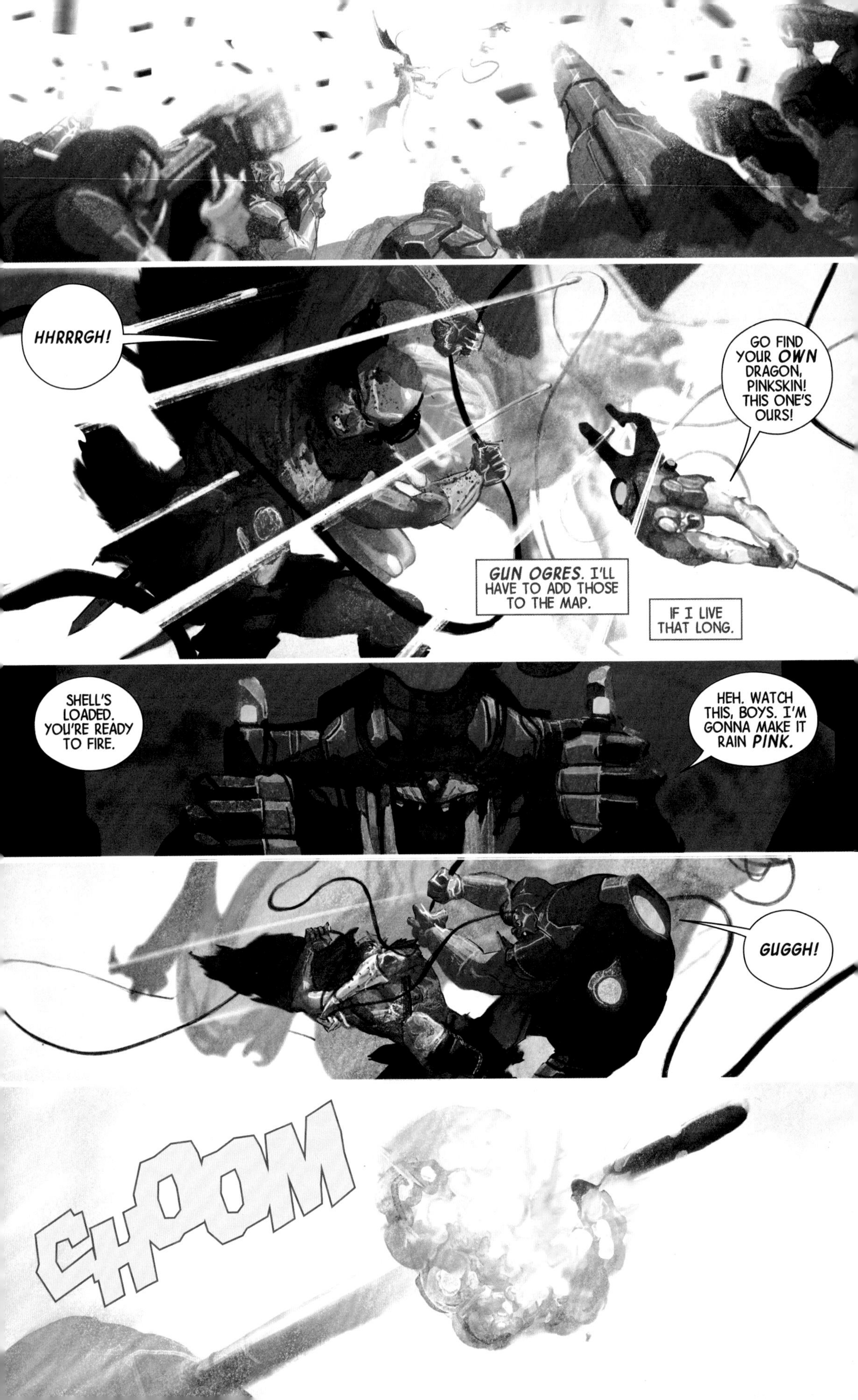
HHRRRGH!
GO FIND YOUR OWN DRAGON, PINKSKIN! THIS ONE'S OURS!
GUN OGRES. I'LL HAVE TO ADD THOSE TO THE MAP.
IF I LIVE THAT LONG.
SHELL'S LOADED. YOU'RE READY TO FIRE.
HEH. WATCH THIS, BOYS. I'M GONNA MAKE IT RAIN PINK.
GUGGH!
CHOOM

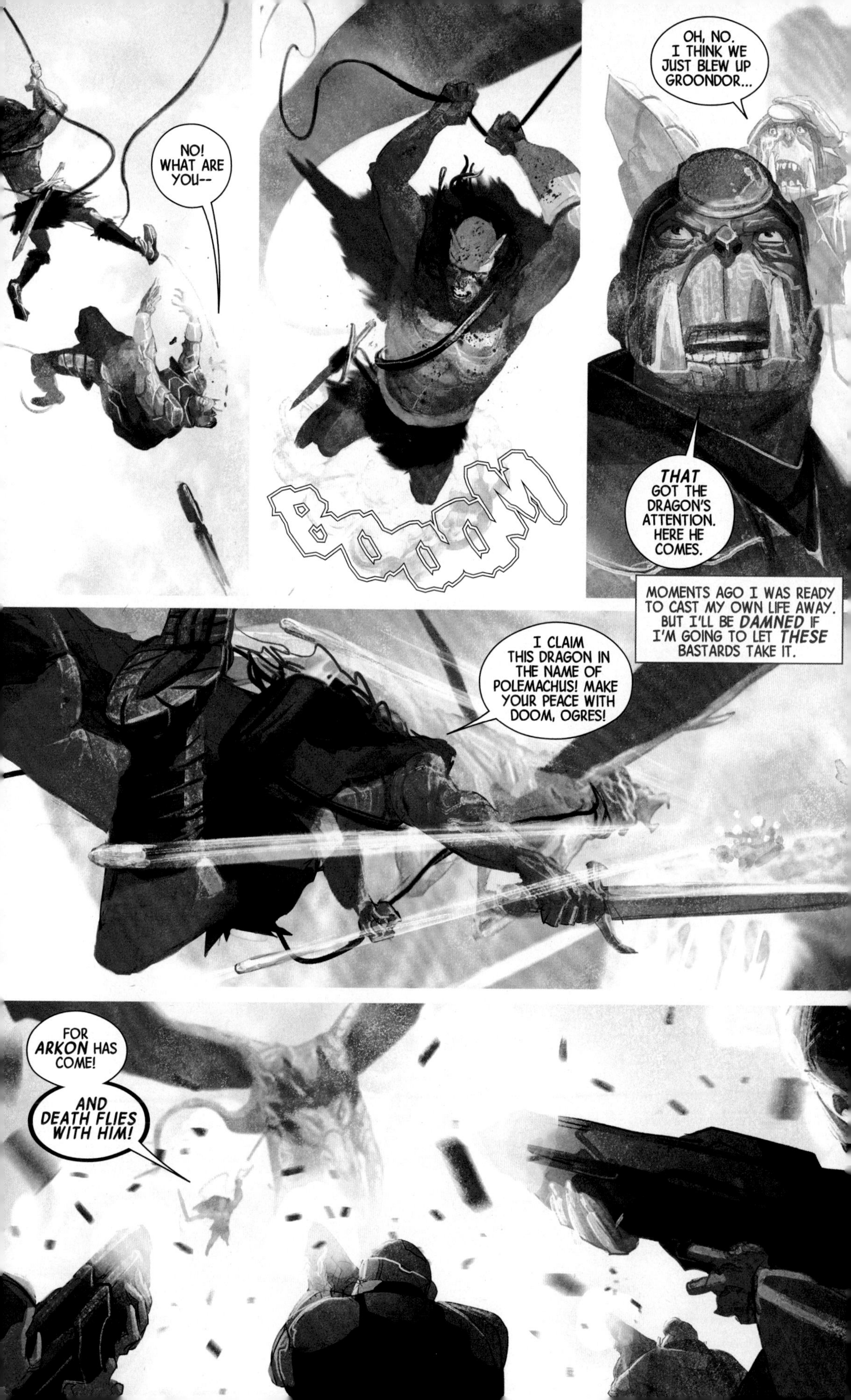
NO! WHAT ARE YOU--
BOOOM
OH, NO. I THINK WE JUST BLEW UP GROONDOR...
THAT GOT THE DRAGON'S ATTENTION. HERE HE COMES.
MOMENTS AGO I WAS READY TO CAST MY OWN LIFE AWAY. BUT I'LL BE DAMNED IF I'M GOING TO LET THESE BASTARDS TAKE IT.
I CLAIM THIS DRAGON IN THE NAME OF POLEMACHUS! MAKE YOUR PEACE WITH DOOM, OGRES!
FOR ARKON HAS COME!
AND DEATH FLIES WITH HIM!

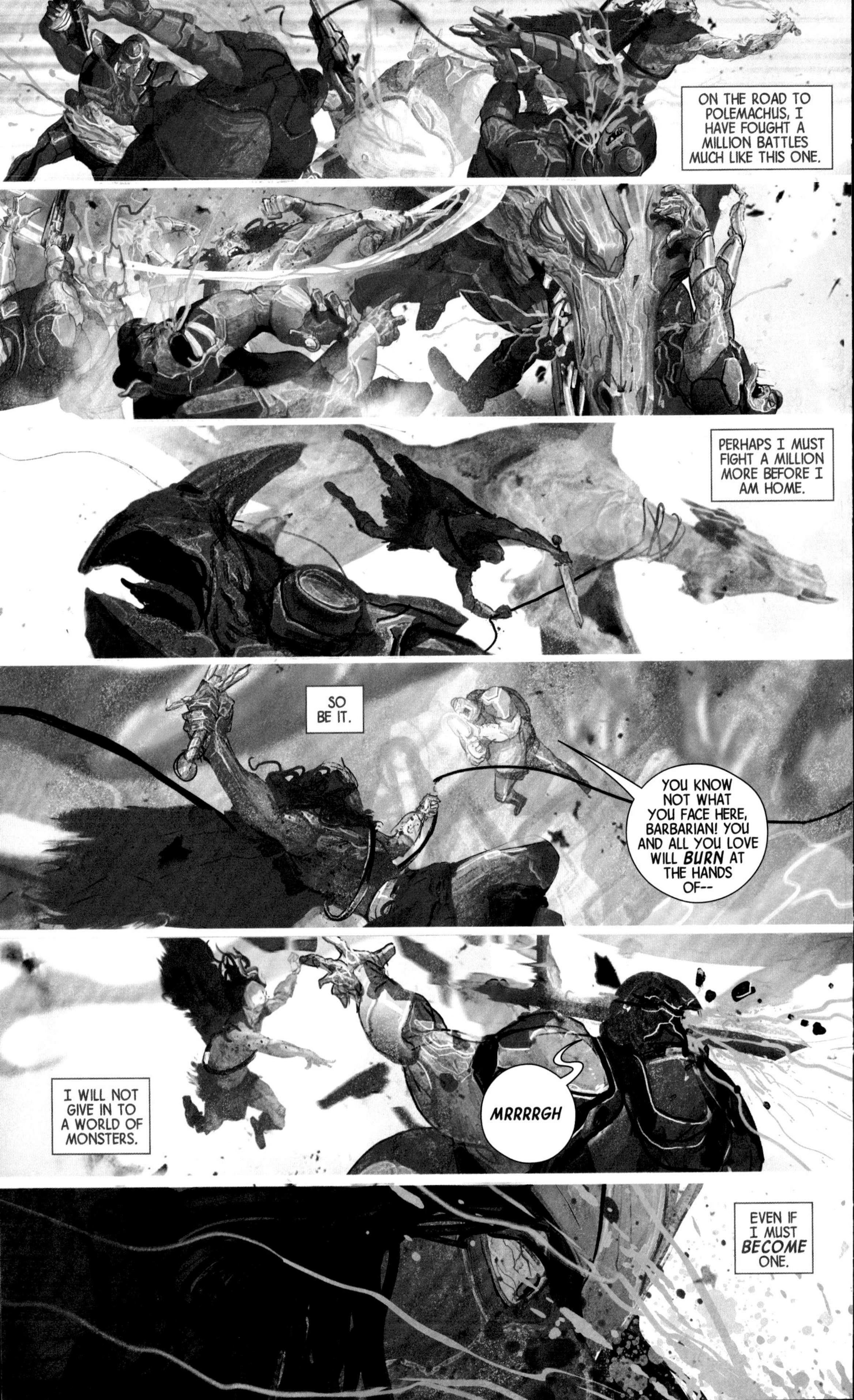
ON THE ROAD TO POLEMACHUS, I HAVE FOUGHT A MILLION BATTLES MUCH LIKE THIS ONE.
PERHAPS I MUST FIGHT A MILLION MORE BEFORE I AM HOME.
SO BE IT.
YOU KNOW NOT WHAT YOU FACE HERE, BARBARIAN! YOU AND ALL YOU LOVE WILL BURN AT THE HANDS OF--
I WILL NOT GIVE IN TO A WORLD OF MONSTERS.
MRRRRGH
EVEN IF I MUST BECOME ONE.

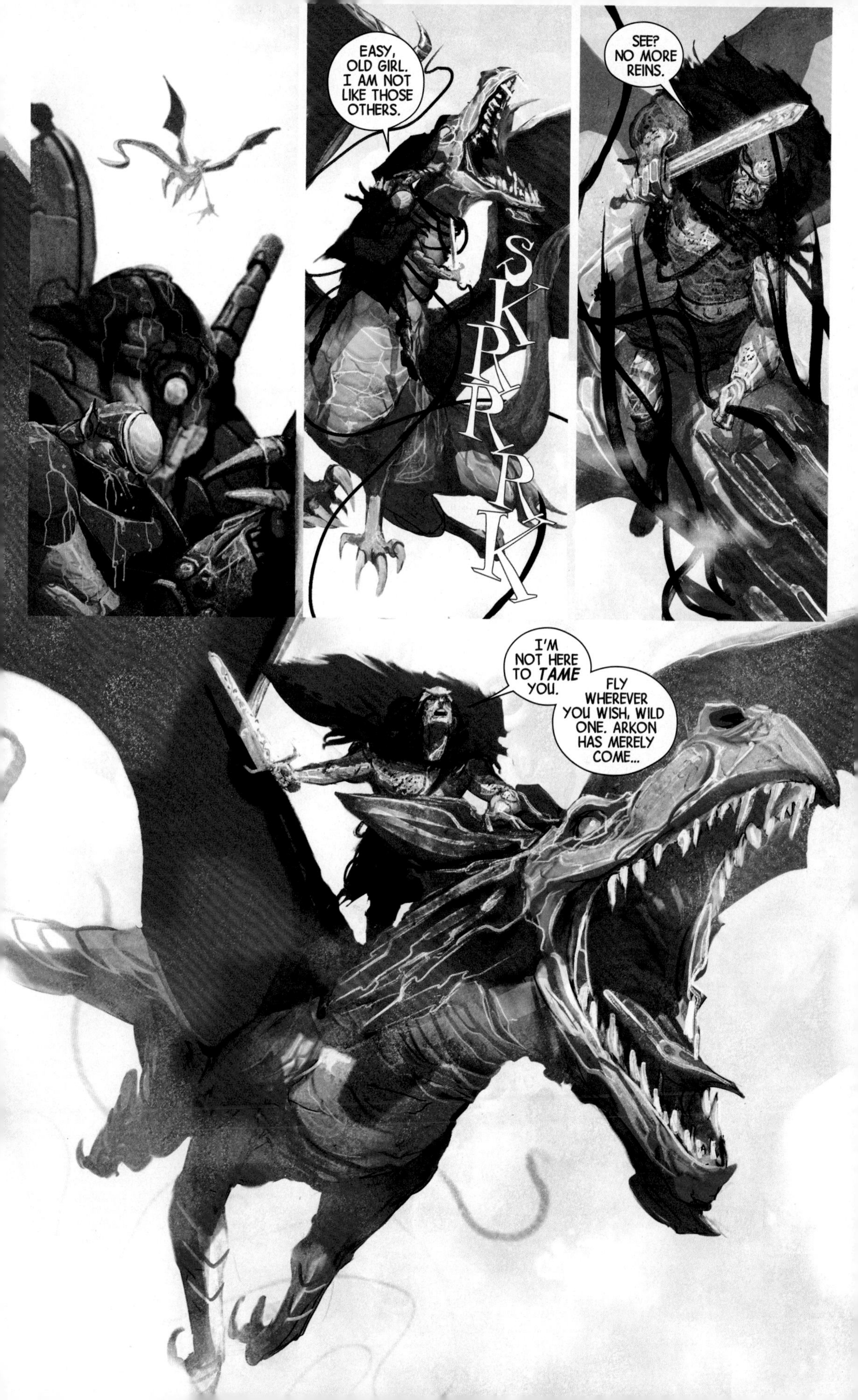
EASY, OLD GIRL. I AM NOT LIKE THOSE OTHERS.
SKRRRRK
SEE? NO MORE REINS.
I'M NOT HERE TO *TAME* YOU.
FLY WHEREVER YOU WISH, WILD ONE. ARKON HAS MERELY COME...

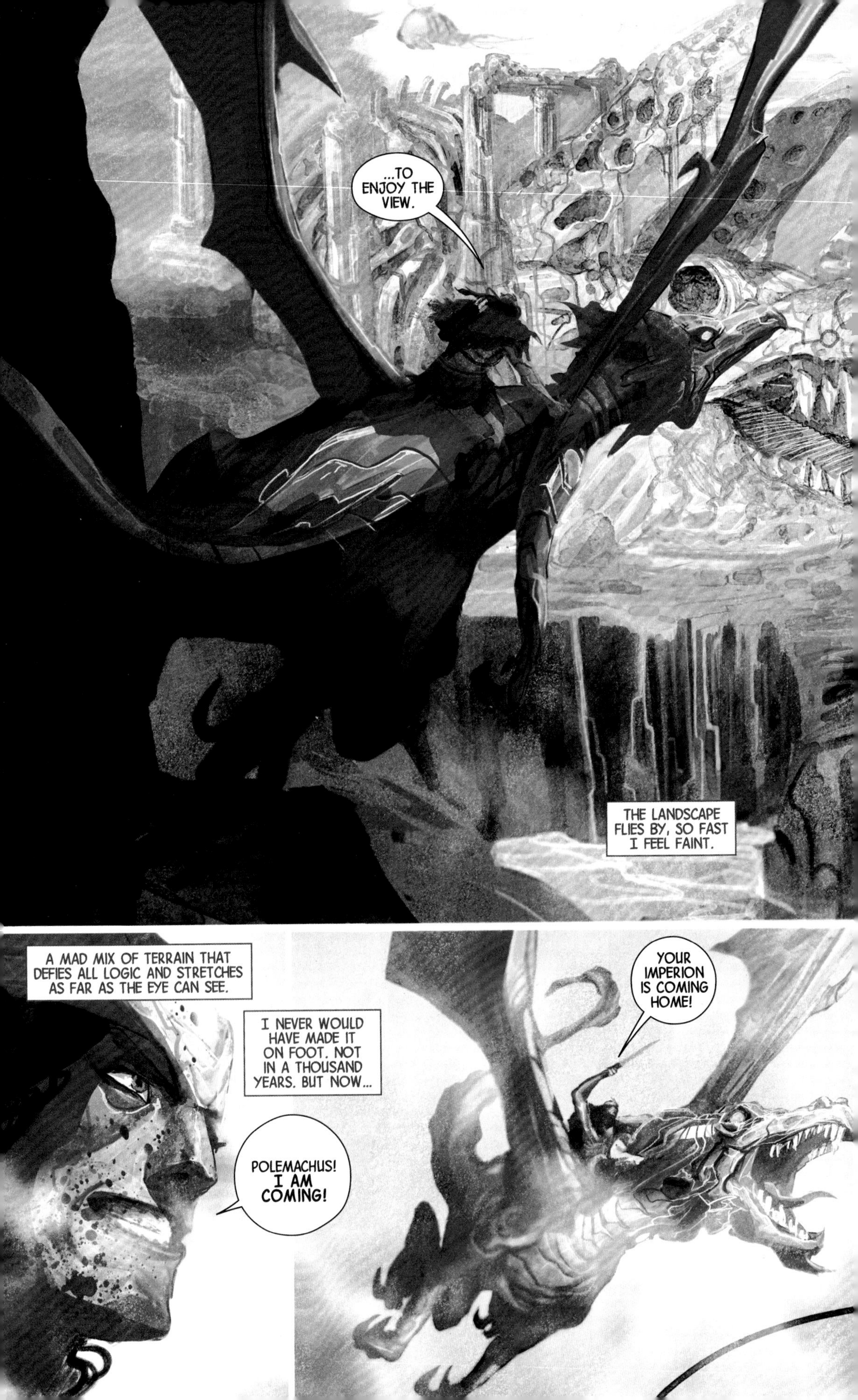
...TO ENJOY THE VIEW.
THE LANDSCAPE FLIES BY, SO FAST I FEEL FAINT.
A MAD MIX OF TERRAIN THAT DEFIES ALL LOGIC AND STRETCHES AS FAR AS THE EYE CAN SEE.
I NEVER WOULD HAVE MADE IT ON FOOT. NOT IN A THOUSAND YEARS. BUT NOW...
POLEMACHUS! I AM COMING!
YOUR IMPERION IS COMING HOME!

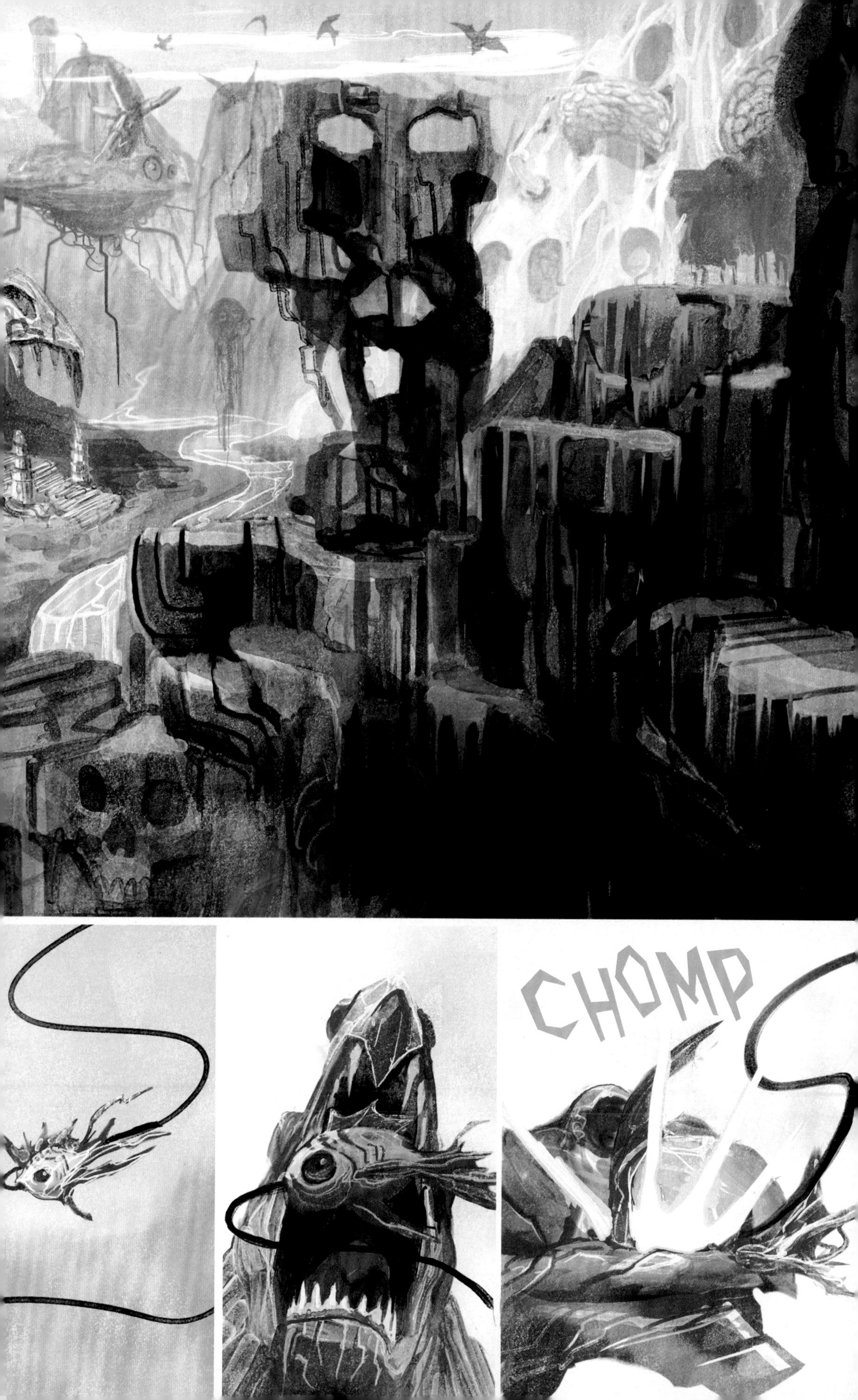
CHOMP

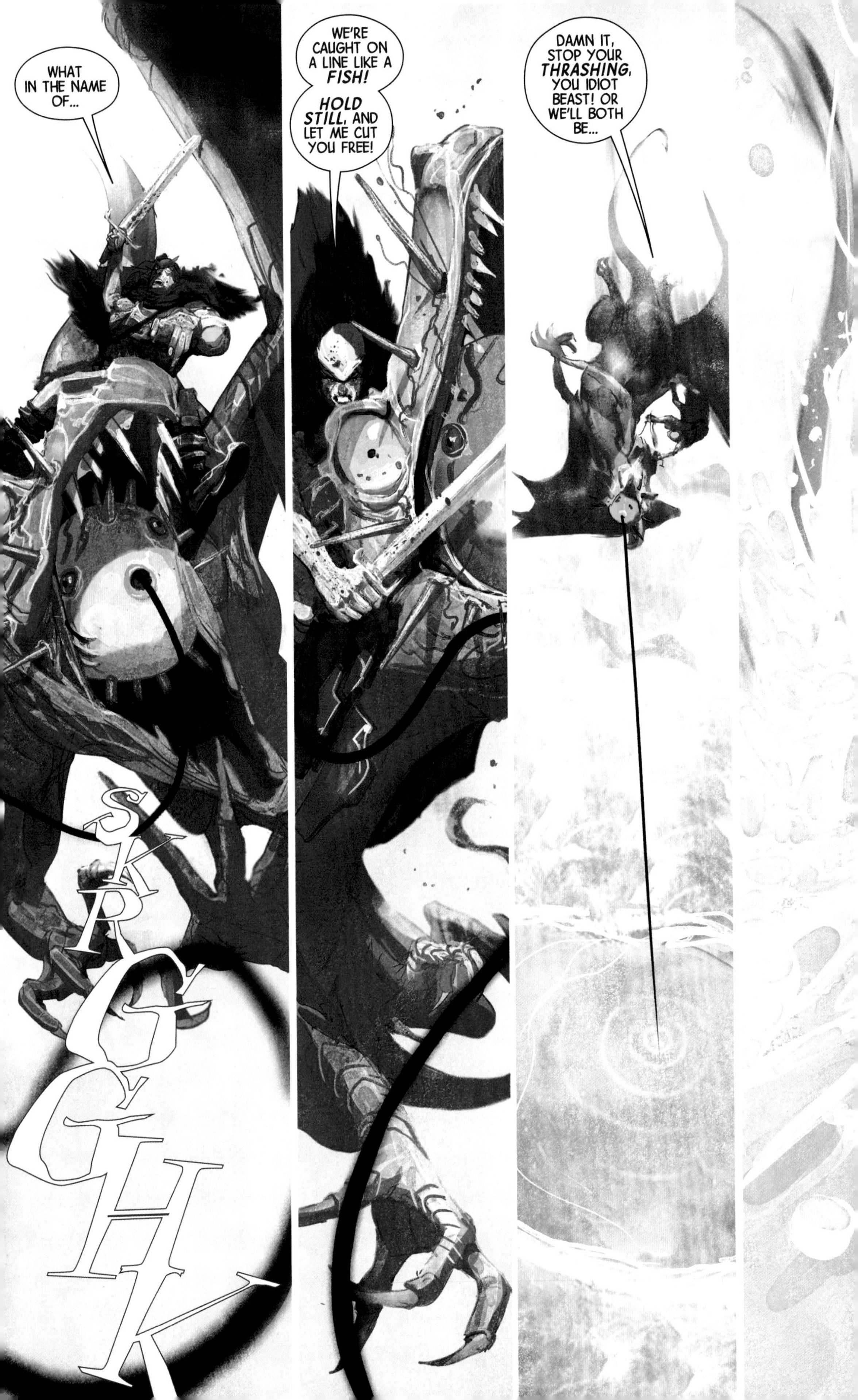
WHAT IN THE NAME OF...
SKRAGGHHK
WE'RE CAUGHT ON A LINE LIKE A FISH!
HOLD STILL, AND LET ME CUT YOU FREE!
DAMN IT, STOP YOUR THRASHING, YOU IDIOT BEAST! OR WE'LL BOTH BE...

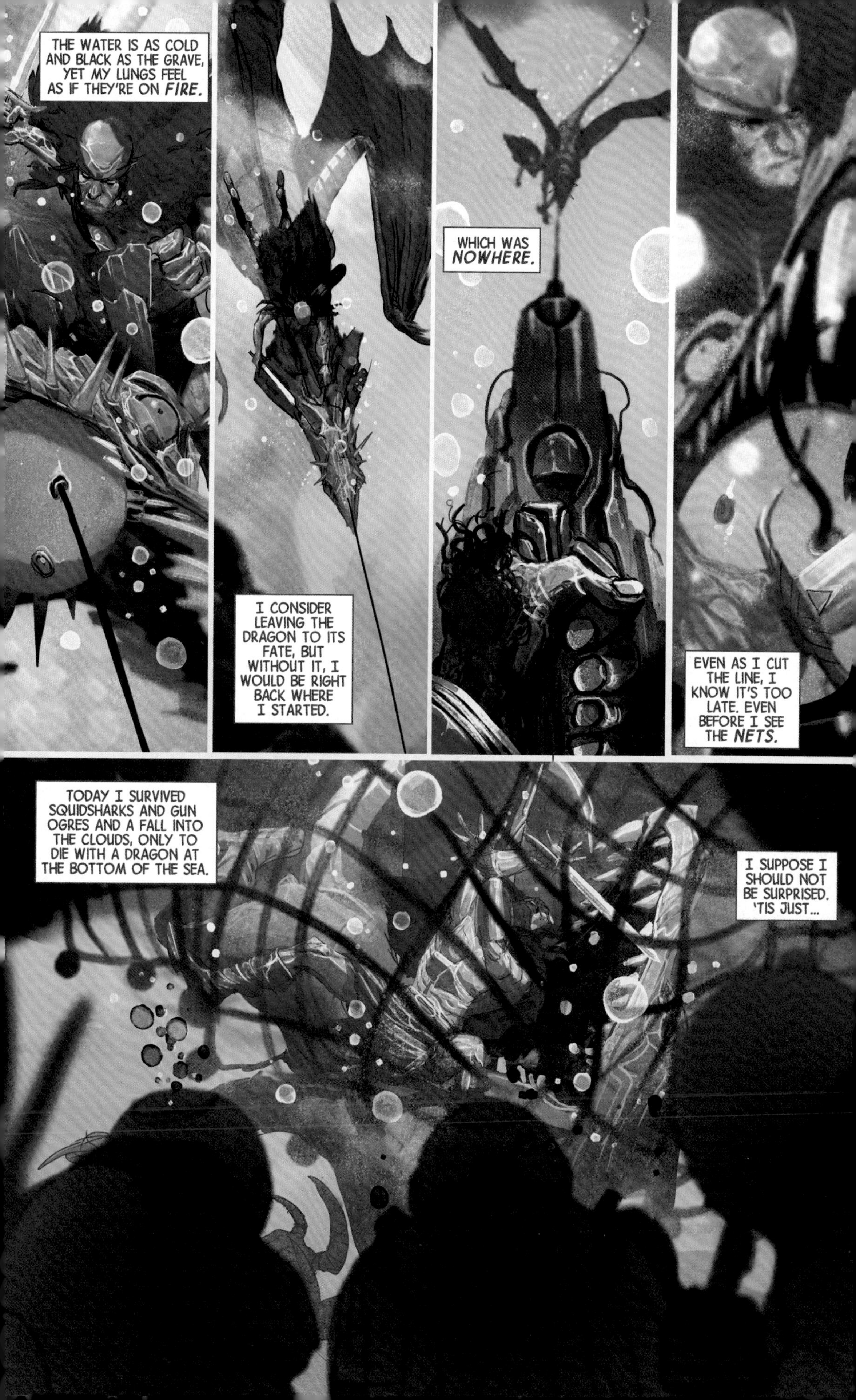
THE WATER IS AS COLD AND BLACK AS THE GRAVE, YET MY LUNGS FEEL AS IF THEY'RE ON *FIRE.*
I CONSIDER LEAVING THE DRAGON TO ITS FATE, BUT WITHOUT IT, I WOULD BE RIGHT BACK WHERE I STARTED.
WHICH WAS *NOWHERE.*
EVEN AS I CUT THE LINE, I KNOW IT'S TOO LATE. EVEN BEFORE I SEE THE *NETS.*
TODAY I SURVIVED SQUIDSHARKS AND GUN OGRES AND A FALL INTO THE CLOUDS, ONLY TO DIE WITH A DRAGON AT THE BOTTOM OF THE SEA.
I SUPPOSE I SHOULD NOT BE SURPRISED. 'TIS JUST...

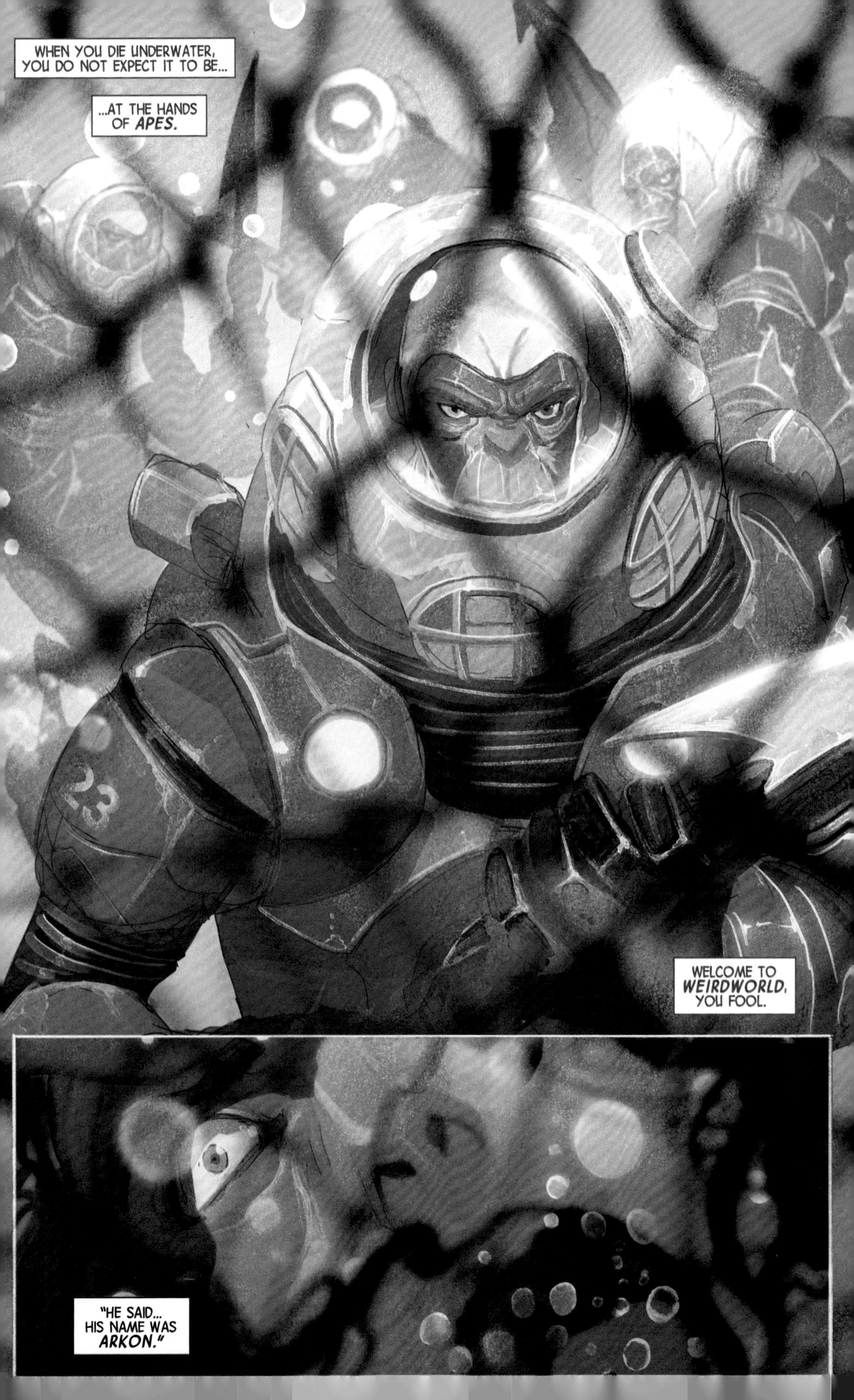
WHEN YOU DIE UNDERWATER, YOU DO NOT EXPECT IT TO BE...
...AT THE HANDS OF APES.
23
WELCOME TO WEIRDWORLD, YOU FOOL.
"HE SAID... HIS NAME WAS ARKON."

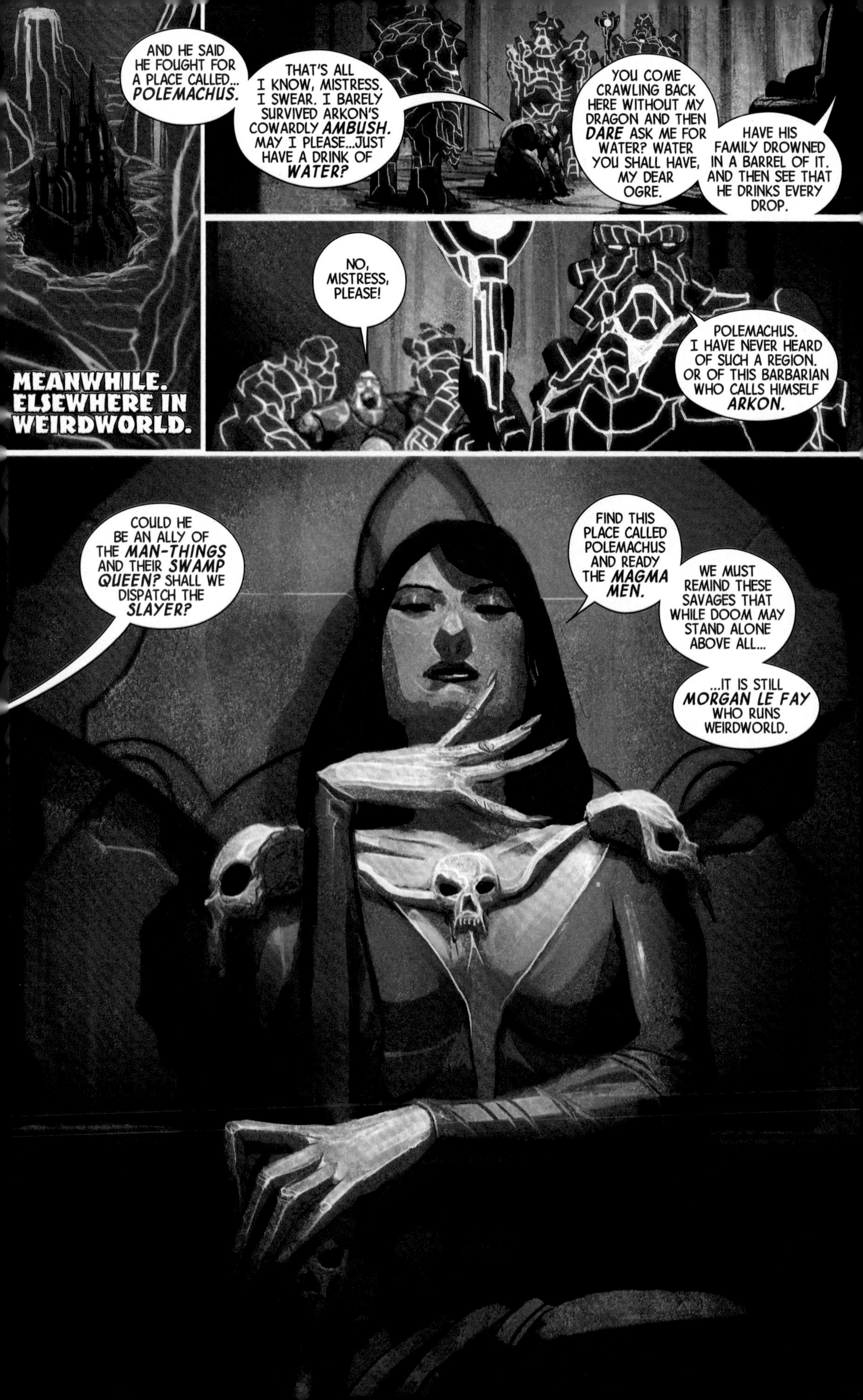
AND HE SAID HE FOUGHT FOR A PLACE CALLED... POLEMACHUS.
THAT'S ALL I KNOW, MISTRESS. I SWEAR. I BARELY SURVIVED ARKON'S COWARDLY AMBUSH. MAY I PLEASE...JUST HAVE A DRINK OF WATER?
YOU COME CRAWLING BACK HERE WITHOUT MY DRAGON AND THEN DARE ASK ME FOR WATER? WATER YOU SHALL HAVE, MY DEAR OGRE.
HAVE HIS FAMILY DROWNED IN A BARREL OF IT. AND THEN SEE THAT HE DRINKS EVERY DROP.
MEANWHILE. ELSEWHERE IN WEIRDWORLD.
NO, MISTRESS, PLEASE!
POLEMACHUS. I HAVE NEVER HEARD OF SUCH A REGION. OR OF THIS BARBARIAN WHO CALLS HIMSELF ARKON.
COULD HE BE AN ALLY OF THE MAN-THINGS AND THEIR SWAMP QUEEN? SHALL WE DISPATCH THE SLAYER?
FIND THIS PLACE CALLED POLEMACHUS AND READY THE MAGMA MEN.
WE MUST REMIND THESE SAVAGES THAT WHILE DOOM MAY STAND ALONE ABOVE ALL...
...IT IS STILL MORGAN LE FAY WHO RUNS WEIRDWORLD.

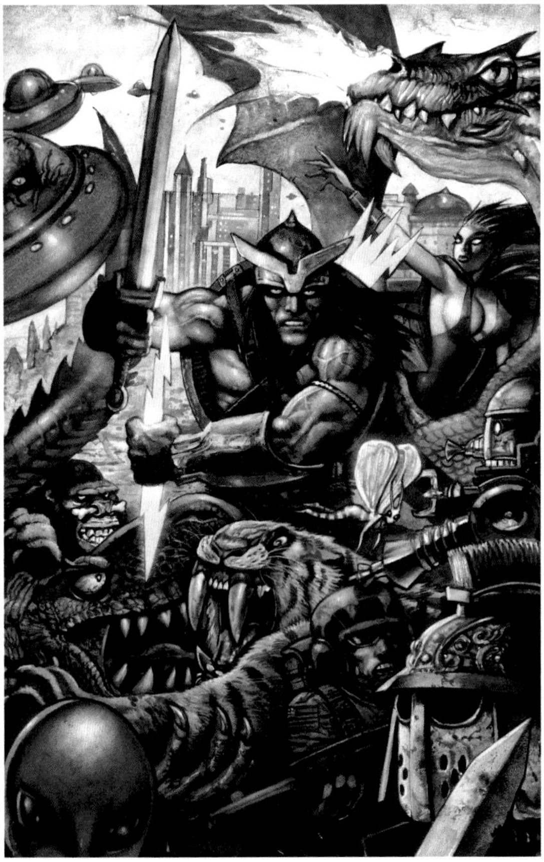

#1 VARIANT BY SIMON BISLEY

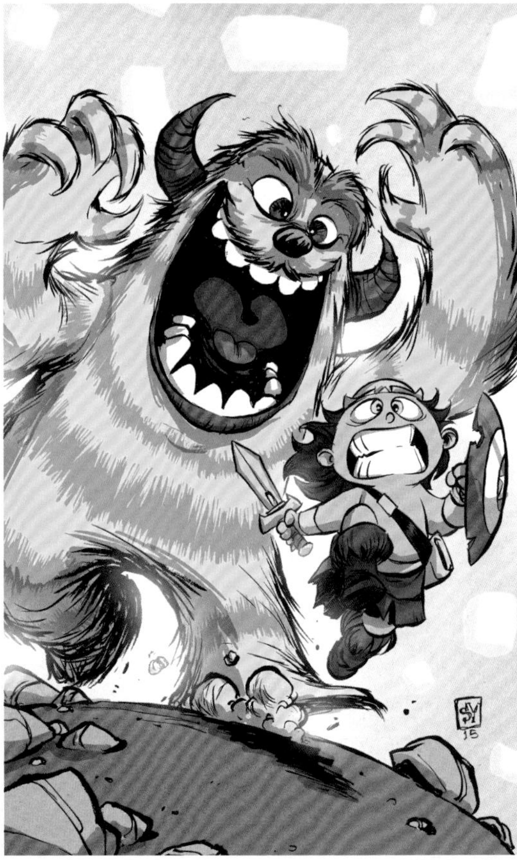

#1 VARIANT BY SKOTTIE YOUNG

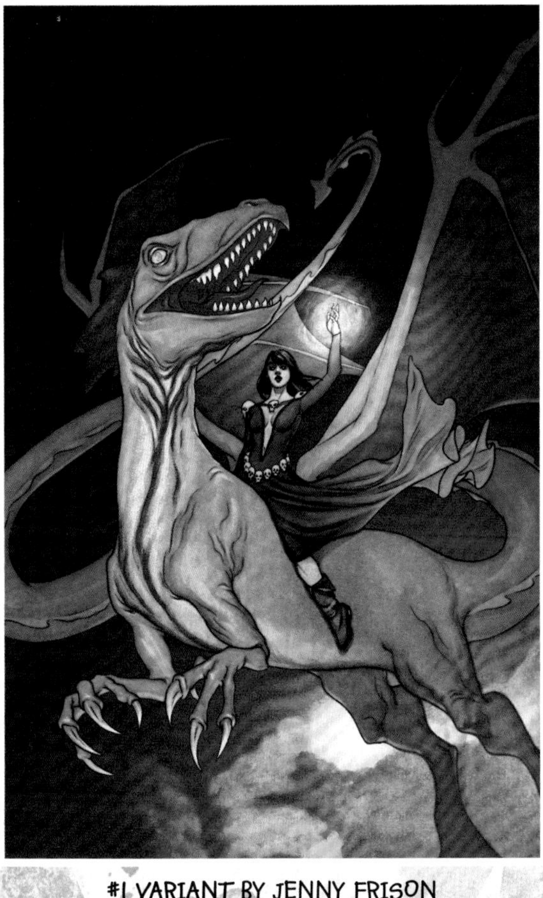

#1 VARIANT BY JENNY FRISON

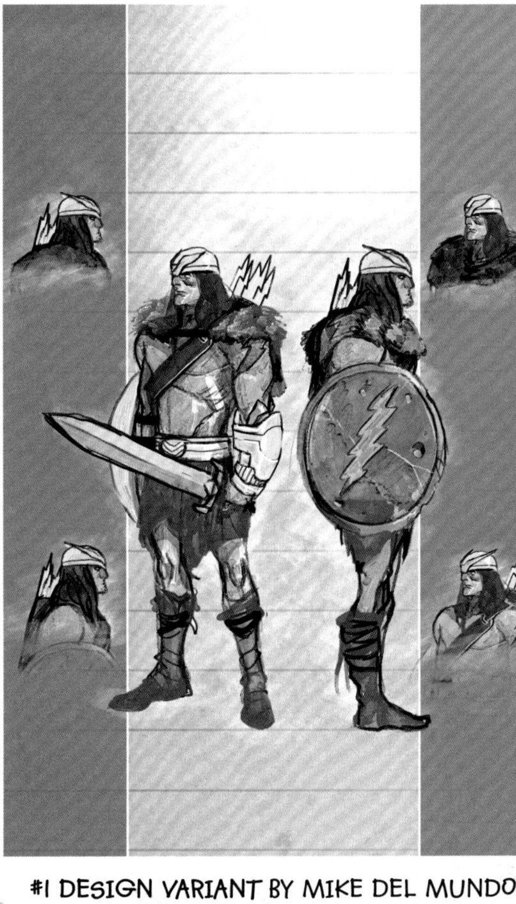

#1 DESIGN VARIANT BY MIKE DEL MUNDO

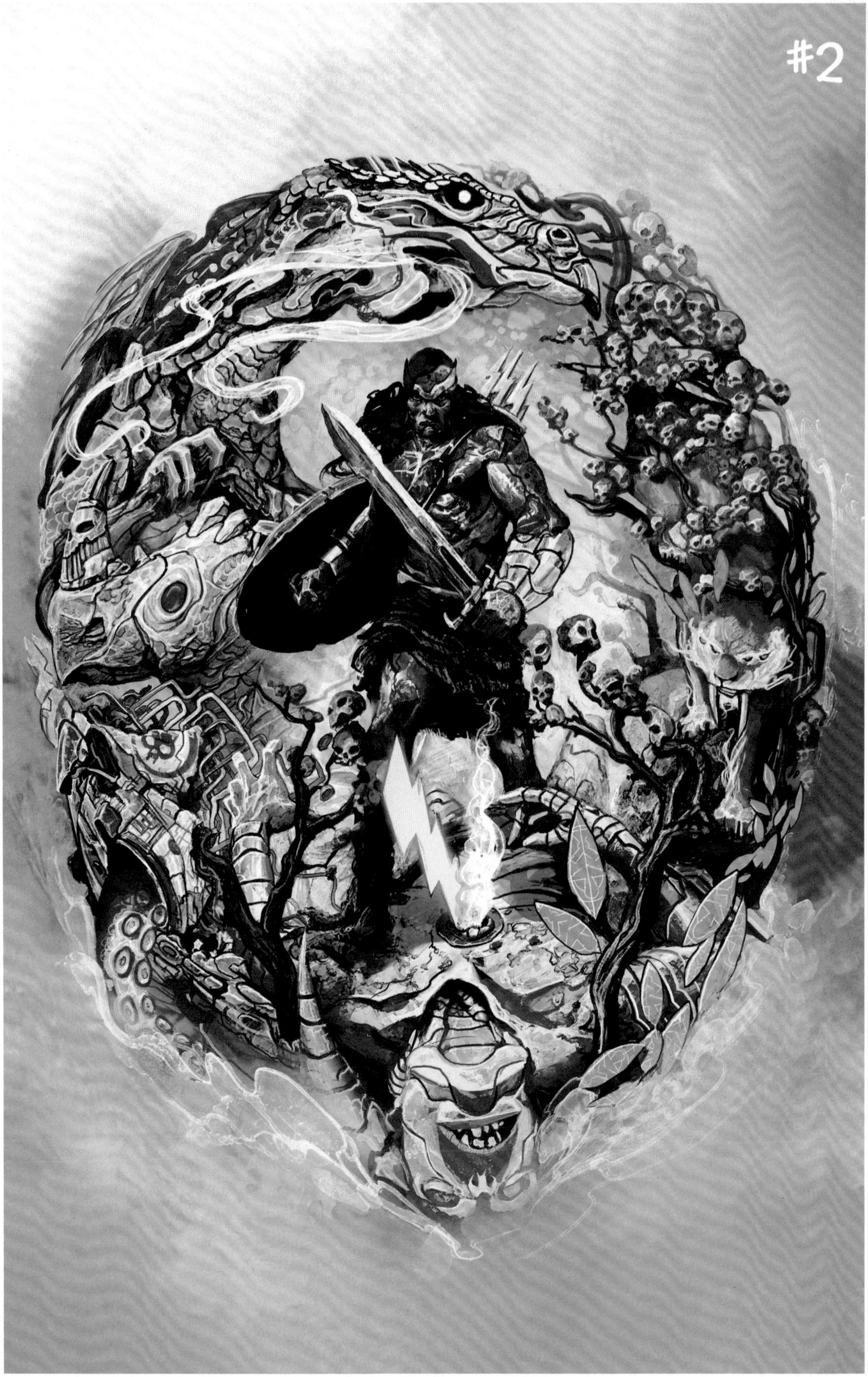
#2

• ESCAPE FROM APELANTIS •

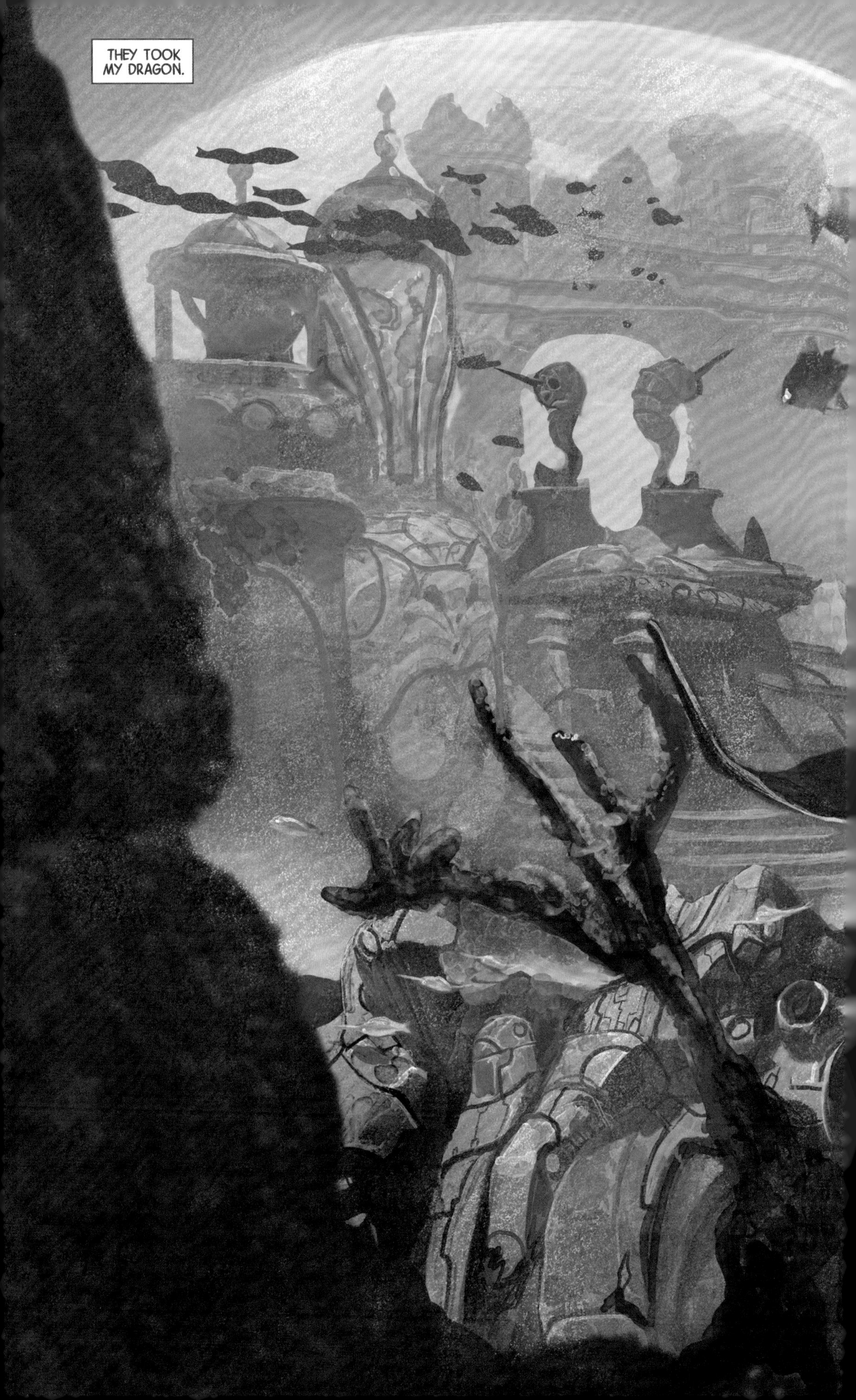
THEY TOOK MY DRAGON.

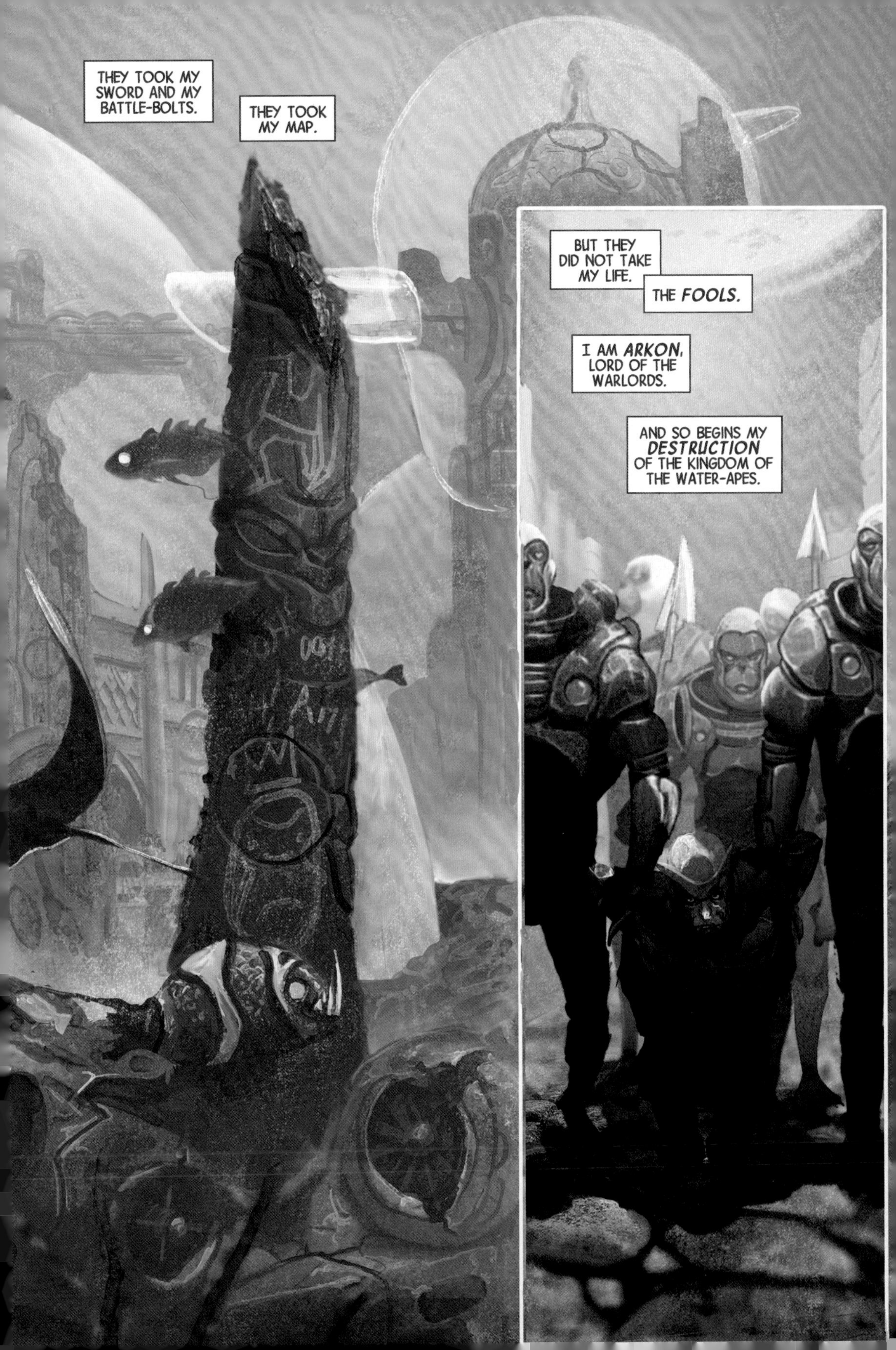
THEY TOOK MY SWORD AND MY BATTLE-BOLTS.
THEY TOOK MY MAP.
BUT THEY DID NOT TAKE MY LIFE.
THE *FOOLS.*
I AM *ARKON,* LORD OF THE WARLORDS.
AND SO BEGINS MY *DESTRUCTION* OF THE KINGDOM OF THE WATER-APES.

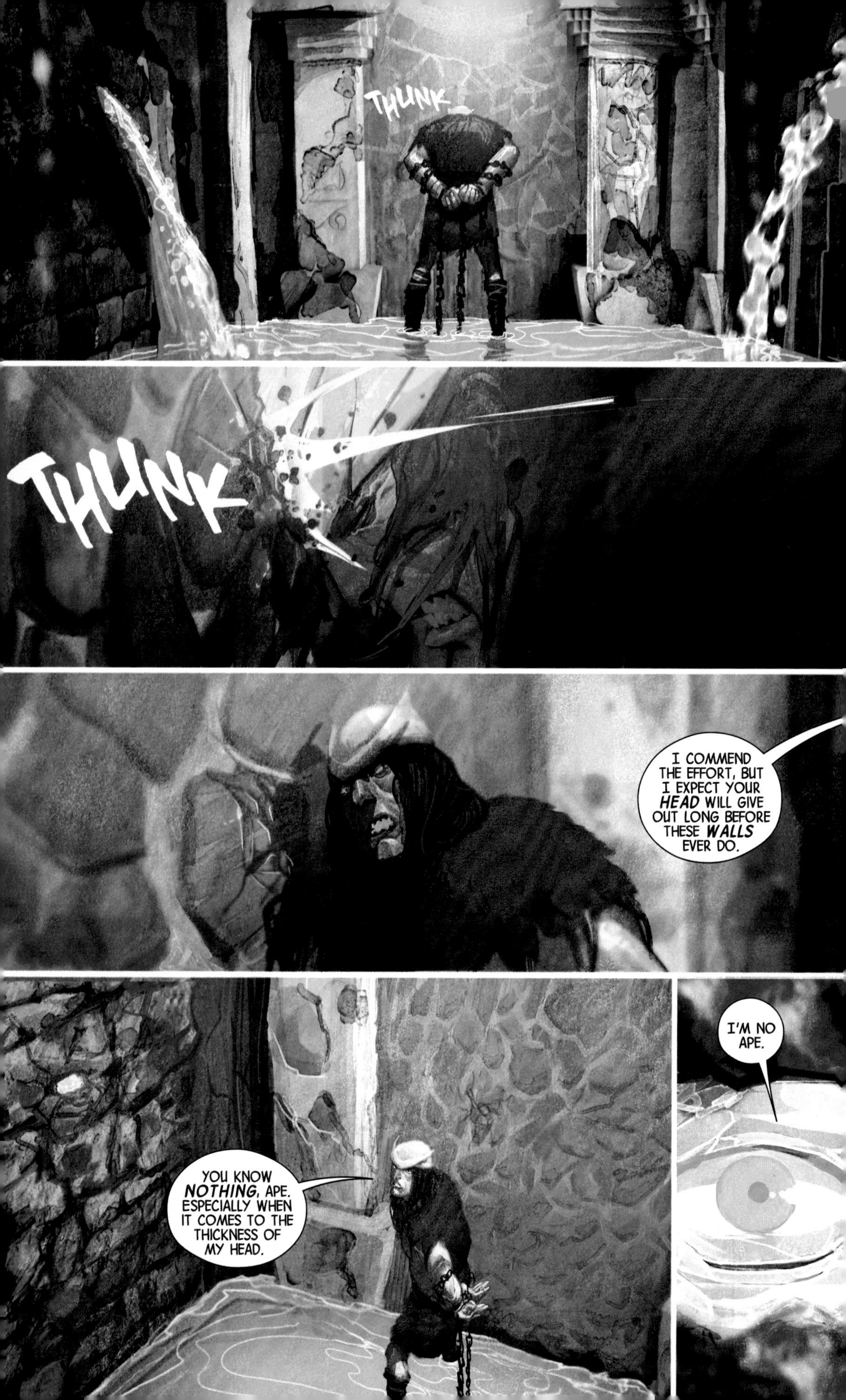
THUNK
THUNK
I COMMEND THE EFFORT, BUT I EXPECT YOUR HEAD WILL GIVE OUT LONG BEFORE THESE WALLS EVER DO.
YOU KNOW NOTHING, APE. ESPECIALLY WHEN IT COMES TO THE THICKNESS OF MY HEAD.
I'M NO APE.

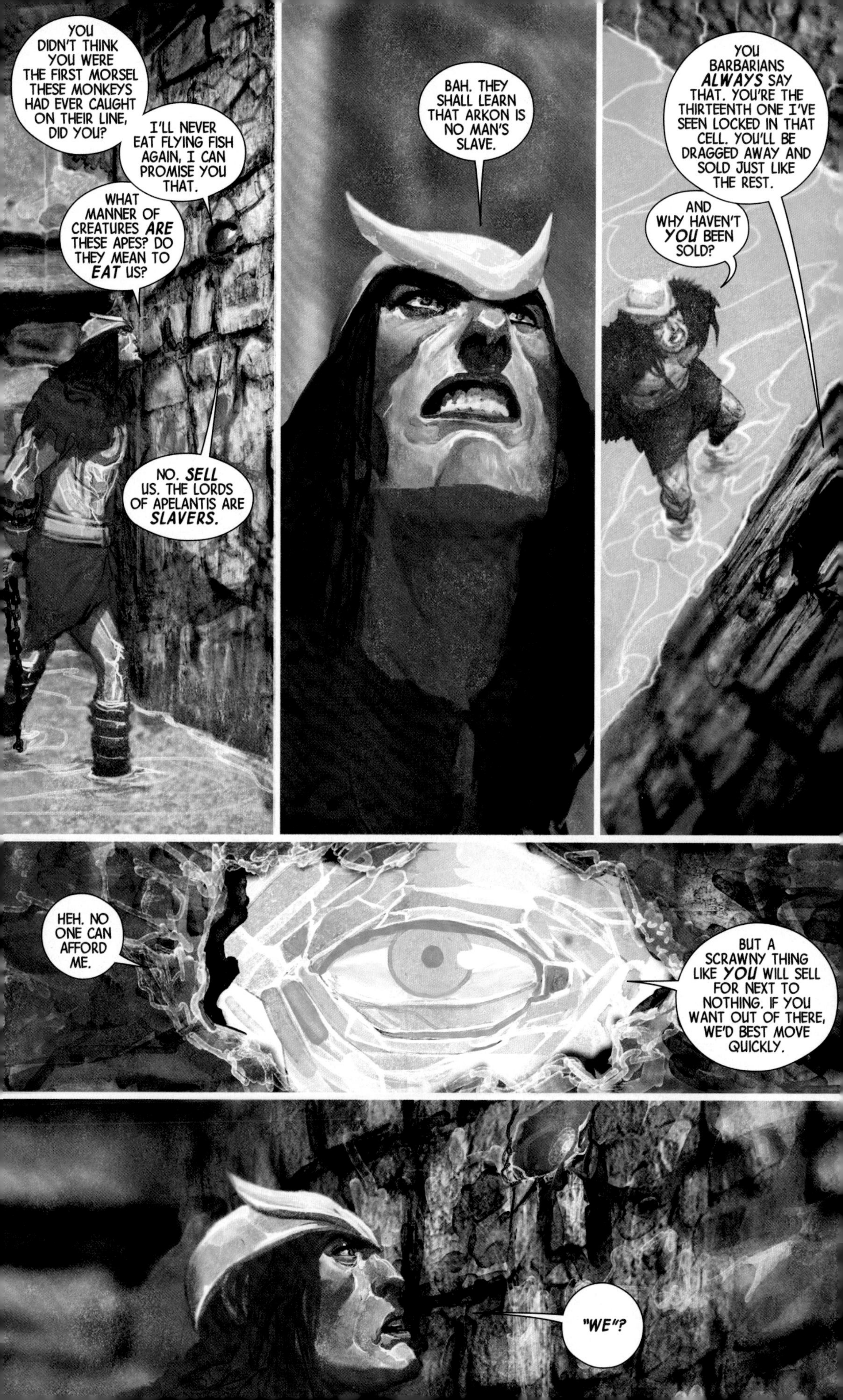
YOU DIDN'T THINK YOU WERE THE FIRST MORSEL THESE MONKEYS HAD EVER CAUGHT ON THEIR LINE, DID YOU?
I'LL NEVER EAT FLYING FISH AGAIN, I CAN PROMISE YOU THAT.
WHAT MANNER OF CREATURES ARE THESE APES? DO THEY MEAN TO EAT US?
NO. SELL US. THE LORDS OF APELANTIS ARE SLAVERS.
BAH. THEY SHALL LEARN THAT ARKON IS NO MAN'S SLAVE.
YOU BARBARIANS ALWAYS SAY THAT. YOU'RE THE THIRTEENTH ONE I'VE SEEN LOCKED IN THAT CELL. YOU'LL BE DRAGGED AWAY AND SOLD JUST LIKE THE REST.
AND WHY HAVEN'T YOU BEEN SOLD?
HEH. NO ONE CAN AFFORD ME.
BUT A SCRAWNY THING LIKE YOU WILL SELL FOR NEXT TO NOTHING. IF YOU WANT OUT OF THERE, WE'D BEST MOVE QUICKLY.
"WE"?

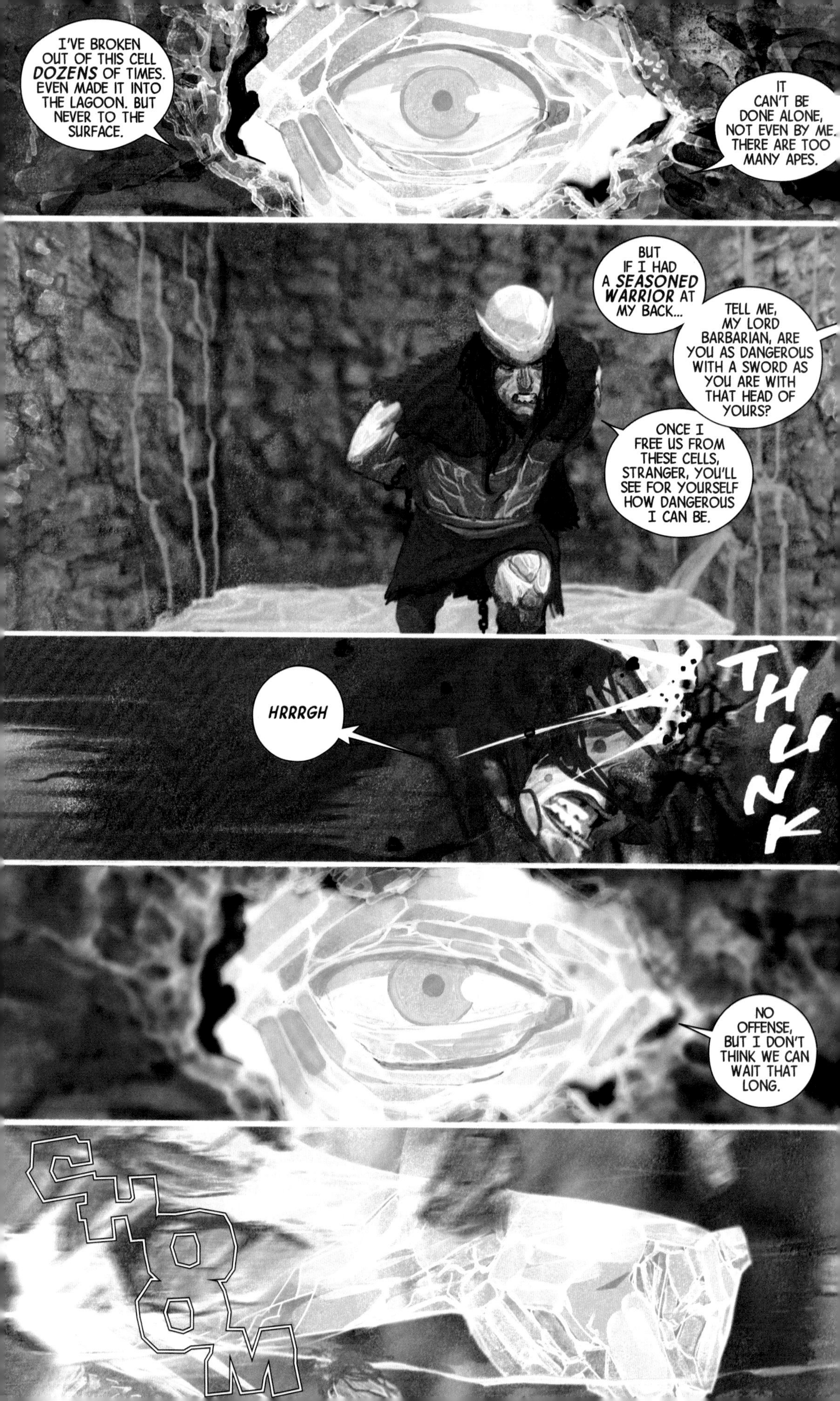
I'VE BROKEN OUT OF THIS CELL *DOZENS* OF TIMES. EVEN MADE IT INTO THE LAGOON. BUT NEVER TO THE SURFACE.
IT CAN'T BE DONE ALONE, NOT EVEN BY ME. THERE ARE TOO MANY APES.
BUT IF I HAD A *SEASONED WARRIOR* AT MY BACK...
TELL ME, MY LORD BARBARIAN, ARE YOU AS DANGEROUS WITH A SWORD AS YOU ARE WITH THAT HEAD OF YOURS?
ONCE I FREE US FROM THESE CELLS, STRANGER, YOU'LL SEE FOR YOURSELF HOW DANGEROUS I CAN BE.
THUNK
HRRRGH
NO OFFENSE, BUT I DON'T THINK WE CAN WAIT THAT LONG.
CHOOM

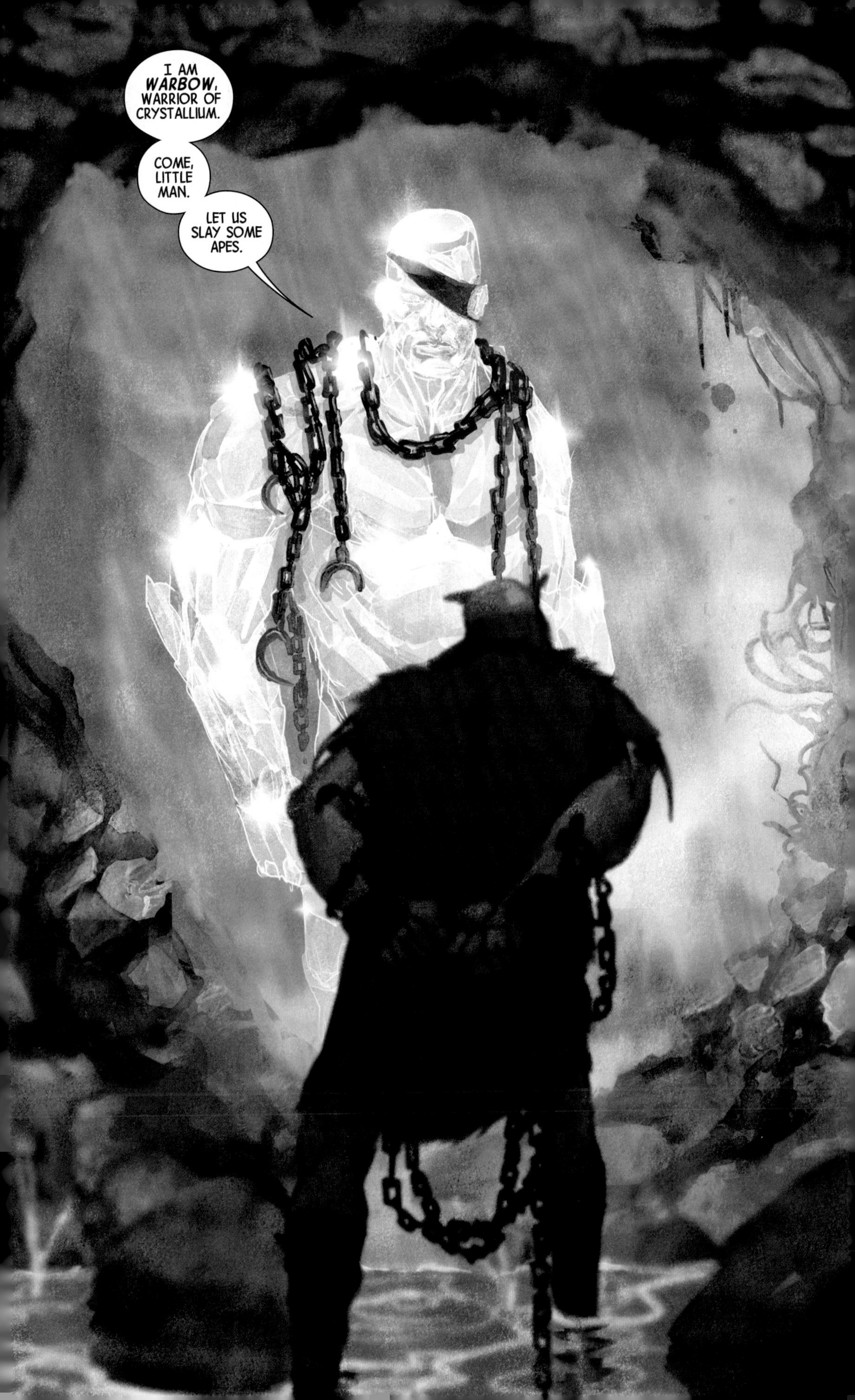
I AM WARBOW, WARRIOR OF CRYSTALLIUM.
COME, LITTLE MAN.
LET US SLAY SOME APES.

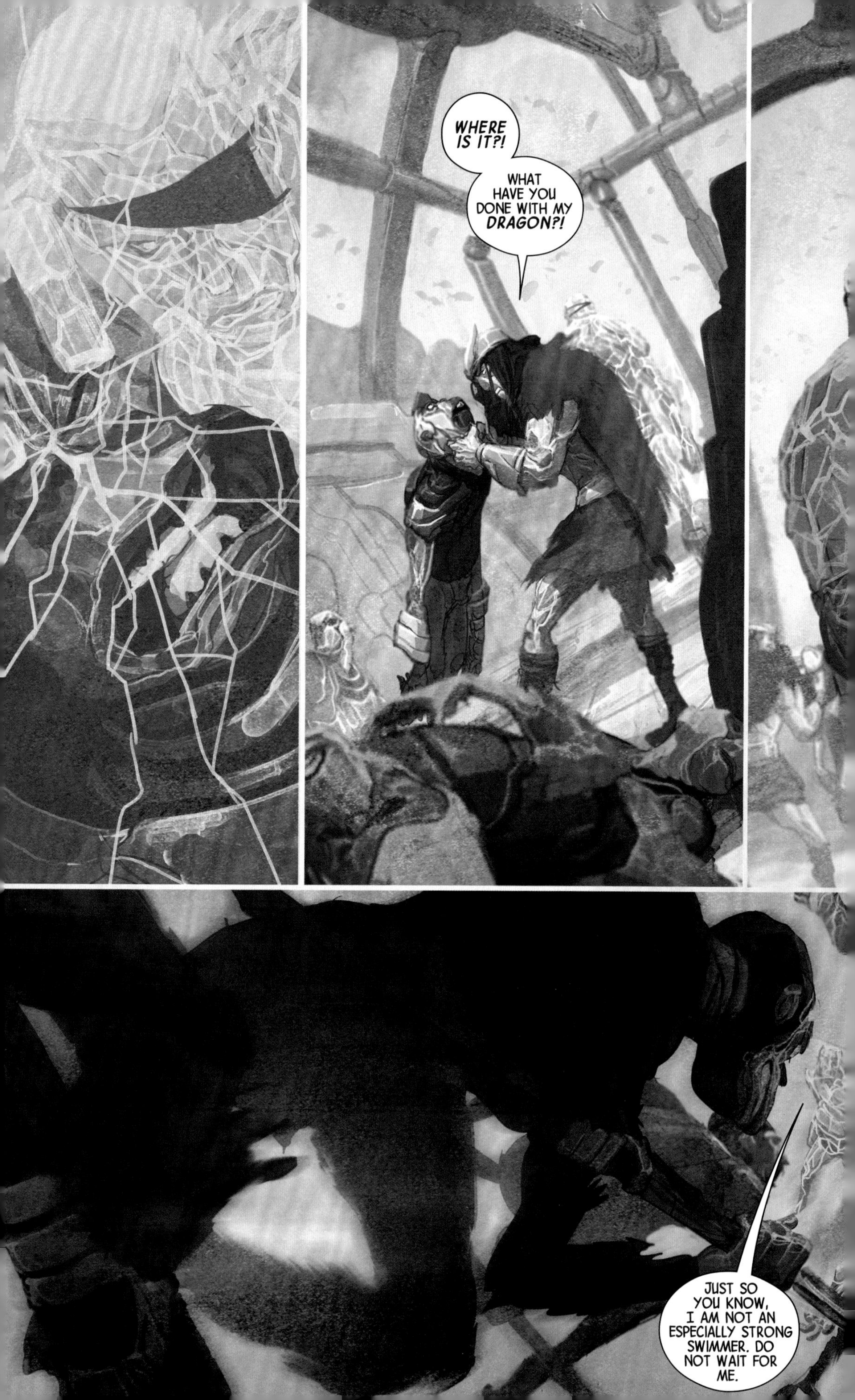
WHERE IS IT?!
WHAT HAVE YOU DONE WITH MY DRAGON?!
JUST SO YOU KNOW, I AM NOT AN ESPECIALLY STRONG SWIMMER. DO NOT WAIT FOR ME.

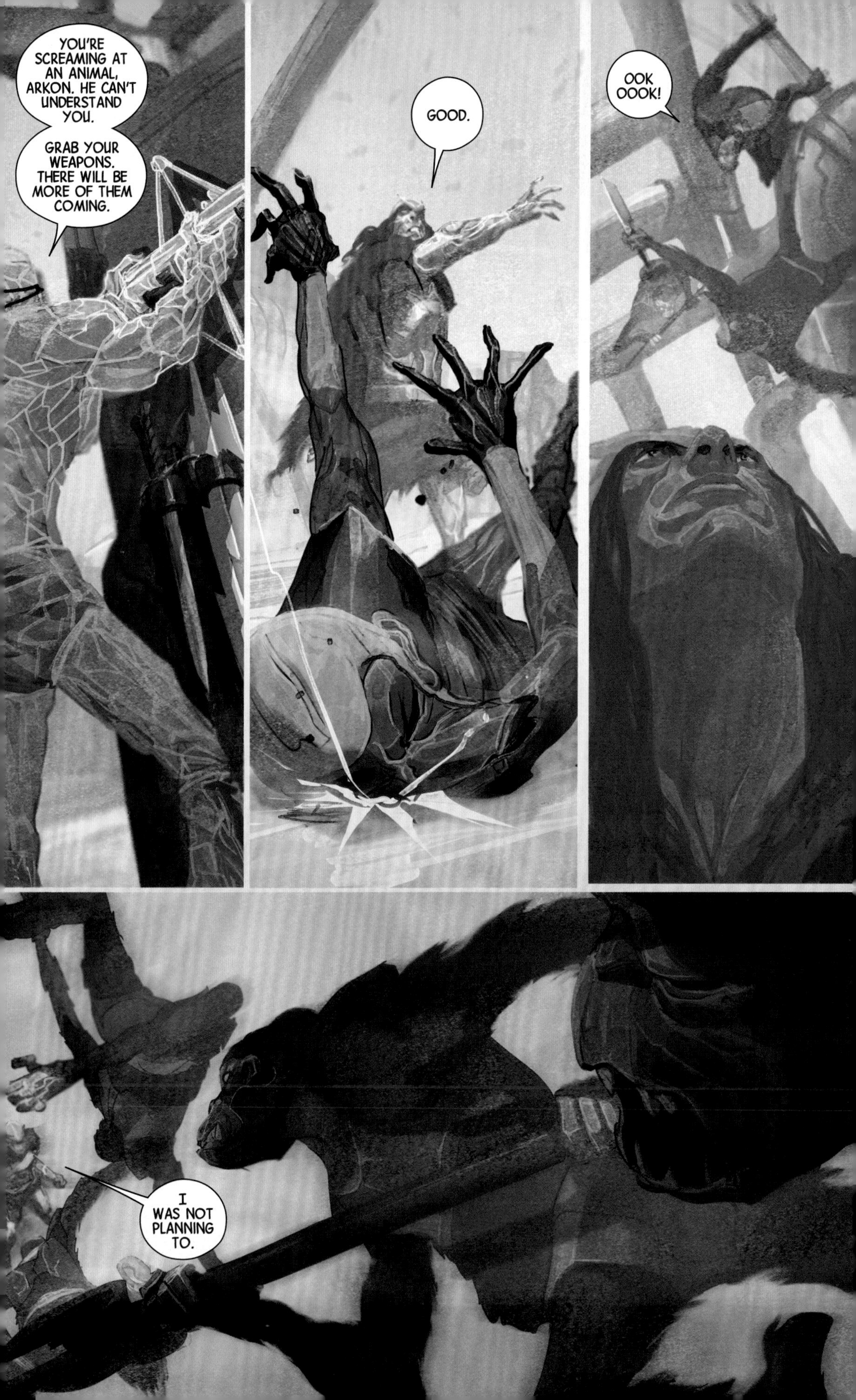
YOU'RE SCREAMING AT AN ANIMAL, ARKON. HE CAN'T UNDERSTAND YOU.
GRAB YOUR WEAPONS. THERE WILL BE MORE OF THEM COMING.
GOOD.
OOK OOOK!
I WAS NOT PLANNING TO.

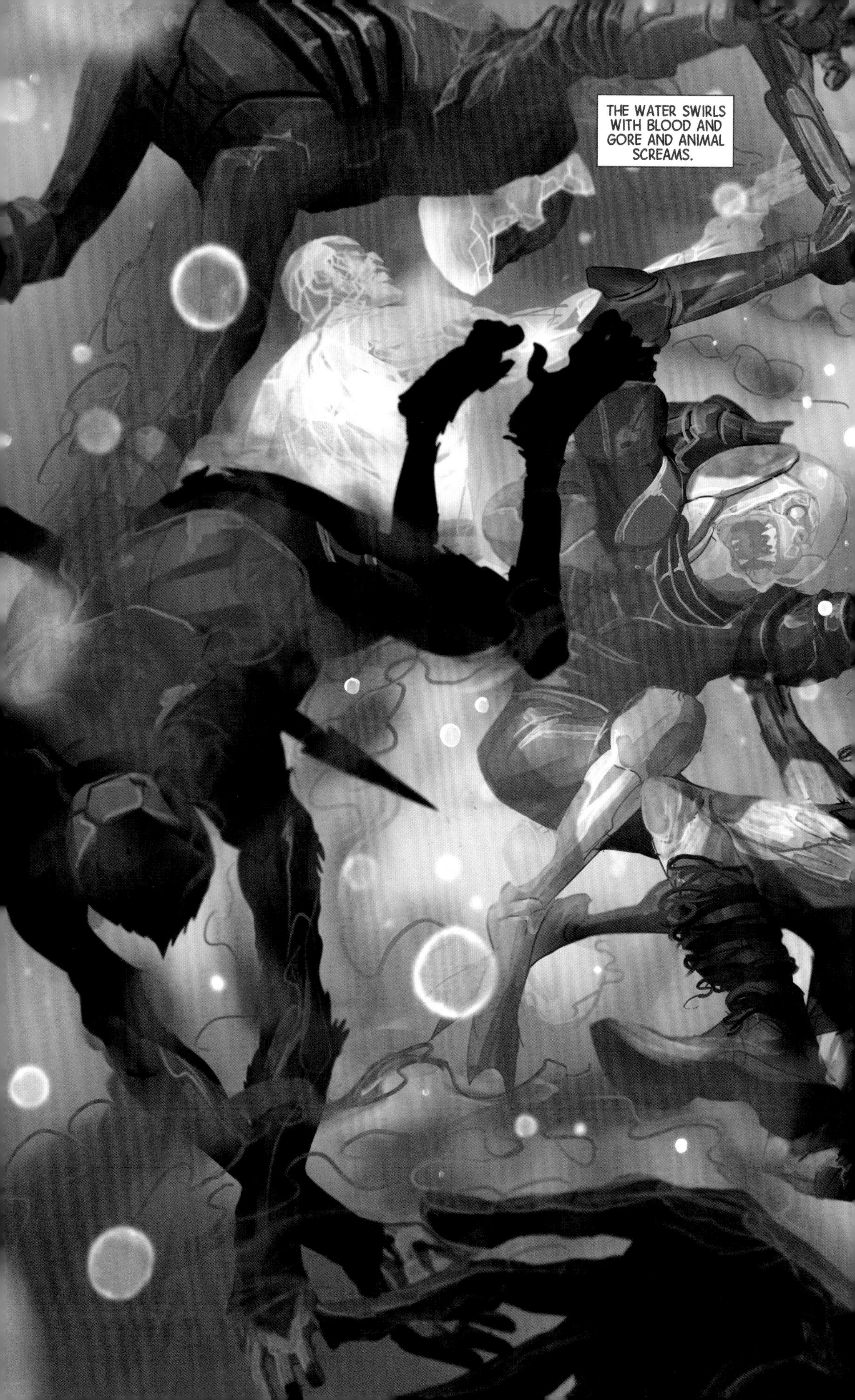
THE WATER SWIRLS WITH BLOOD AND GORE AND ANIMAL SCREAMS.

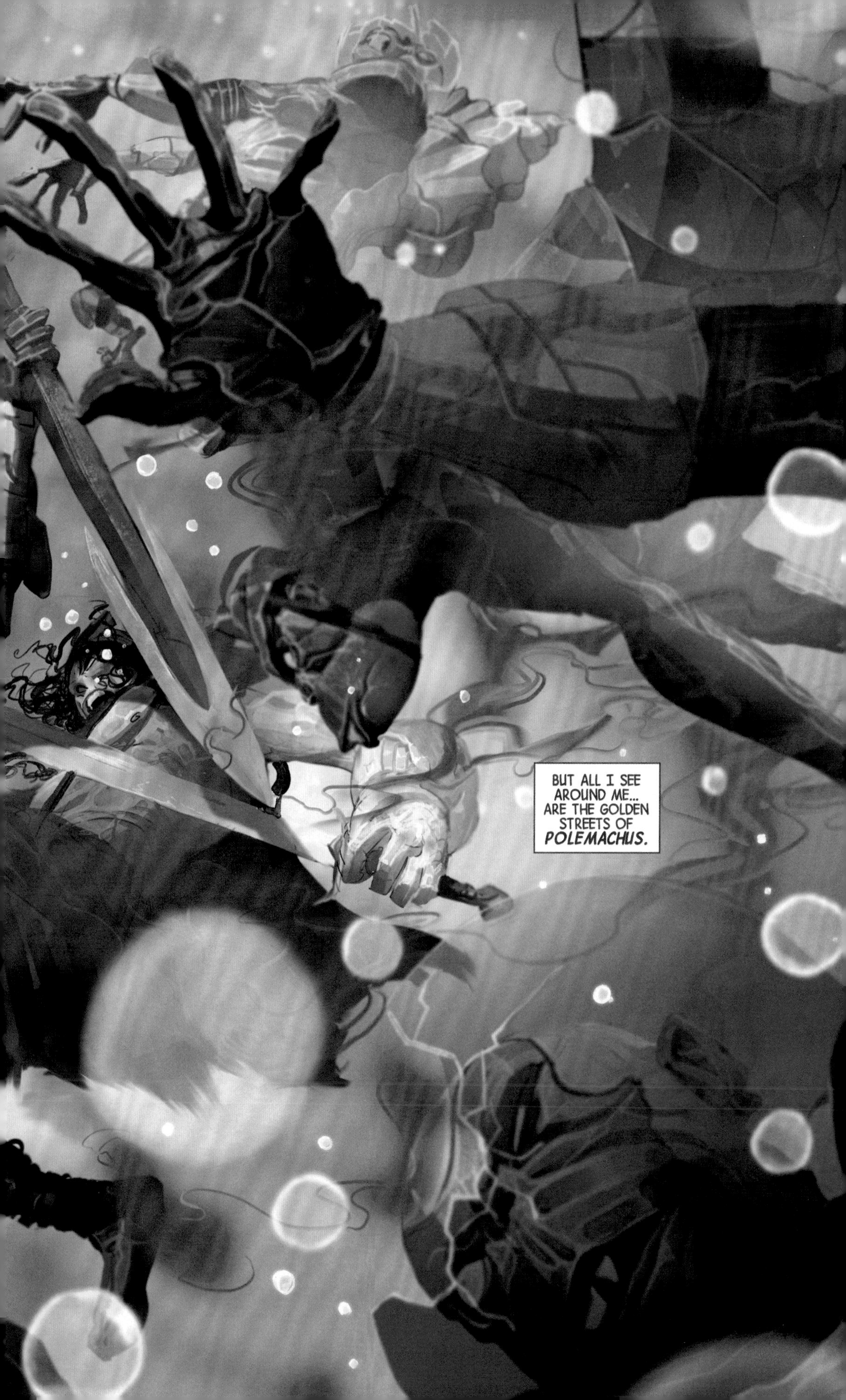
BUT ALL I SEE AROUND ME... ARE THE GOLDEN STREETS OF POLEMACHUS.

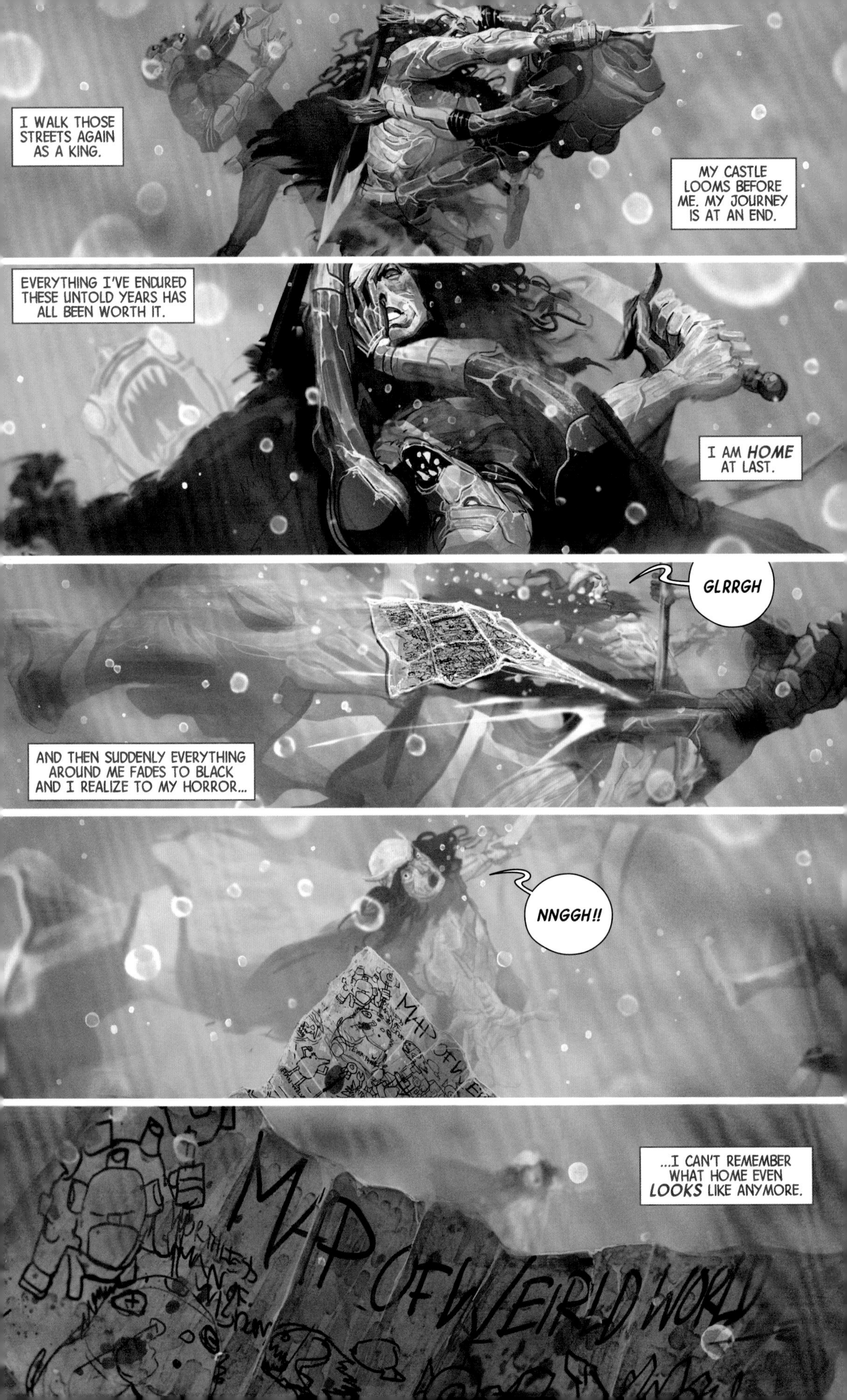
I WALK THOSE STREETS AGAIN AS A KING.
MY CASTLE LOOMS BEFORE ME. MY JOURNEY IS AT AN END.
EVERYTHING I'VE ENDURED THESE UNTOLD YEARS HAS ALL BEEN WORTH IT.
I AM *HOME* AT LAST.
GLRRGH
AND THEN SUDDENLY EVERYTHING AROUND ME FADES TO BLACK AND I REALIZE TO MY HORROR...
NNGGH!!
...I CAN'T REMEMBER WHAT HOME EVEN *LOOKS* LIKE ANYMORE.

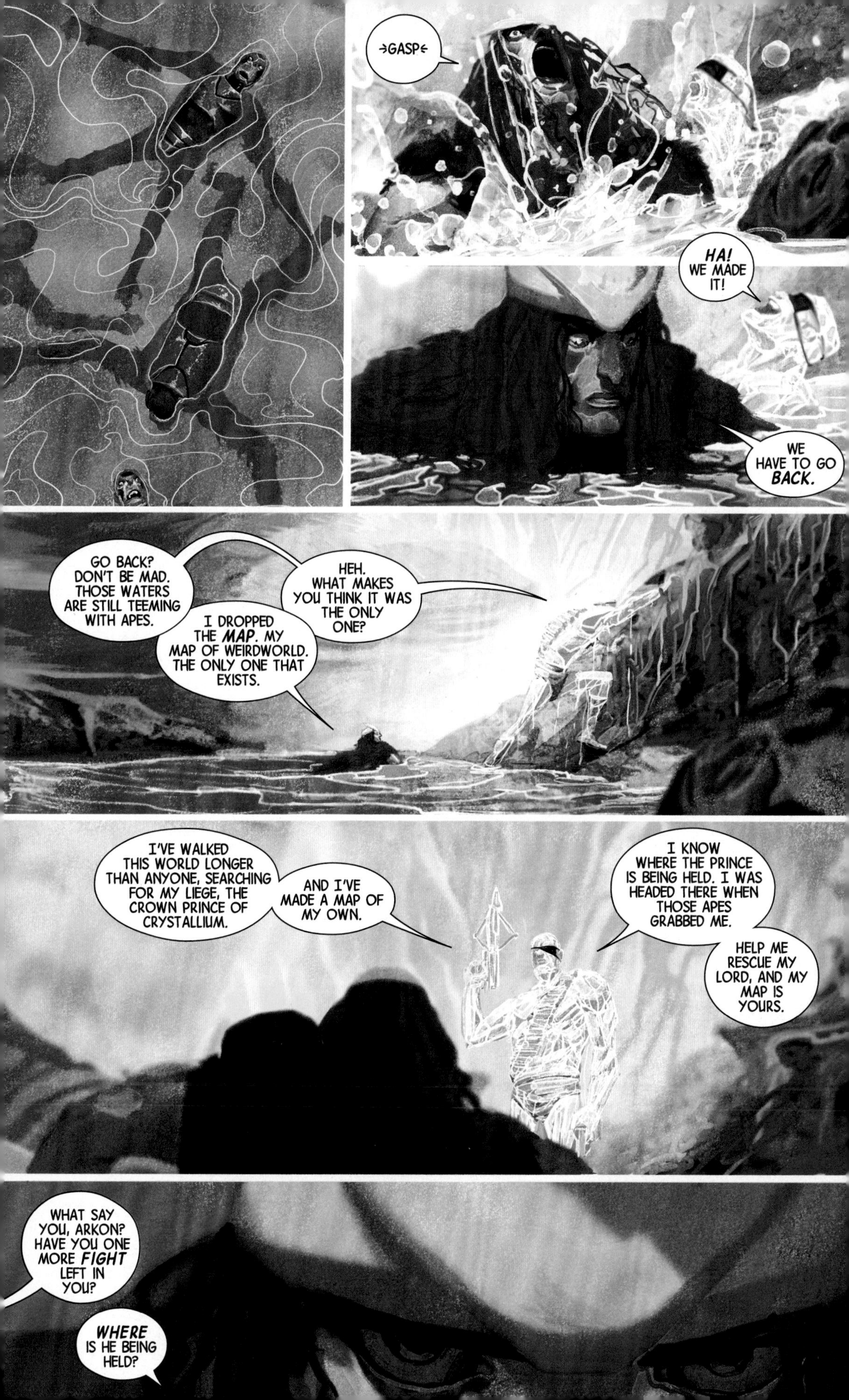

GASP
HA! WE MADE IT!
WE HAVE TO GO BACK.
GO BACK? DON'T BE MAD. THOSE WATERS ARE STILL TEEMING WITH APES.
I DROPPED THE MAP. MY MAP OF WEIRDWORLD. THE ONLY ONE THAT EXISTS.
HEH. WHAT MAKES YOU THINK IT WAS THE ONLY ONE?
I'VE WALKED THIS WORLD LONGER THAN ANYONE, SEARCHING FOR MY LIEGE, THE CROWN PRINCE OF CRYSTALLIUM.
AND I'VE MADE A MAP OF MY OWN.
I KNOW WHERE THE PRINCE IS BEING HELD. I WAS HEADED THERE WHEN THOSE APES GRABBED ME.
HELP ME RESCUE MY LORD, AND MY MAP IS YOURS.
WHAT SAY YOU, ARKON? HAVE YOU ONE MORE FIGHT LEFT IN YOU?
WHERE IS HE BEING HELD?

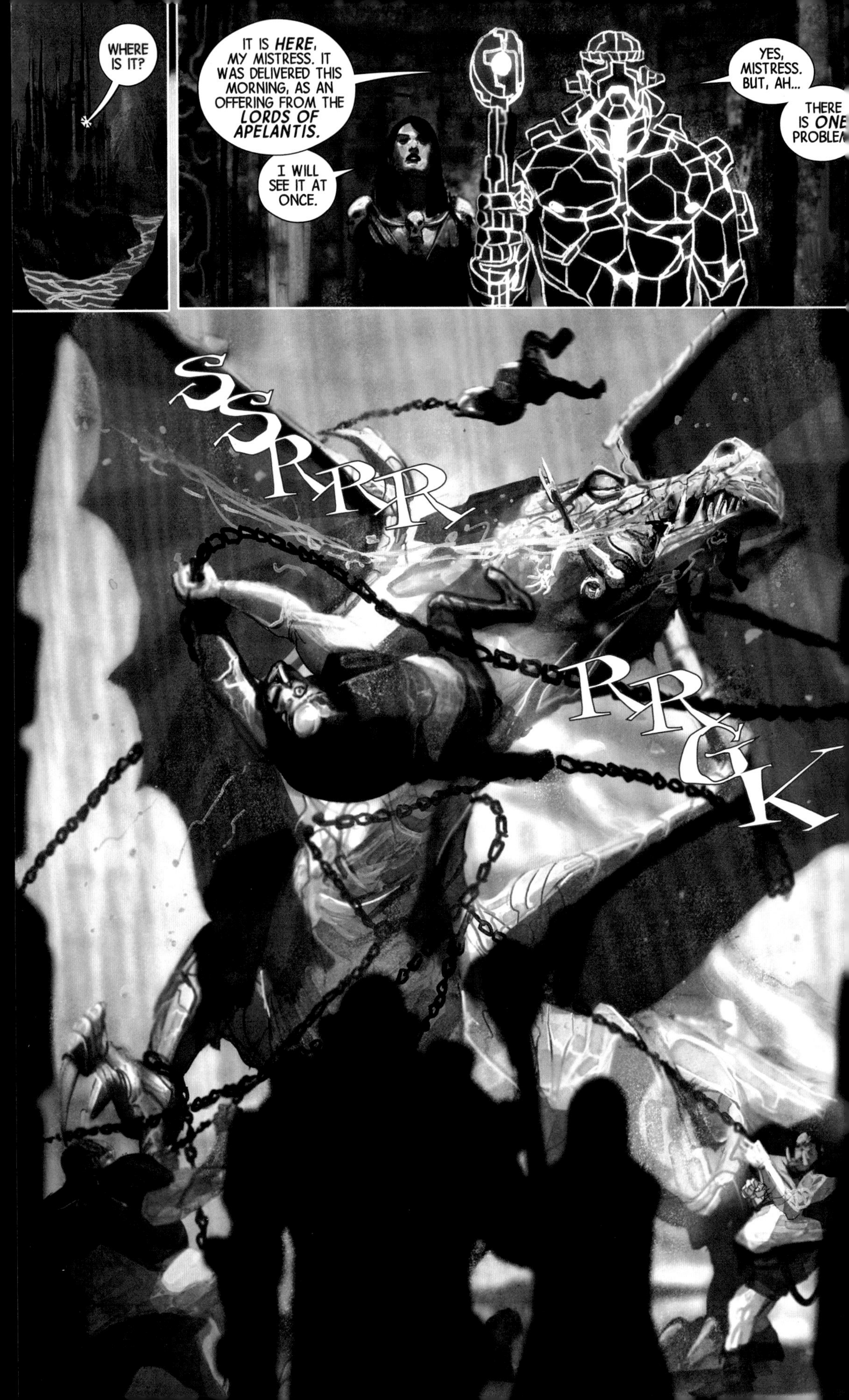
WHERE IS IT?
IT IS HERE, MY MISTRESS. IT WAS DELIVERED THIS MORNING, AS AN OFFERING FROM THE LORDS OF APELANTIS.
I WILL SEE IT AT ONCE.
YES, MISTRESS. BUT, AH...
THERE IS ONE PROBLEM
SSRRRR
RRRGK

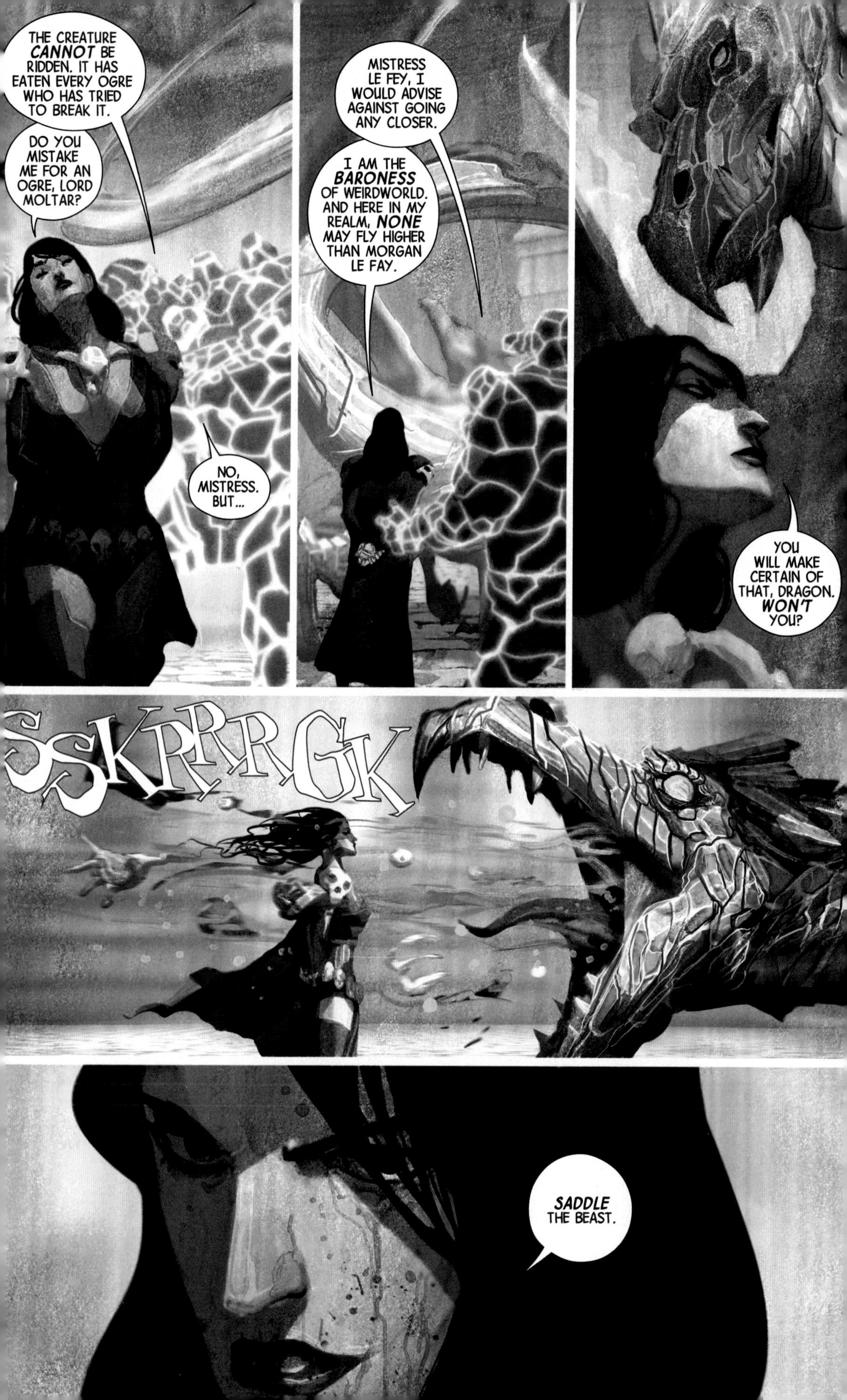
THE CREATURE CANNOT BE RIDDEN. IT HAS EATEN EVERY OGRE WHO HAS TRIED TO BREAK IT.
DO YOU MISTAKE ME FOR AN OGRE, LORD MOLTAR?
NO, MISTRESS. BUT...
MISTRESS LE FEY, I WOULD ADVISE AGAINST GOING ANY CLOSER.
I AM THE BARONESS OF WEIRDWORLD. AND HERE IN MY REALM, NONE MAY FLY HIGHER THAN MORGAN LE FAY.
YOU WILL MAKE CERTAIN OF THAT, DRAGON. WON'T YOU?
SSKRRRRGK
SADDLE THE BEAST.

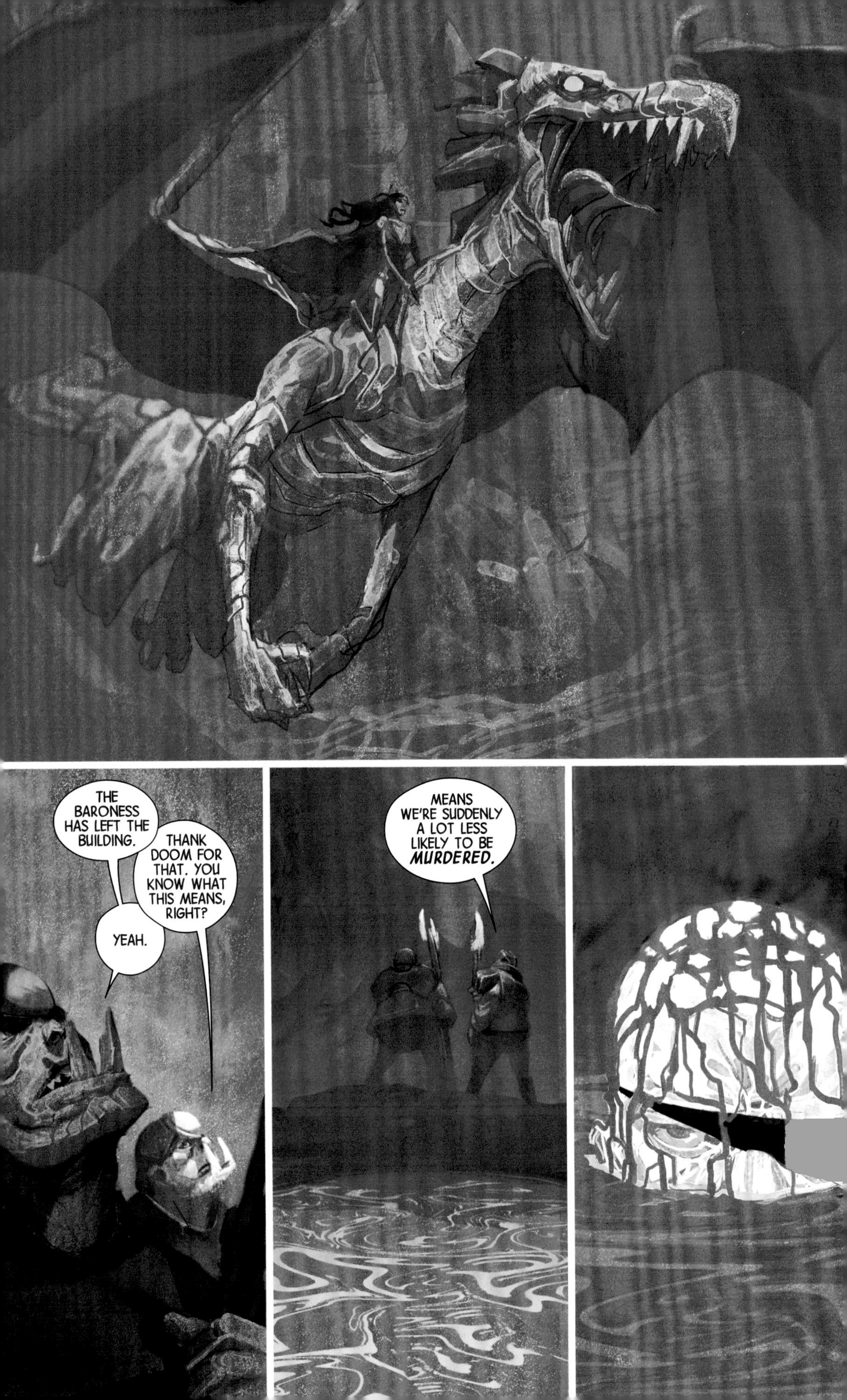
THE BARONESS HAS LEFT THE BUILDING.
THANK DOOM FOR THAT. YOU KNOW WHAT THIS MEANS, RIGHT?
YEAH.
MEANS WE'RE SUDDENLY A LOT LESS LIKELY TO BE *MURDERED.*

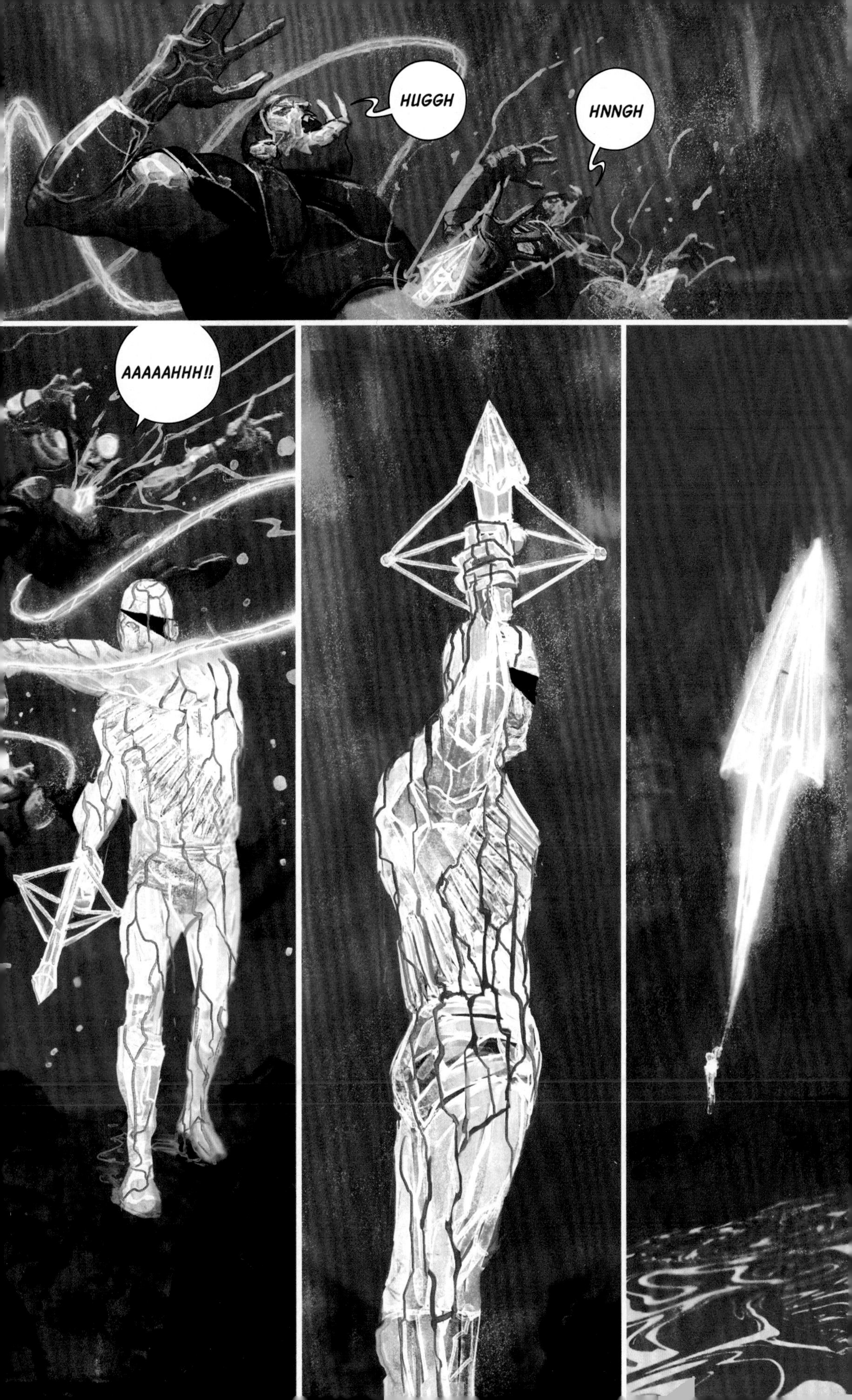
HUGGH
HNNGH
AAAAAHHH!!

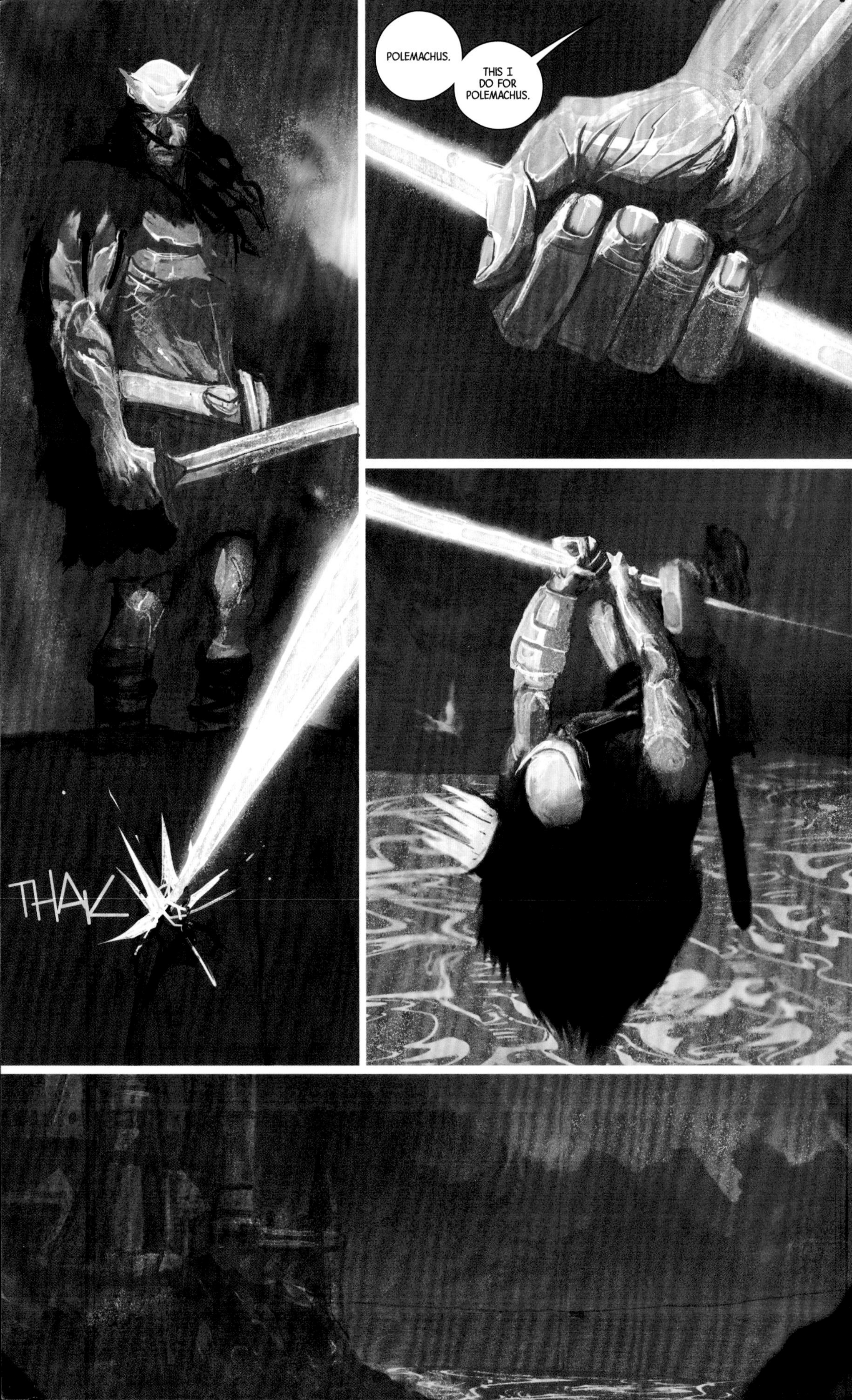
POLEMACHUS.
THIS I DO FOR POLEMACHUS.
THAK

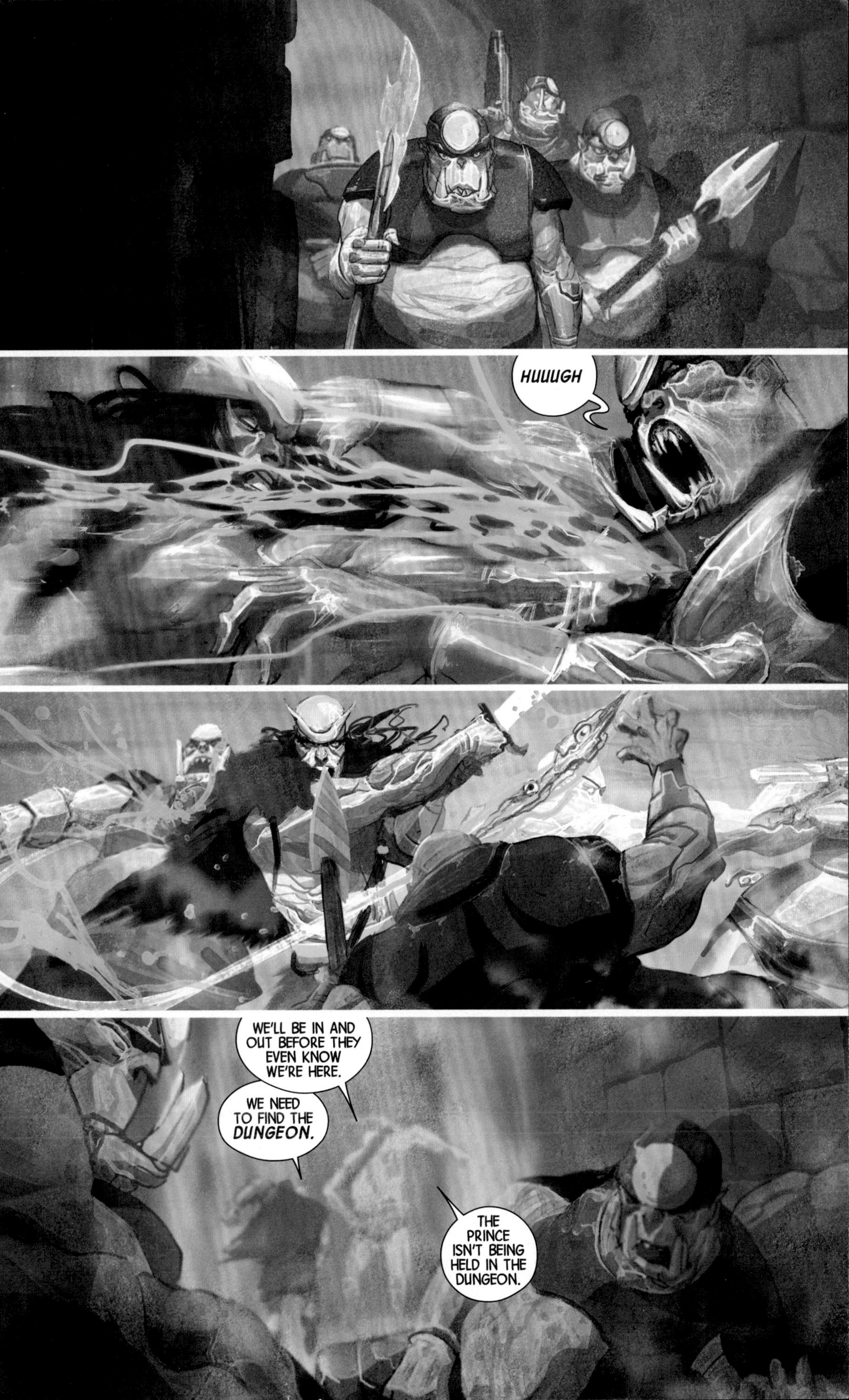
HUUUGH
WE'LL BE IN AND OUT BEFORE THEY EVEN KNOW WE'RE HERE.
WE NEED TO FIND THE DUNGEON.
THE PRINCE ISN'T BEING HELD IN THE DUNGEON.

THIS IS THE TREASURE VAULT.

I THOUGHT YOU SAID WE WERE HERE FOR A--

THERE HE IS!

AT LAST! WE ARE REUNITED, MY PRINCE.

THAT...IS THE FRIEND WE RISKED OUR LIVES TO SAVE? THAT LOOKS LIKE A BAG OF...

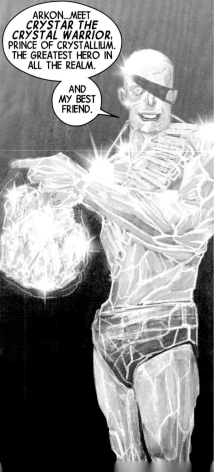

ARKON...MEET CRYSTAR THE CRYSTAL WARRIOR, PRINCE OF CRYSTALLIUM, THE GREATEST HERO IN ALL THE REALM.

AND MY BEST FRIEND.

OH, DOOM.

THIS IS WHY I HAVE TO FIND MY WAY HOME. QUICKLY.

THIS IS WHAT HAPPENS WHEN YOU'RE LOST IN WEIRDWORLD FOR FAR TOO LONG.

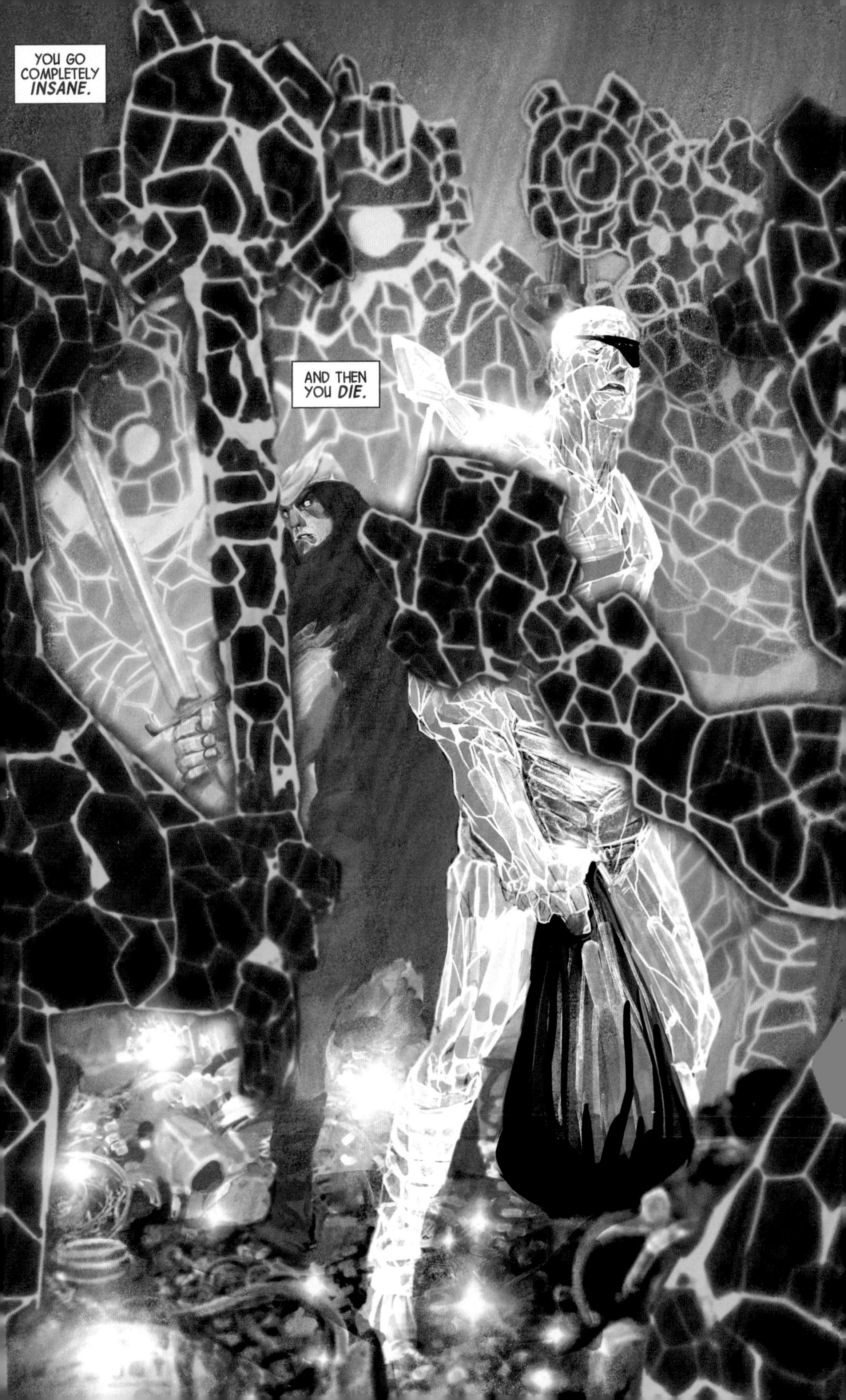
YOU GO COMPLETELY *INSANE.*
AND THEN YOU *DIE.*

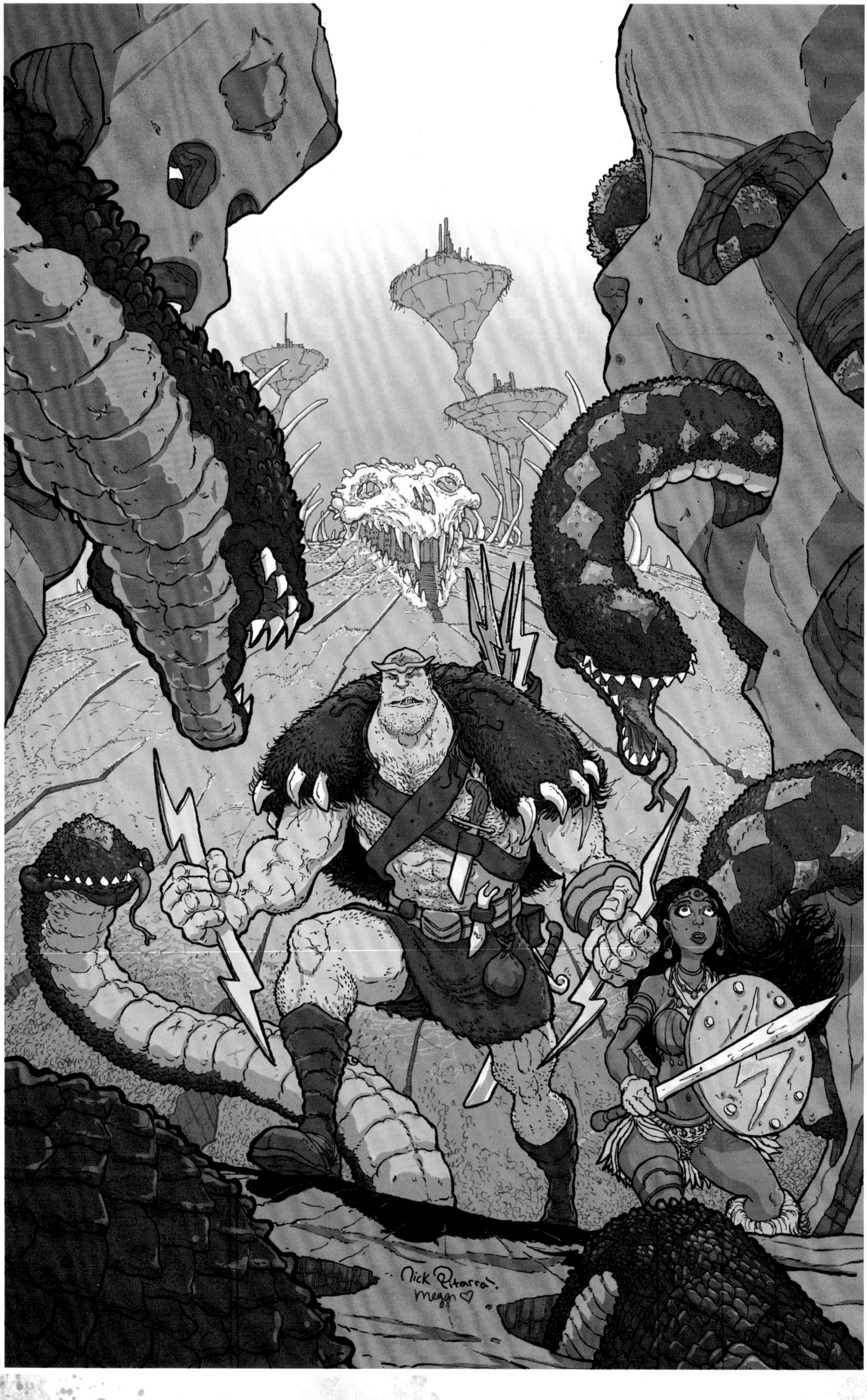
Nick Pitarra
megan

#2 VARIANT BY NICK PITARRA & MEGAN WILSON

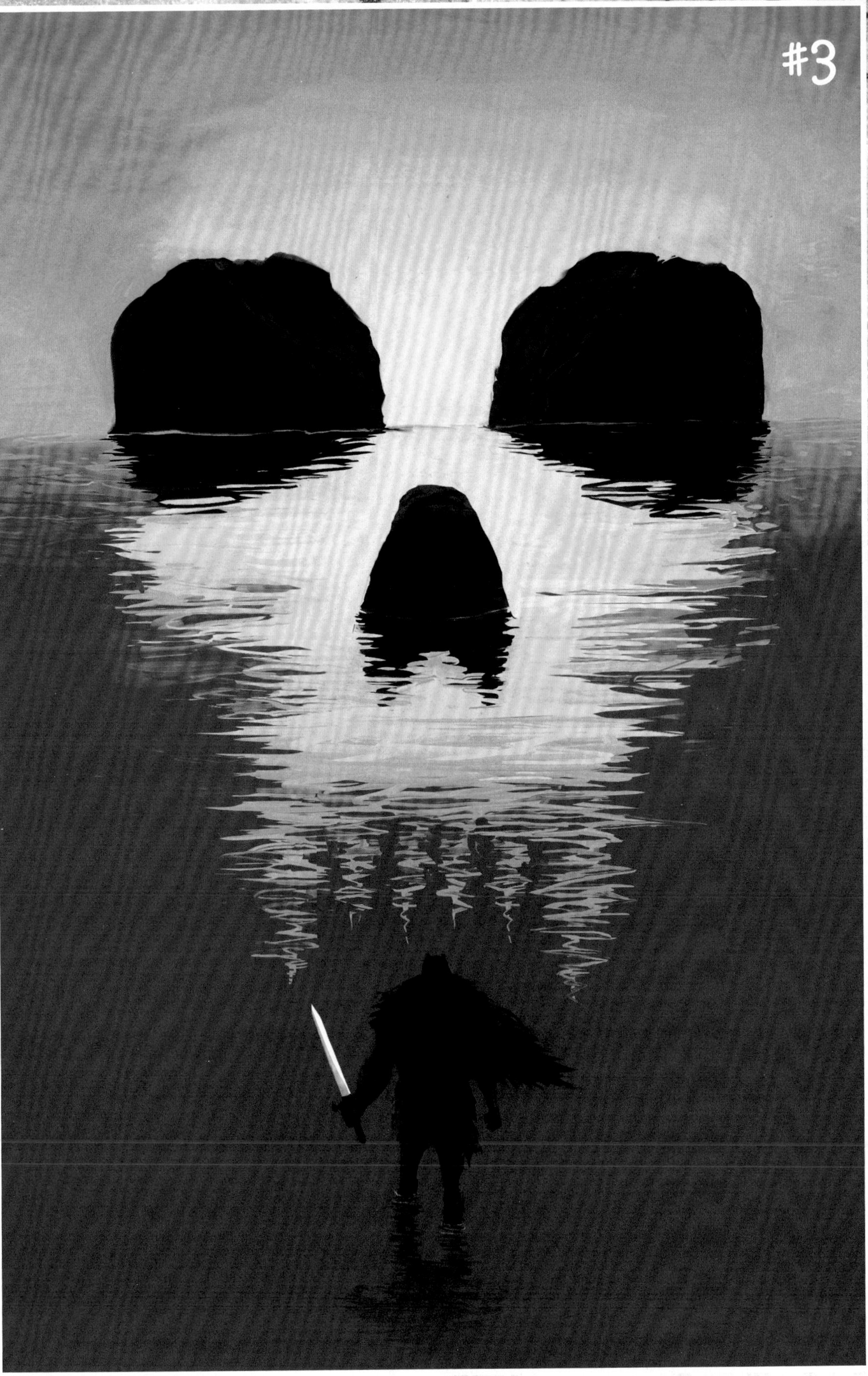
#3

• THE COMING OF THE SLAYER •

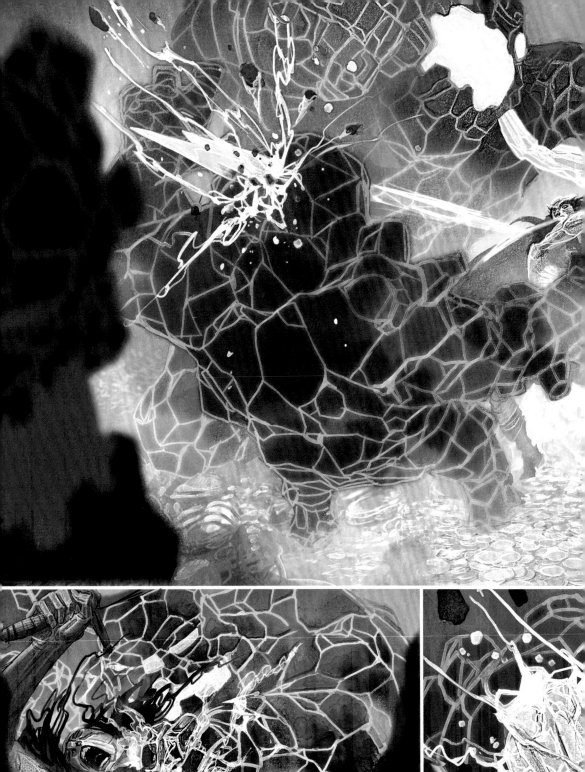

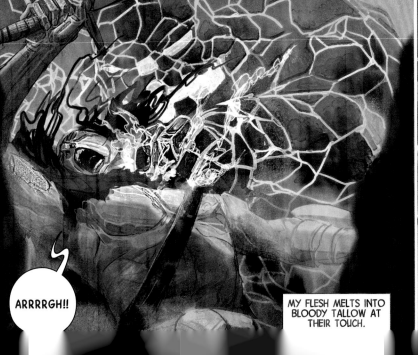

ARRRRGH!!

MY FLESH MELTS INTO
BLOODY TALLOW AT
THEIR TOUCH.

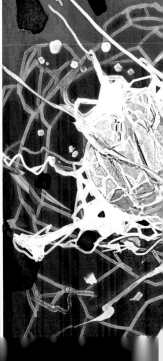

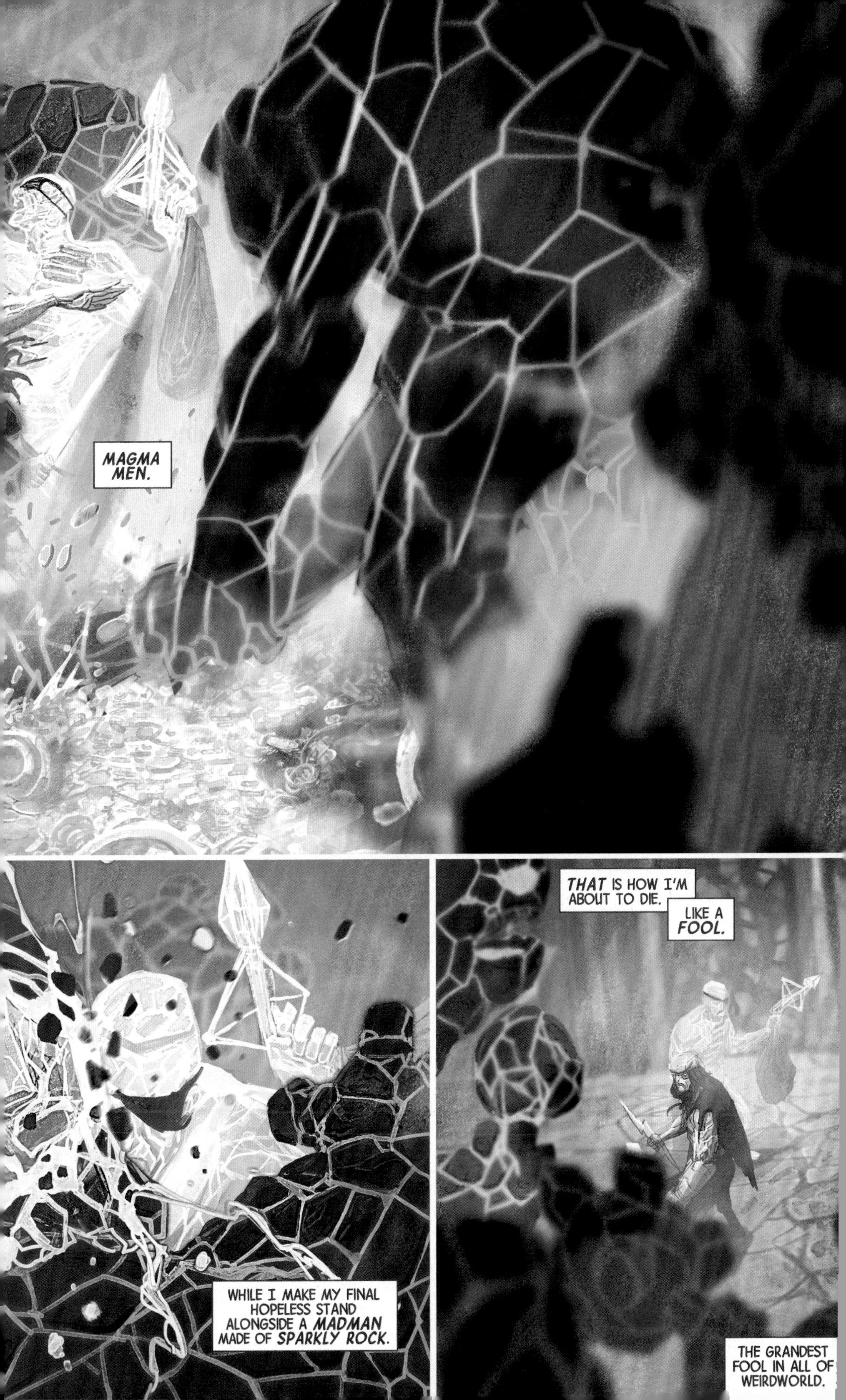
MAGMA MEN.
WHILE I MAKE MY FINAL HOPELESS STAND ALONGSIDE A MADMAN MADE OF SPARKLY ROCK.
THAT IS HOW I'M ABOUT TO DIE.
LIKE A FOOL.
THE GRANDEST FOOL IN ALL OF WEIRDWORLD.

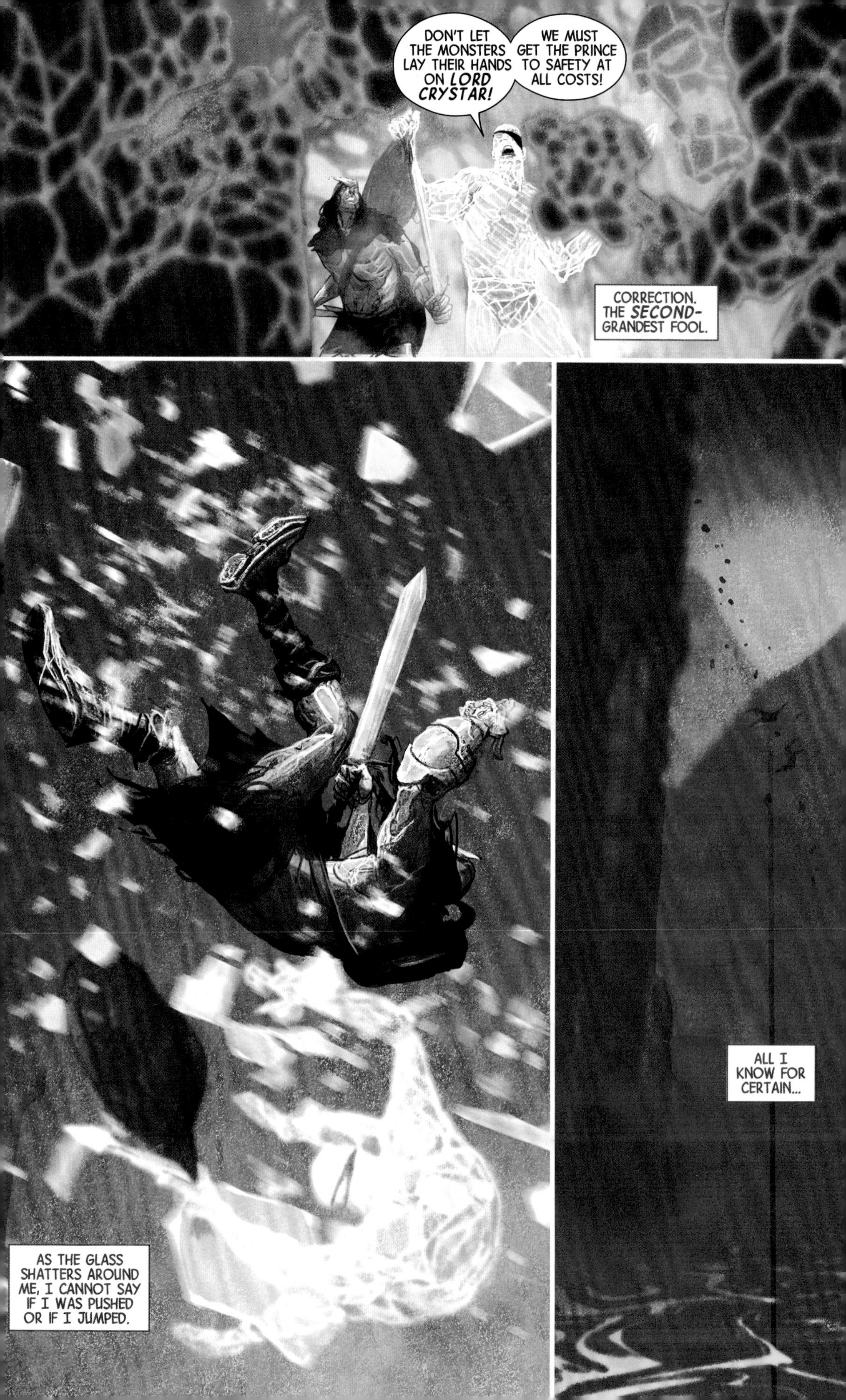
DON'T LET THE MONSTERS LAY THEIR HANDS ON LORD CRYSTAR!
WE MUST GET THE PRINCE TO SAFETY AT ALL COSTS!
CORRECTION. THE SECOND-GRANDEST FOOL.
AS THE GLASS SHATTERS AROUND ME, I CANNOT SAY IF I WAS PUSHED OR IF I JUMPED.
ALL I KNOW FOR CERTAIN...

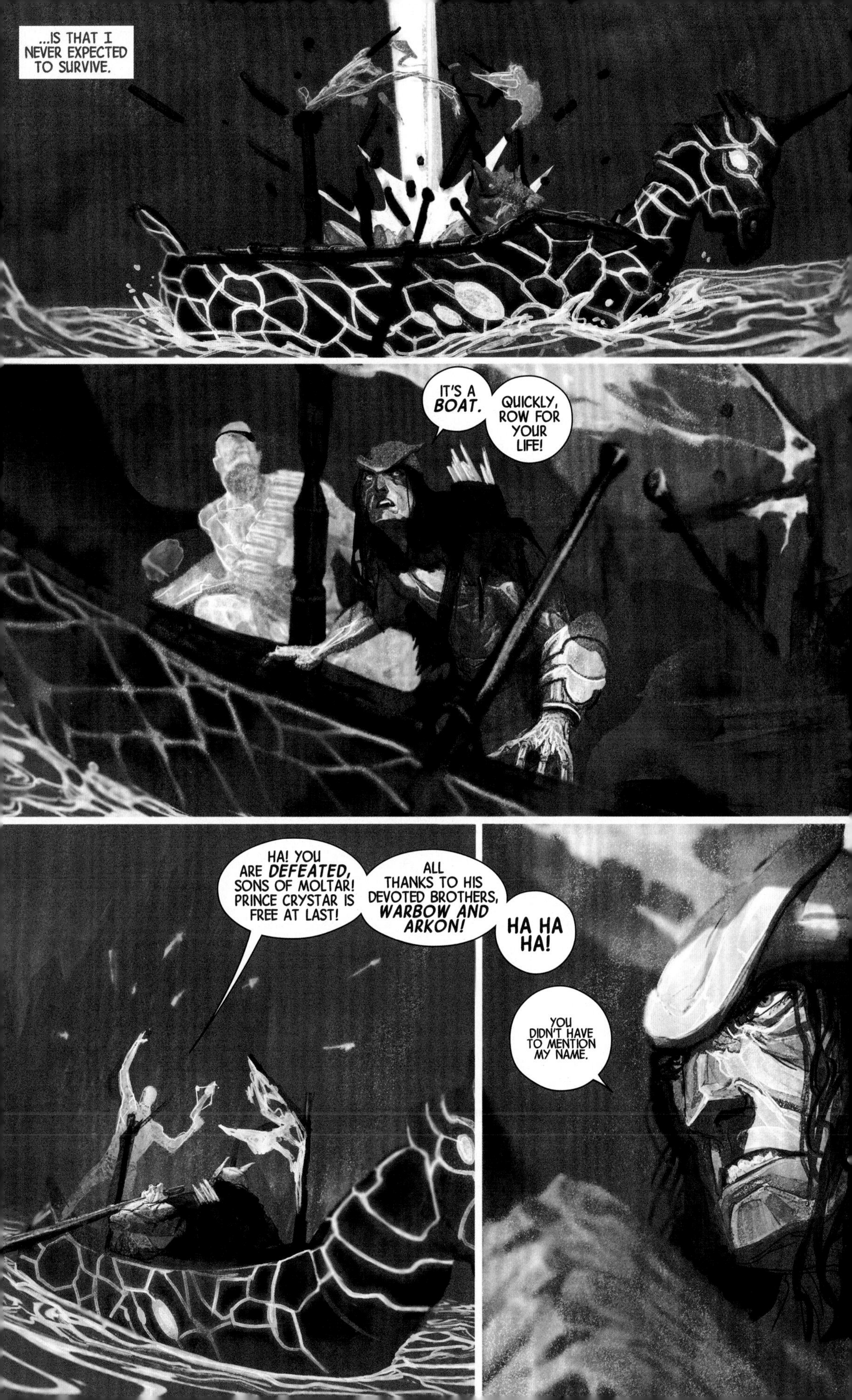
...IS THAT I NEVER EXPECTED TO SURVIVE.
IT'S A BOAT.
QUICKLY, ROW FOR YOUR LIFE!
HA! YOU ARE DEFEATED, SONS OF MOLTAR! PRINCE CRYSTAR IS FREE AT LAST!
ALL THANKS TO HIS DEVOTED BROTHERS, WARBOW AND ARKON!
HA HA HA!
YOU DIDN'T HAVE TO MENTION MY NAME.

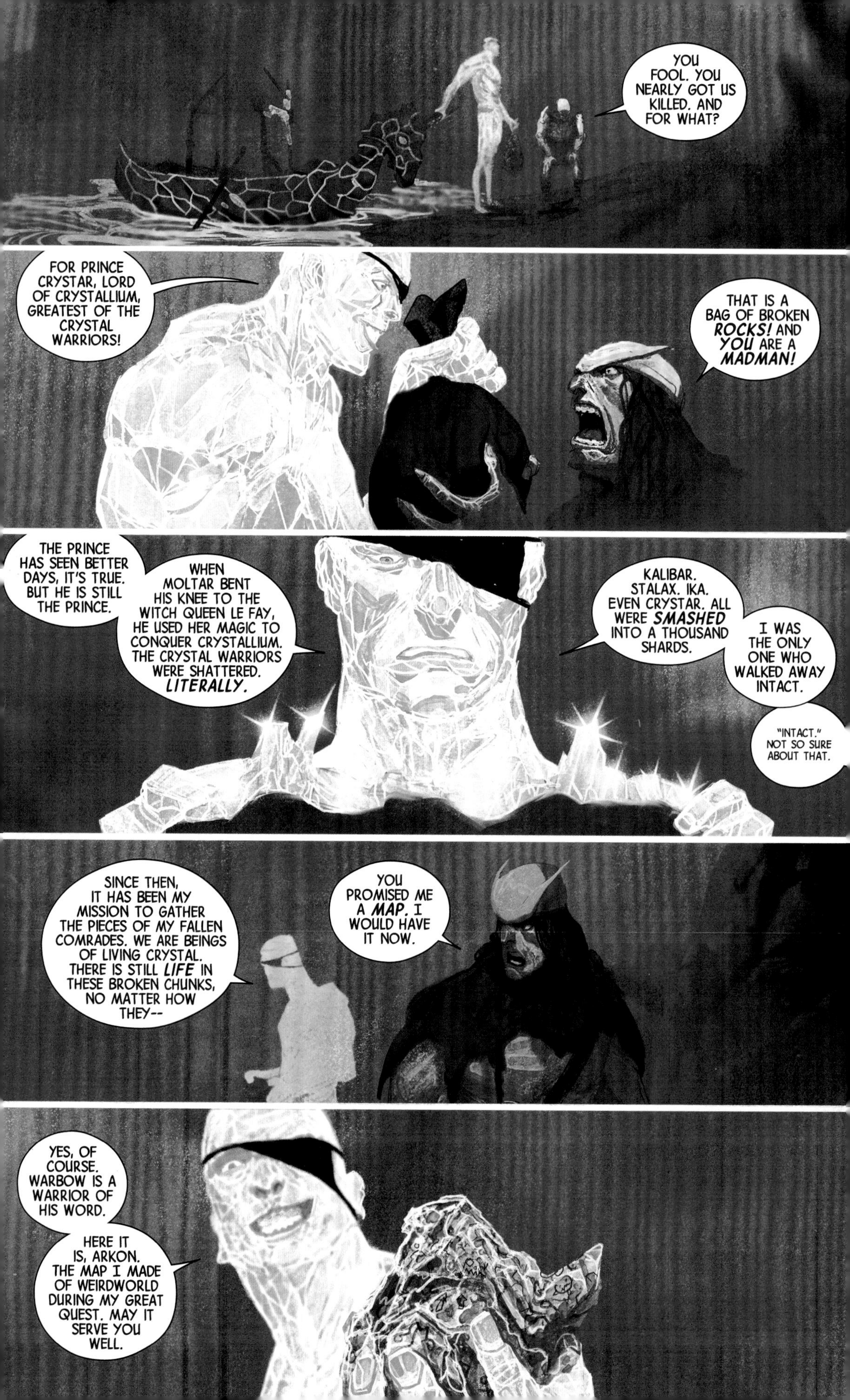
YOU FOOL. YOU NEARLY GOT US KILLED. AND FOR WHAT?
FOR PRINCE CRYSTAR, LORD OF CRYSTALLIUM, GREATEST OF THE CRYSTAL WARRIORS!
THAT IS A BAG OF BROKEN ROCKS! AND YOU ARE A MADMAN!
THE PRINCE HAS SEEN BETTER DAYS, IT'S TRUE. BUT HE IS STILL THE PRINCE.
WHEN MOLTAR BENT HIS KNEE TO THE WITCH QUEEN LE FAY, HE USED HER MAGIC TO CONQUER CRYSTALLIUM. THE CRYSTAL WARRIORS WERE SHATTERED. LITERALLY.
KALIBAR. STALAX. IKA. EVEN CRYSTAR. ALL WERE SMASHED INTO A THOUSAND SHARDS.
I WAS THE ONLY ONE WHO WALKED AWAY INTACT.
"INTACT." NOT SO SURE ABOUT THAT.
SINCE THEN, IT HAS BEEN MY MISSION TO GATHER THE PIECES OF MY FALLEN COMRADES. WE ARE BEINGS OF LIVING CRYSTAL. THERE IS STILL LIFE IN THESE BROKEN CHUNKS, NO MATTER HOW THEY--
YOU PROMISED ME A MAP. I WOULD HAVE IT NOW.
YES, OF COURSE. WARBOW IS A WARRIOR OF HIS WORD.
HERE IT IS, ARKON. THE MAP I MADE OF WEIRDWORLD DURING MY GREAT QUEST. MAY IT SERVE YOU WELL.

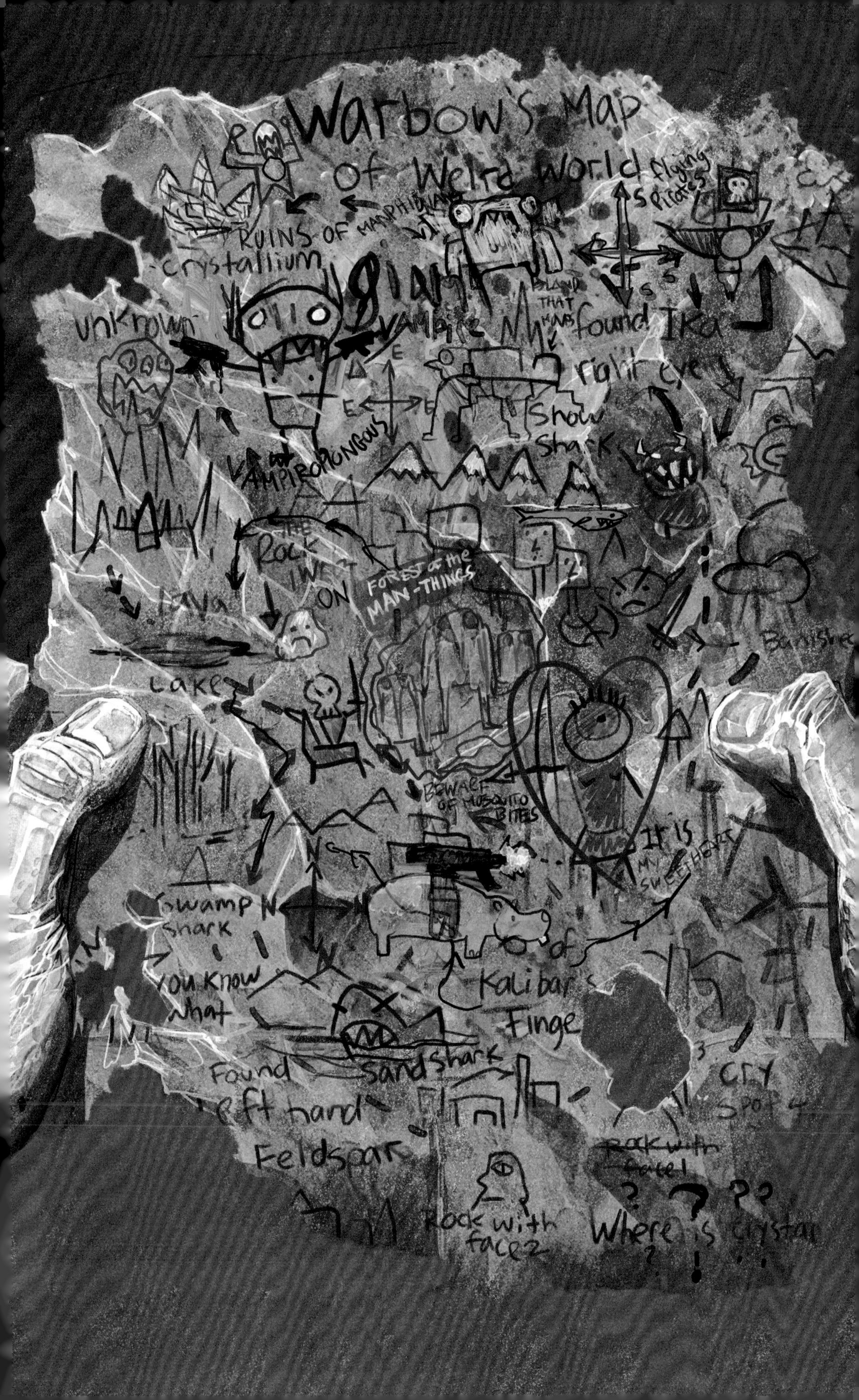
Warbow's Map
of Weird World
flying pirates
crystallium
giant
vampire
found Ika
right eye
unknown
Snow Shark
THE ROCK I WEPT ON
lava
FOREST OF THE MAN-THINGS
Lake
Banshee
BEWARE OF MOSQUITO BITES
It is my sweetheart
swamp shark
of Kalibar's
Finge
You know what
Sand shark
Found left hand
Feldspar
cry spot
Rock with face 1
Rock with face 2
Where is crystal

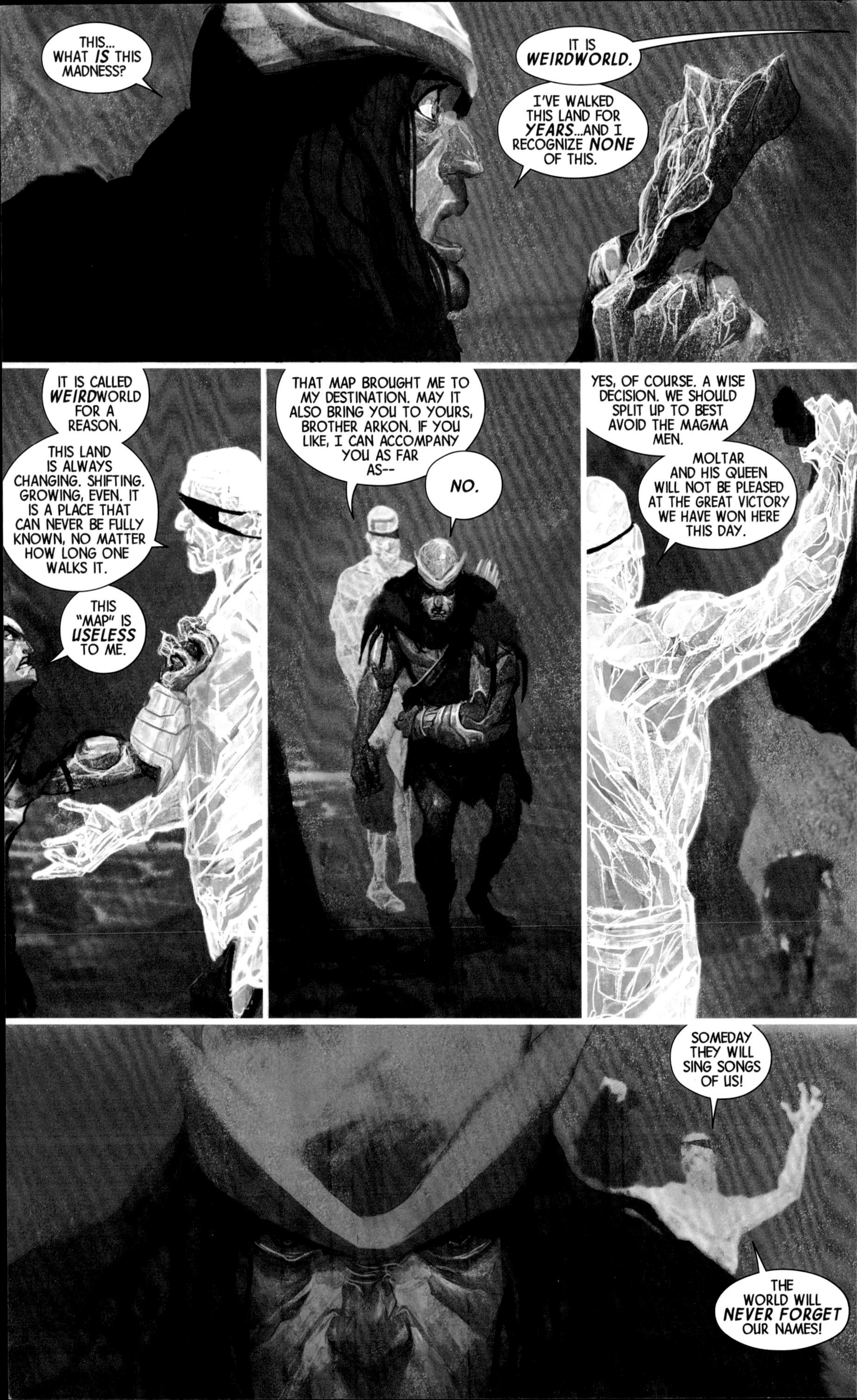
THIS... WHAT IS THIS MADNESS?
IT IS WEIRDWORLD.
I'VE WALKED THIS LAND FOR YEARS...AND I RECOGNIZE NONE OF THIS.
IT IS CALLED WEIRDWORLD FOR A REASON.
THIS LAND IS ALWAYS CHANGING. SHIFTING. GROWING, EVEN. IT IS A PLACE THAT CAN NEVER BE FULLY KNOWN, NO MATTER HOW LONG ONE WALKS IT.
THIS "MAP" IS USELESS TO ME.
THAT MAP BROUGHT ME TO MY DESTINATION. MAY IT ALSO BRING YOU TO YOURS, BROTHER ARKON. IF YOU LIKE, I CAN ACCOMPANY YOU AS FAR AS--
NO.
YES, OF COURSE. A WISE DECISION. WE SHOULD SPLIT UP TO BEST AVOID THE MAGMA MEN.
MOLTAR AND HIS QUEEN WILL NOT BE PLEASED AT THE GREAT VICTORY WE HAVE WON HERE THIS DAY.
SOMEDAY THEY WILL SING SONGS OF US!
THE WORLD WILL NEVER FORGET OUR NAMES!

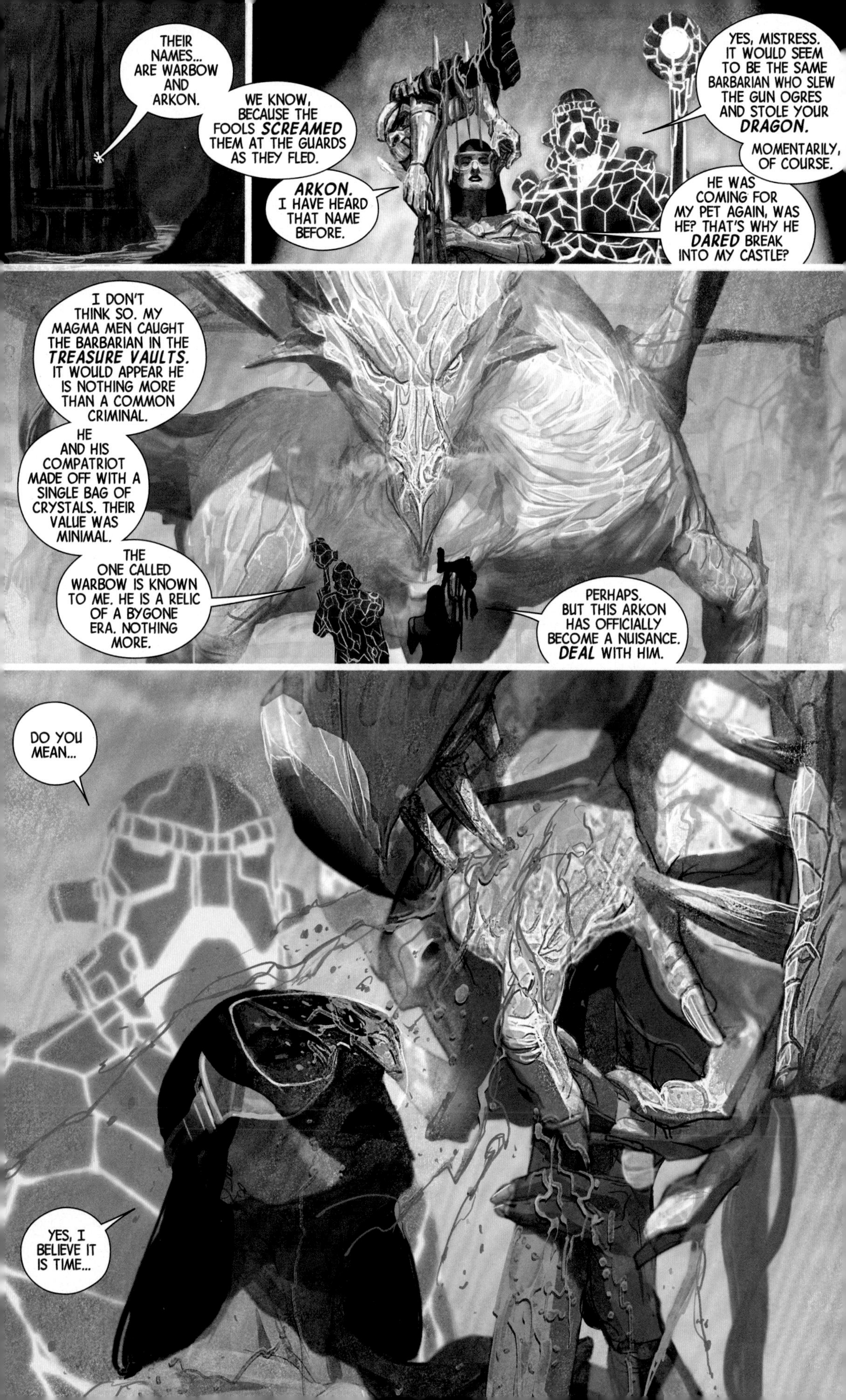
THEIR NAMES... ARE WARBOW AND ARKON.
WE KNOW, BECAUSE THE FOOLS SCREAMED THEM AT THE GUARDS AS THEY FLED.
ARKON. I HAVE HEARD THAT NAME BEFORE.
YES, MISTRESS. IT WOULD SEEM TO BE THE SAME BARBARIAN WHO SLEW THE GUN OGRES AND STOLE YOUR DRAGON.
MOMENTARILY, OF COURSE.
HE WAS COMING FOR MY PET AGAIN, WAS HE? THAT'S WHY HE DARED BREAK INTO MY CASTLE?
I DON'T THINK SO. MY MAGMA MEN CAUGHT THE BARBARIAN IN THE TREASURE VAULTS. IT WOULD APPEAR HE IS NOTHING MORE THAN A COMMON CRIMINAL.
HE AND HIS COMPATRIOT MADE OFF WITH A SINGLE BAG OF CRYSTALS. THEIR VALUE WAS MINIMAL.
THE ONE CALLED WARBOW IS KNOWN TO ME. HE IS A RELIC OF A BYGONE ERA. NOTHING MORE.
PERHAPS. BUT THIS ARKON HAS OFFICIALLY BECOME A NUISANCE. DEAL WITH HIM.
DO YOU MEAN...
YES, I BELIEVE IT IS TIME...

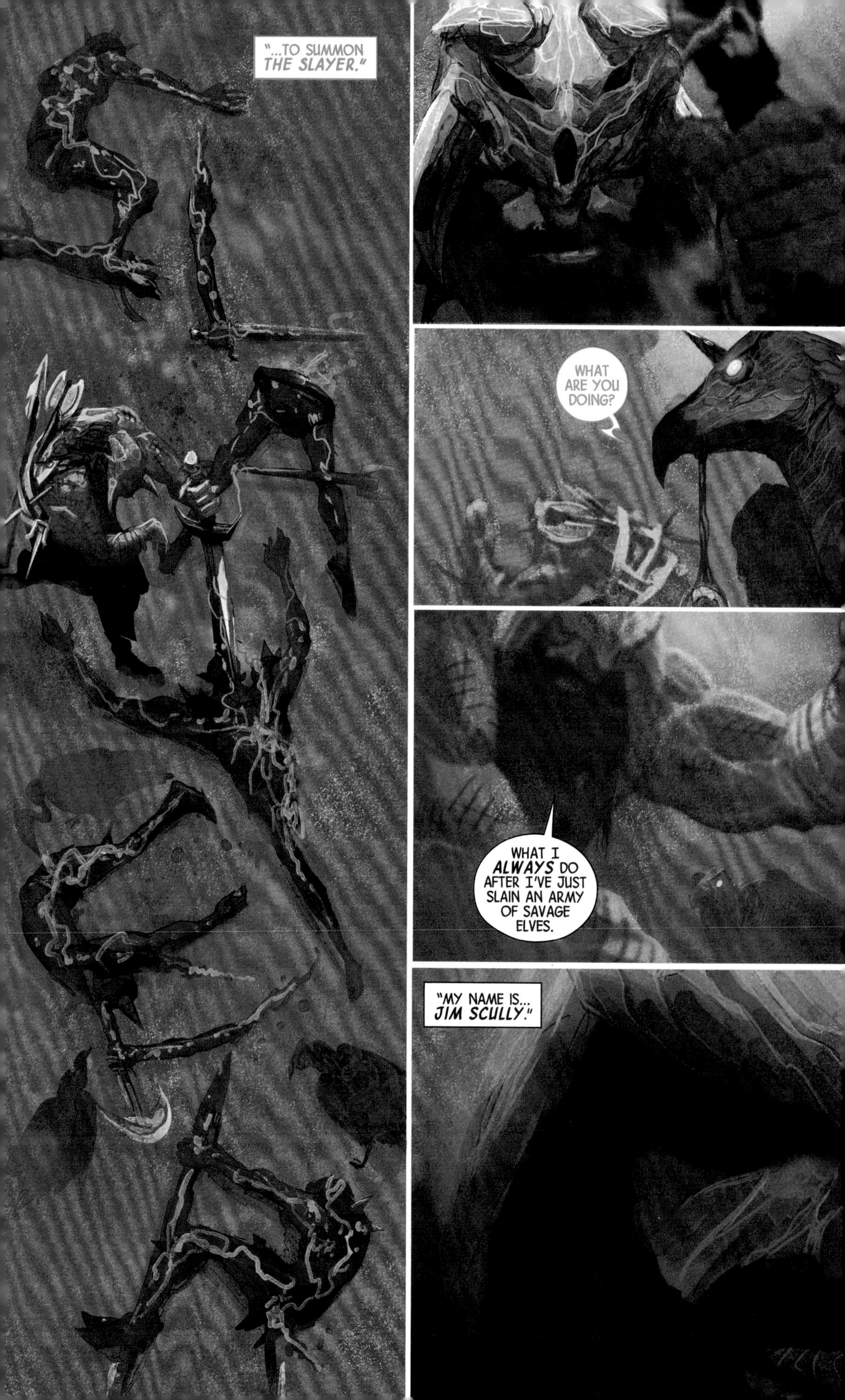
"...TO SUMMON THE SLAYER."
WHAT ARE YOU DOING?
WHAT I ALWAYS DO AFTER I'VE JUST SLAIN AN ARMY OF SAVAGE ELVES.
"MY NAME IS... JIM SCULLY."

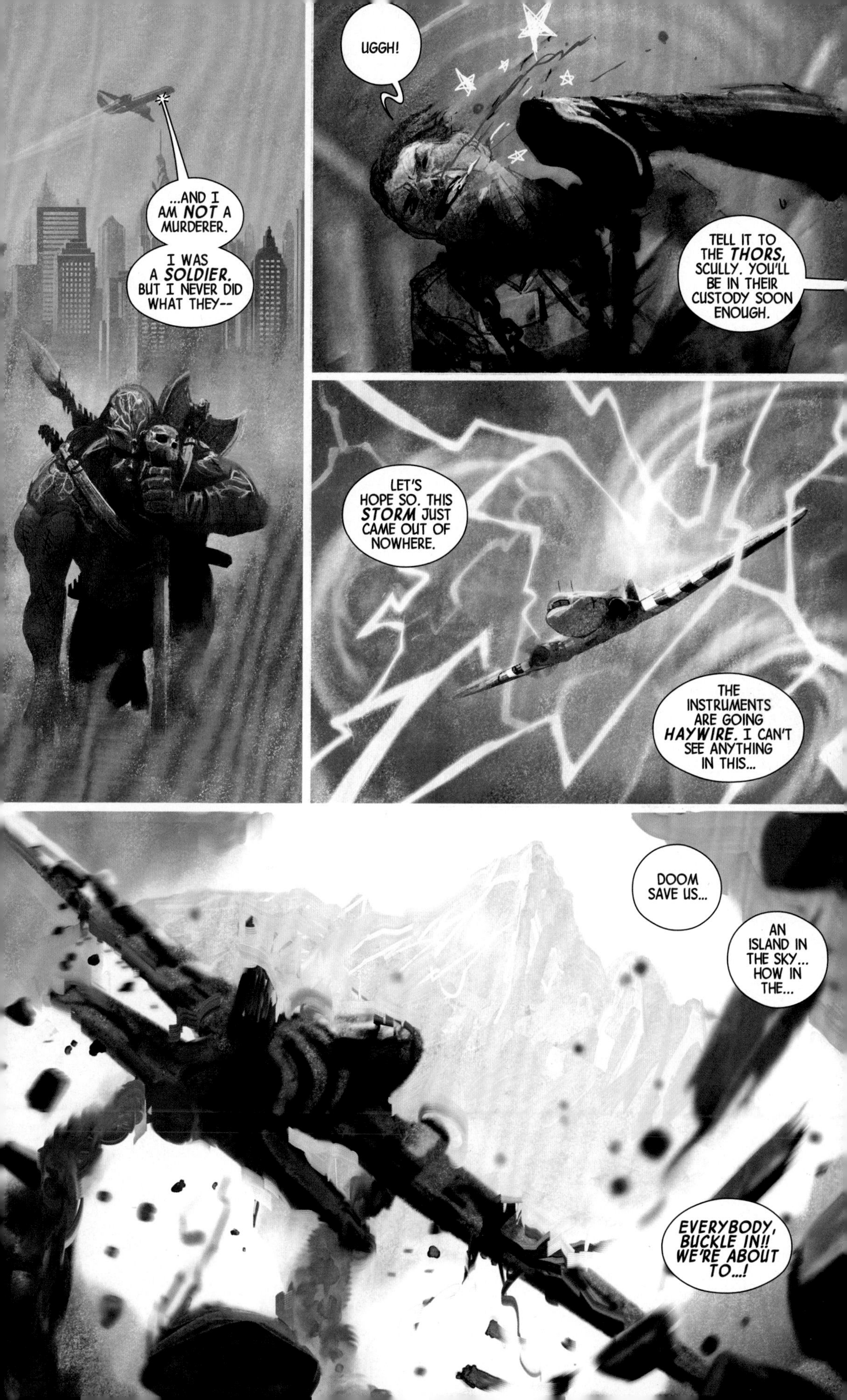
...AND I AM NOT A MURDERER.
I WAS A SOLDIER. BUT I NEVER DID WHAT THEY--
UGGH!
TELL IT TO THE THORS, SCULLY. YOU'LL BE IN THEIR CUSTODY SOON ENOUGH.
LET'S HOPE SO. THIS STORM JUST CAME OUT OF NOWHERE.
THE INSTRUMENTS ARE GOING HAYWIRE. I CAN'T SEE ANYTHING IN THIS...
DOOM SAVE US...
AN ISLAND IN THE SKY... HOW IN THE...
EVERYBODY, BUCKLE IN!! WE'RE ABOUT TO...!

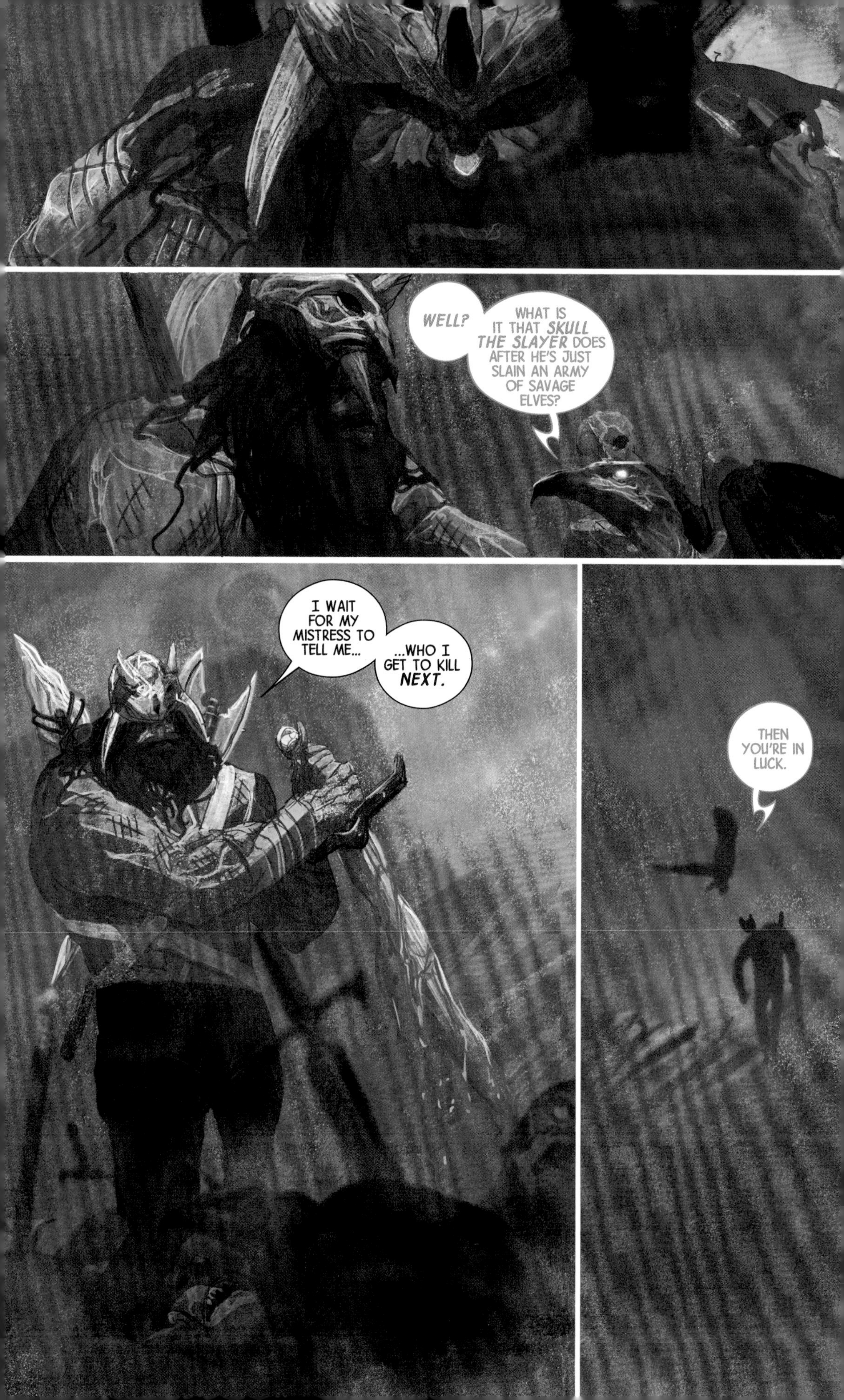
WELL?
WHAT IS IT THAT SKULL THE SLAYER DOES AFTER HE'S JUST SLAIN AN ARMY OF SAVAGE ELVES?
I WAIT FOR MY MISTRESS TO TELL ME...
...WHO I GET TO KILL NEXT.
THEN YOU'RE IN LUCK.

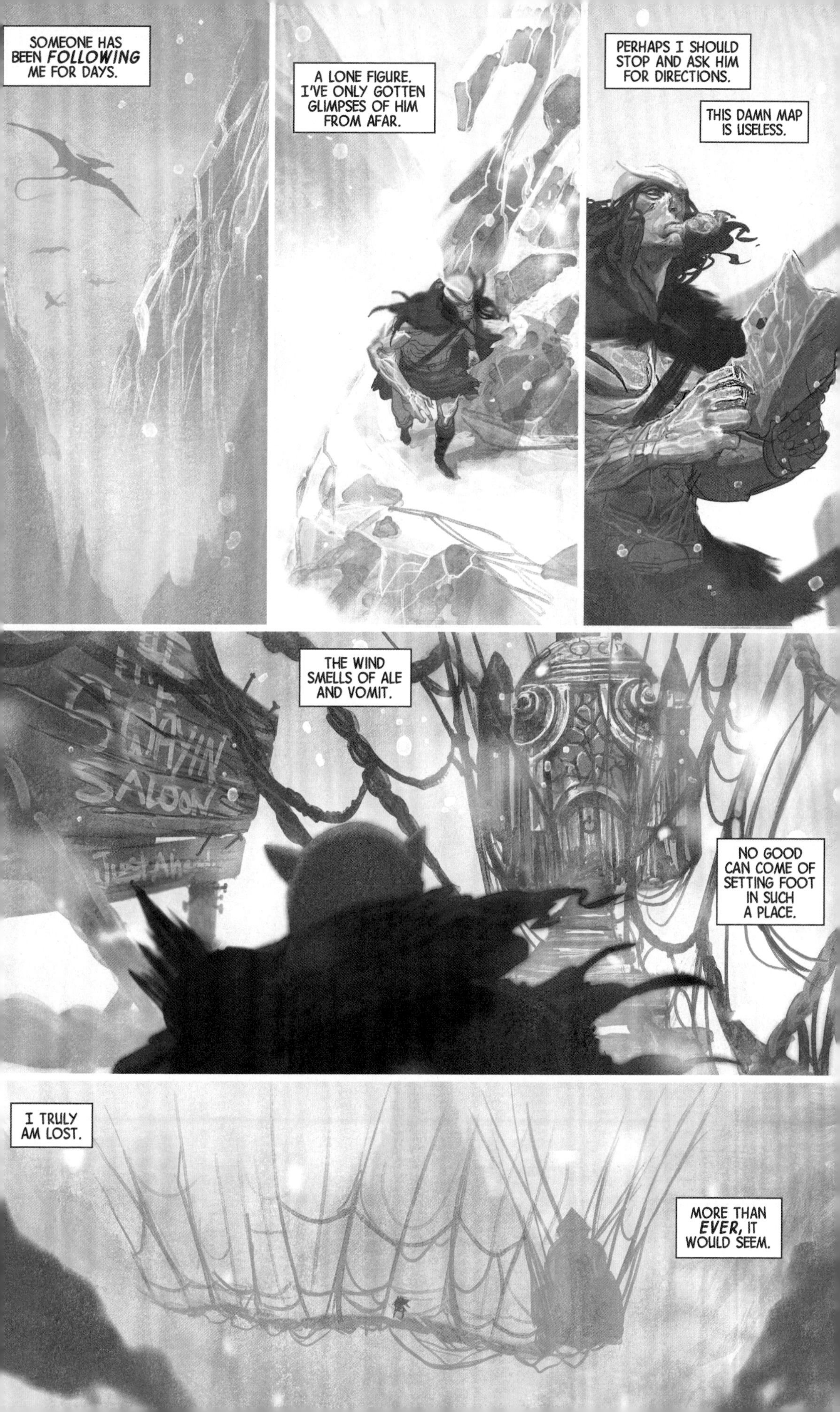
SOMEONE HAS BEEN *FOLLOWING* ME FOR DAYS.
A LONE FIGURE. I'VE ONLY GOTTEN GLIMPSES OF HIM FROM AFAR.
PERHAPS I SHOULD STOP AND ASK HIM FOR DIRECTIONS.
THIS DAMN MAP IS USELESS.
THE WIND SMELLS OF ALE AND VOMIT.
SALOON
NO GOOD CAN COME OF SETTING FOOT IN SUCH A PLACE.
I TRULY AM LOST.
MORE THAN *EVER,* IT WOULD SEEM.

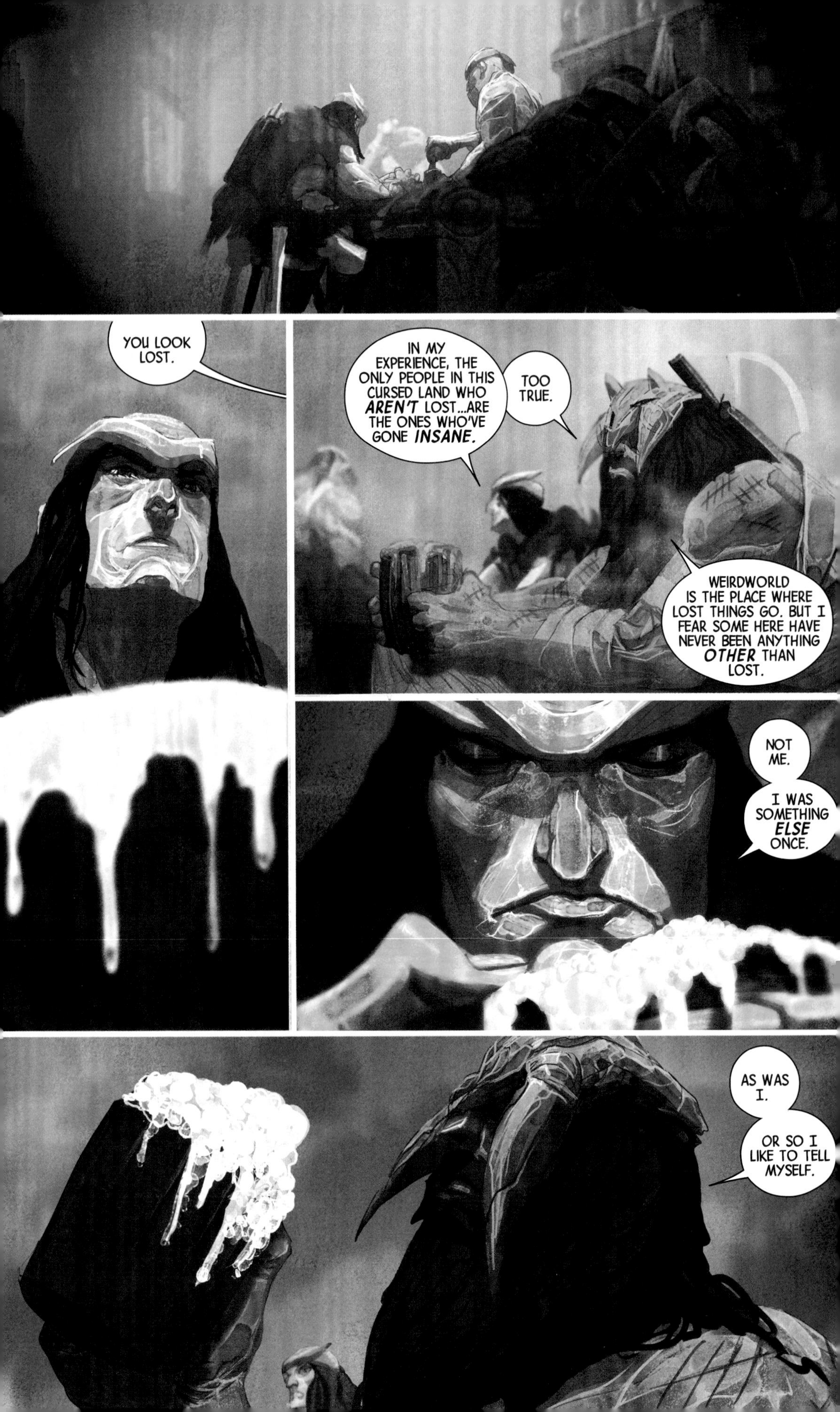
YOU LOOK LOST.
IN MY EXPERIENCE, THE ONLY PEOPLE IN THIS CURSED LAND WHO AREN'T LOST...ARE THE ONES WHO'VE GONE INSANE.
TOO TRUE.
WEIRDWORLD IS THE PLACE WHERE LOST THINGS GO. BUT I FEAR SOME HERE HAVE NEVER BEEN ANYTHING OTHER THAN LOST.
NOT ME.
I WAS SOMETHING ELSE ONCE.
AS WAS I.
OR SO I LIKE TO TELL MYSELF.

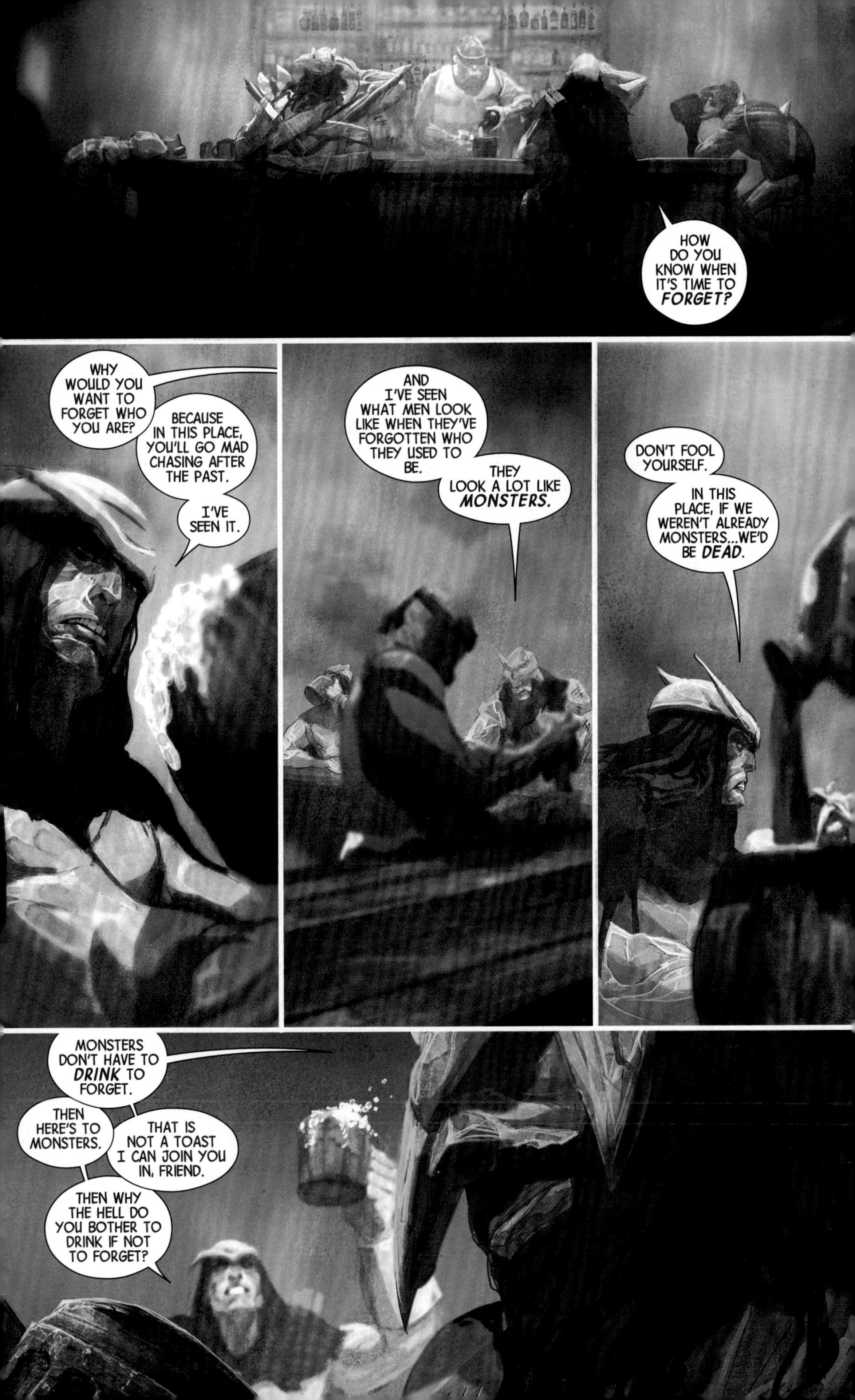
HOW DO YOU KNOW WHEN IT'S TIME TO *FORGET?*
WHY WOULD YOU WANT TO FORGET WHO YOU ARE?
BECAUSE IN THIS PLACE, YOU'LL GO MAD CHASING AFTER THE PAST.
I'VE SEEN IT.
AND I'VE SEEN WHAT MEN LOOK LIKE WHEN THEY'VE FORGOTTEN WHO THEY USED TO BE.
THEY LOOK A LOT LIKE *MONSTERS.*
DON'T FOOL YOURSELF.
IN THIS PLACE, IF WE WEREN'T ALREADY MONSTERS...WE'D BE *DEAD.*
MONSTERS DON'T HAVE TO *DRINK* TO FORGET.
THEN HERE'S TO MONSTERS.
THAT IS NOT A TOAST I CAN JOIN YOU IN, FRIEND.
THEN WHY THE HELL DO YOU BOTHER TO DRINK IF NOT TO FORGET?

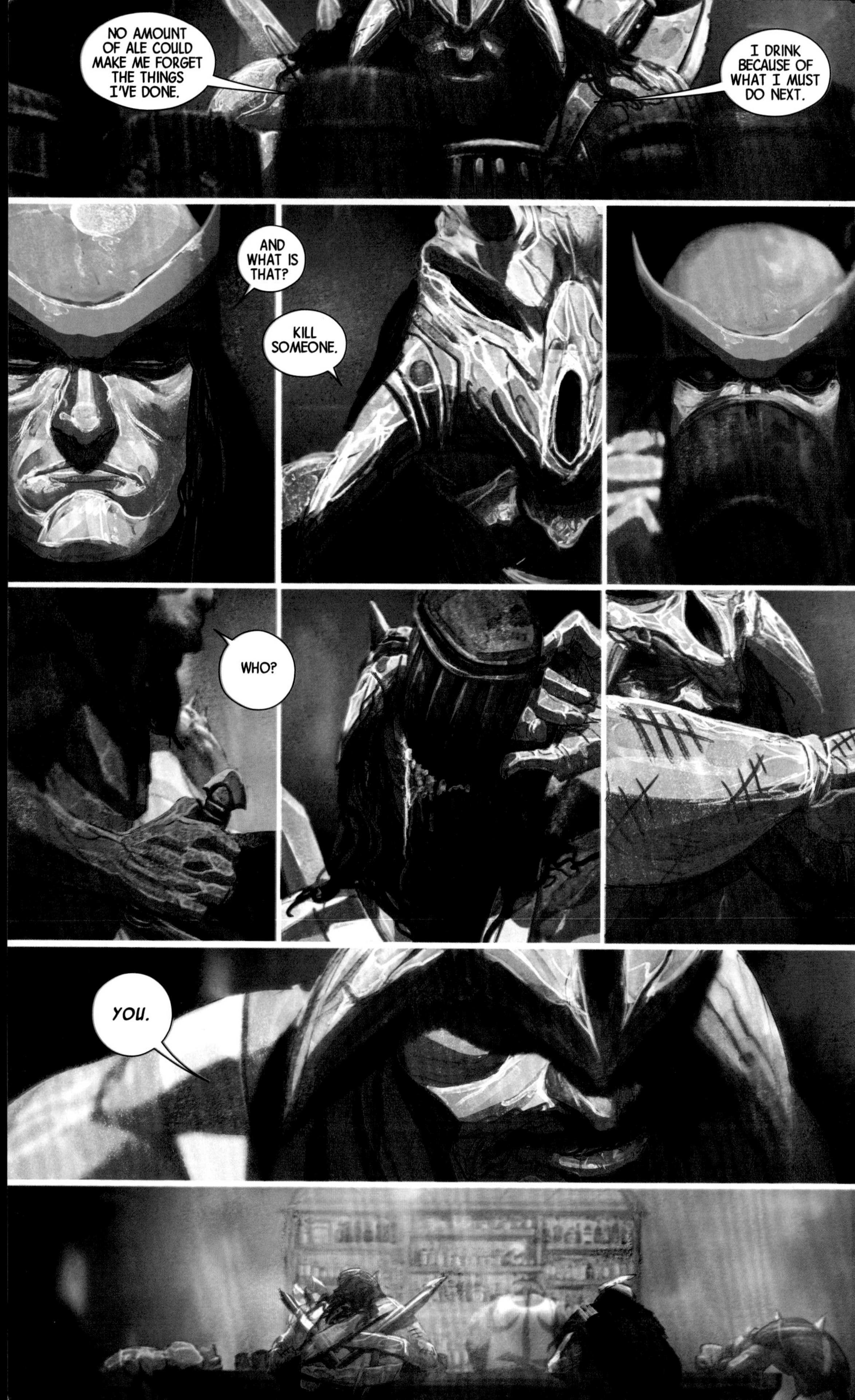
NO AMOUNT OF ALE COULD MAKE ME FORGET THE THINGS I'VE DONE.
I DRINK BECAUSE OF WHAT I MUST DO NEXT.
AND WHAT IS THAT?
KILL SOMEONE.
WHO?
YOU.

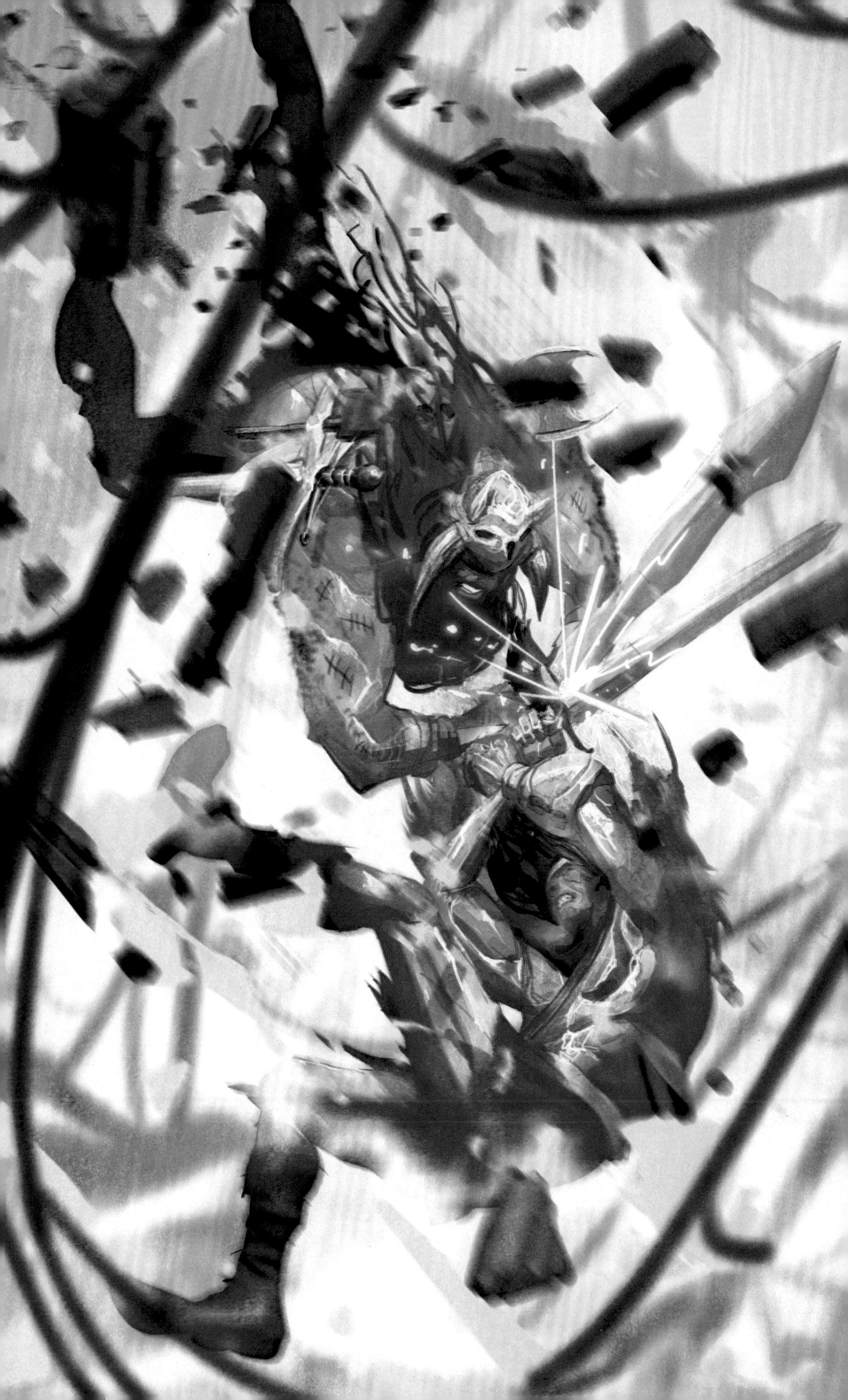

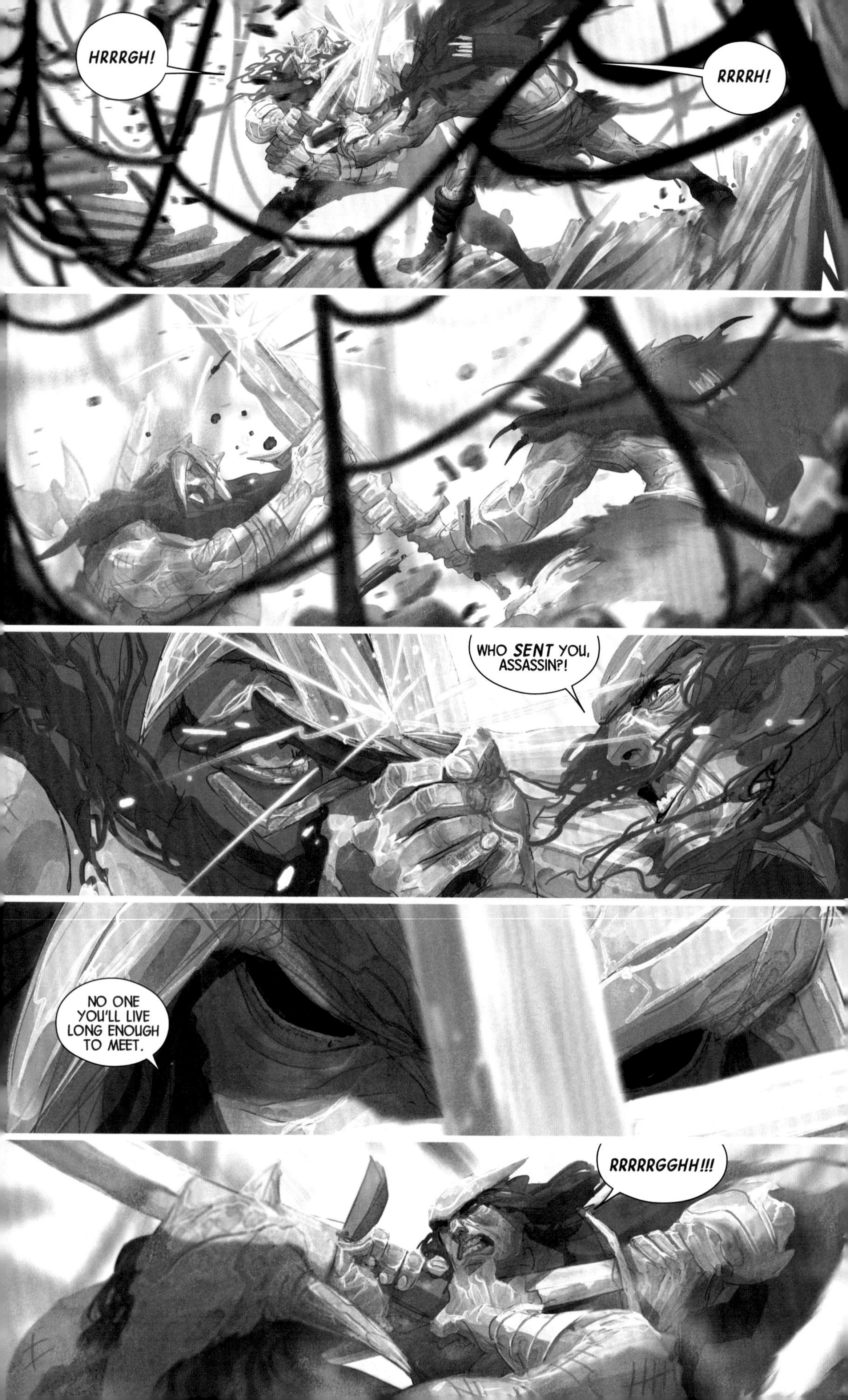
HRRRGH!
RRRRH!
WHO SENT YOU, ASSASSIN?!
NO ONE YOU'LL LIVE LONG ENOUGH TO MEET.
RRRRRGGHH!!!

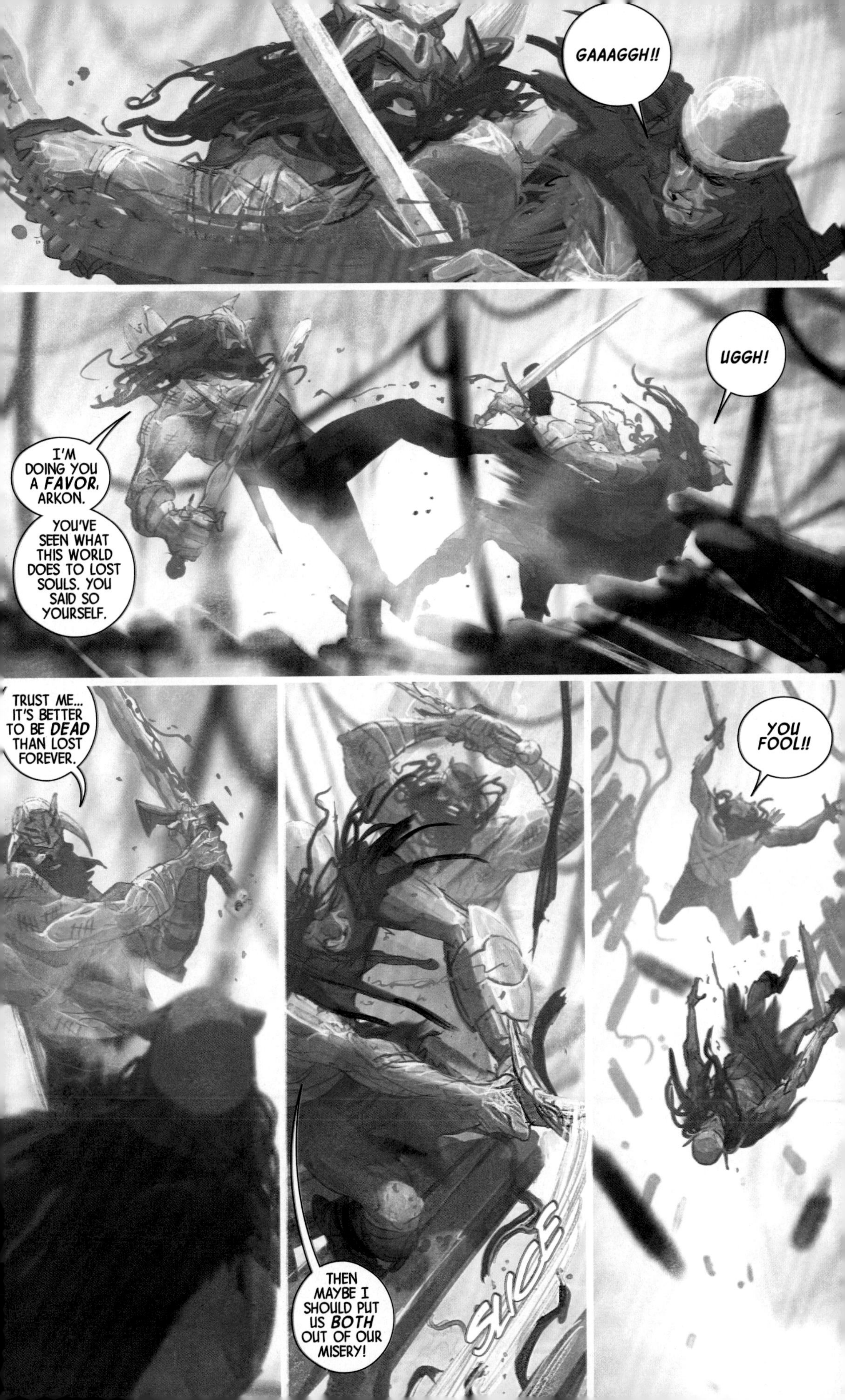
GAAAGGH!!
UGGH!
I'M DOING YOU A *FAVOR*, ARKON.
YOU'VE SEEN WHAT THIS WORLD DOES TO LOST SOULS. YOU SAID SO YOURSELF.
TRUST ME... IT'S BETTER TO BE *DEAD* THAN LOST FOREVER.
THEN MAYBE I SHOULD PUT US *BOTH* OUT OF OUR MISERY!
SLICE
YOU FOOL!!

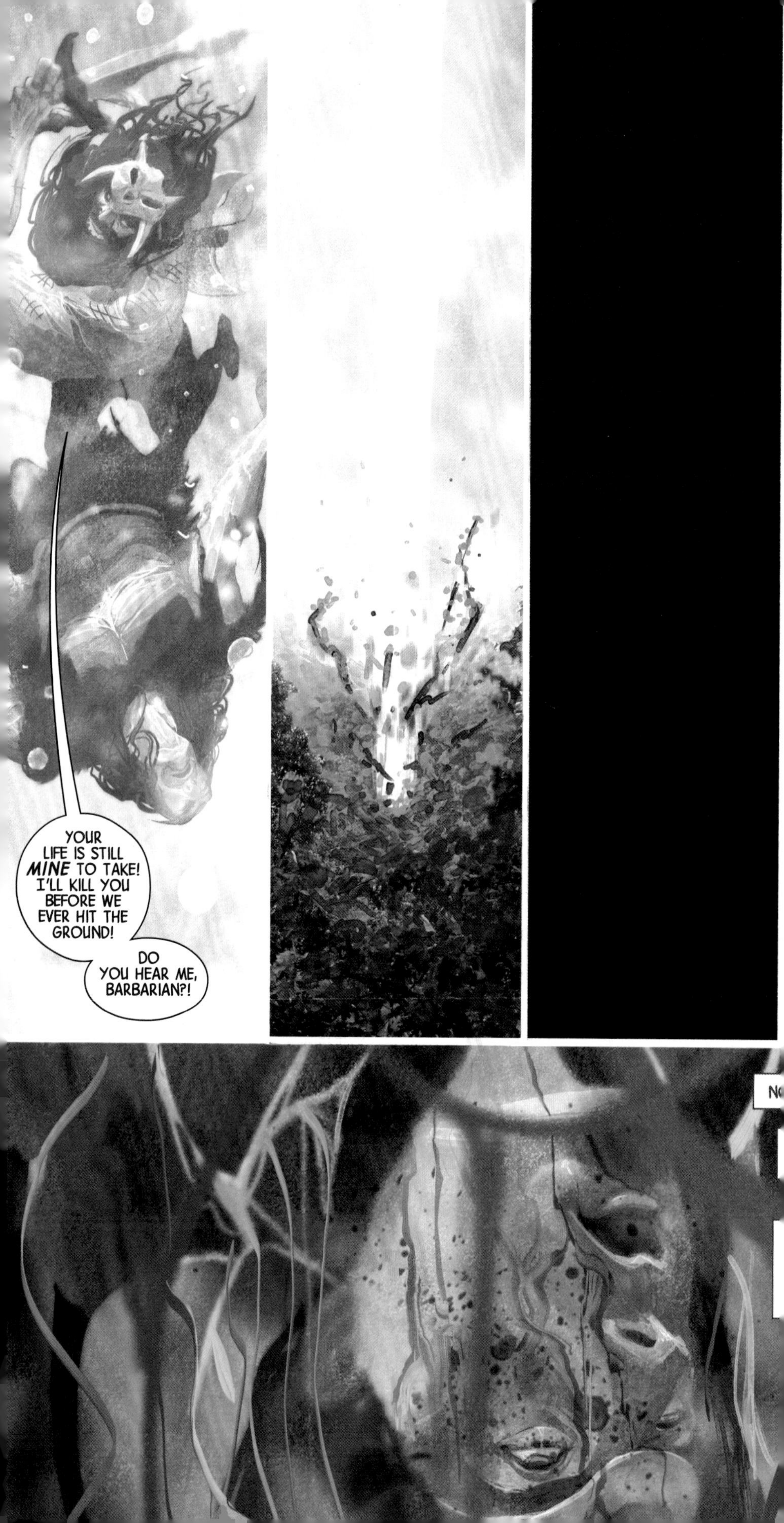
YOUR LIFE IS STILL MINE TO TAKE! I'LL KILL YOU BEFORE WE EVER HIT THE GROUND!
DO YOU HEAR ME, BARBARIAN?!

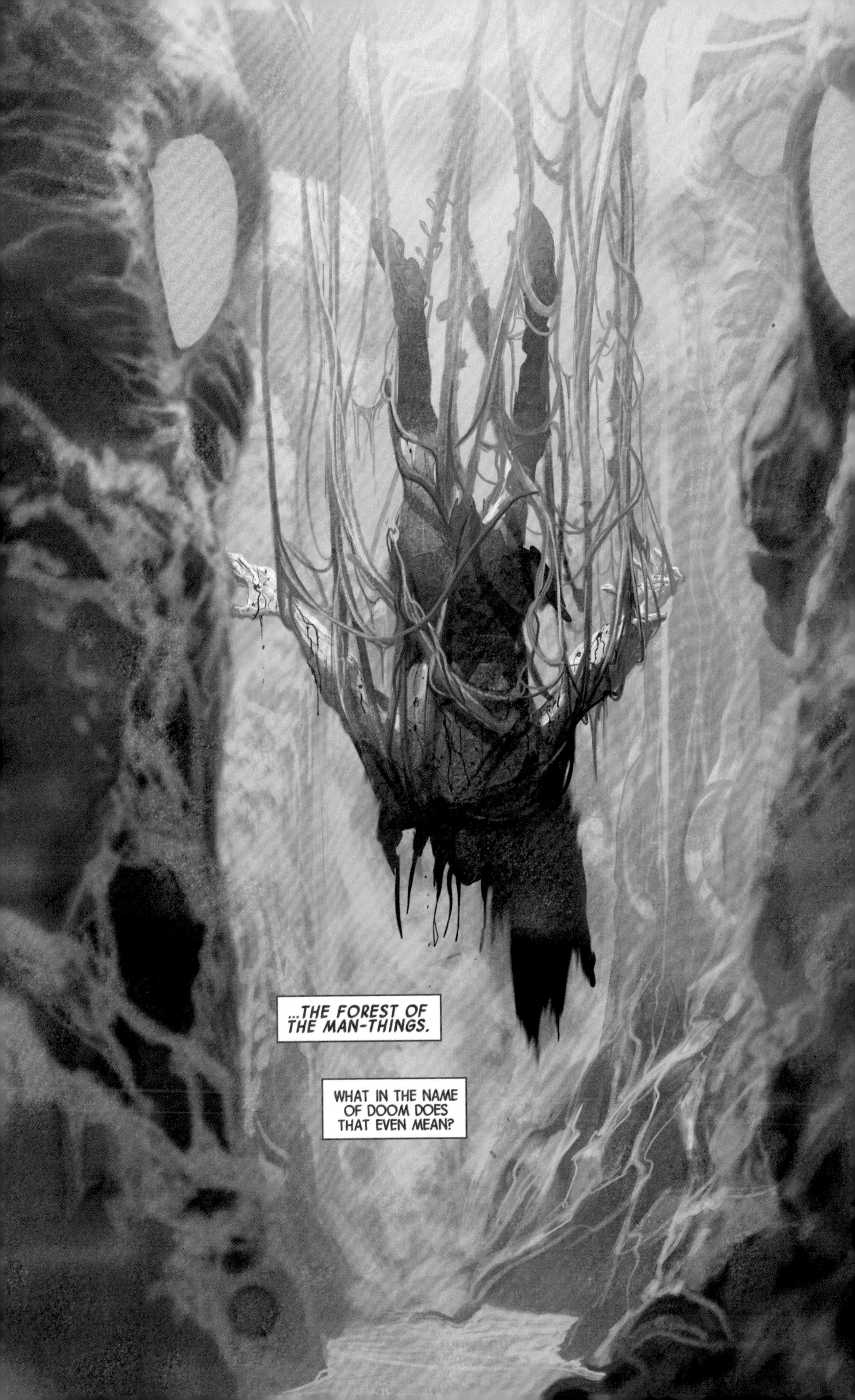
...THE FOREST OF THE MAN-THINGS.
WHAT IN THE NAME OF DOOM DOES THAT EVEN MEAN?

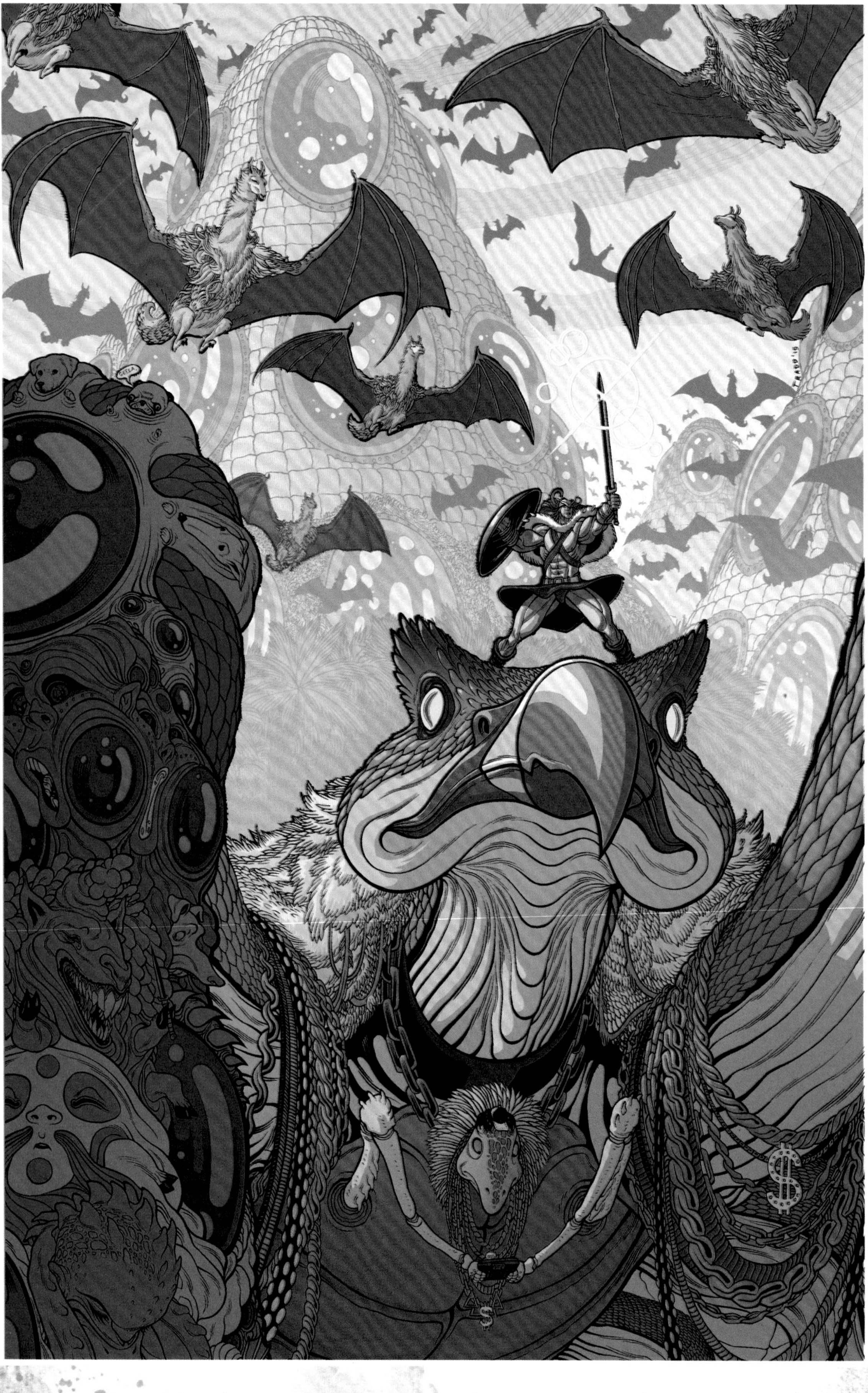

#3 VARIANT BY TRADD MOORE & MATTHEW WILSON

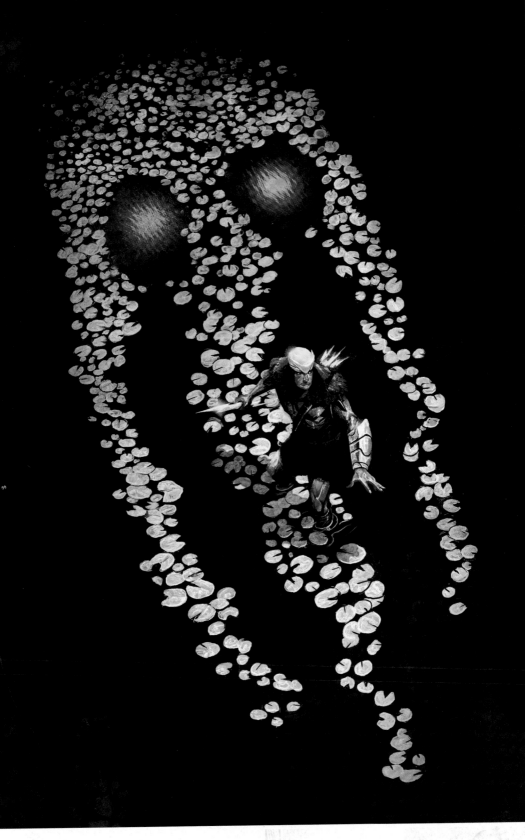

◆ QUEEN OF THE MAN-THINGS ◆

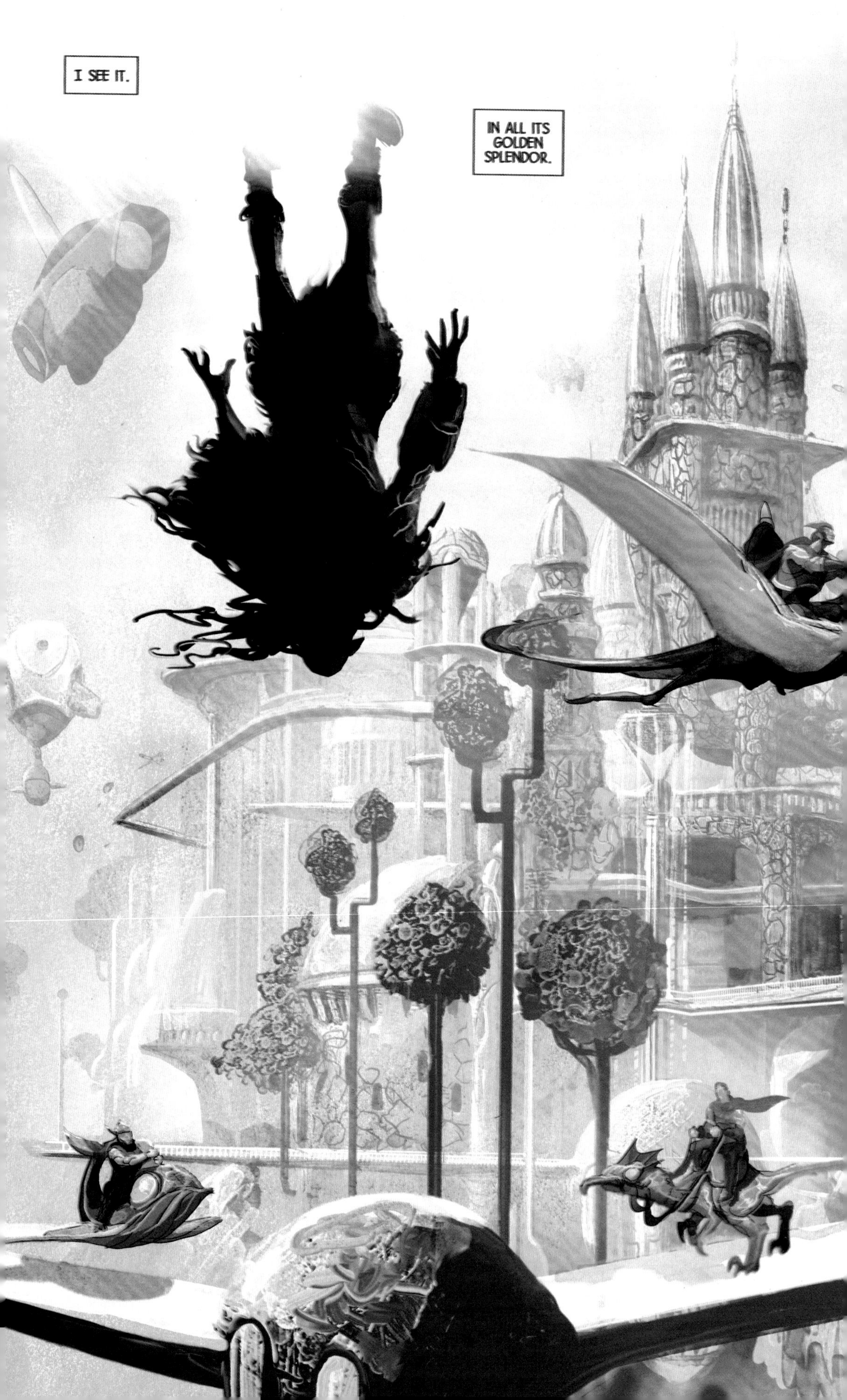
I SEE IT.
IN ALL ITS GOLDEN SPLENDOR.

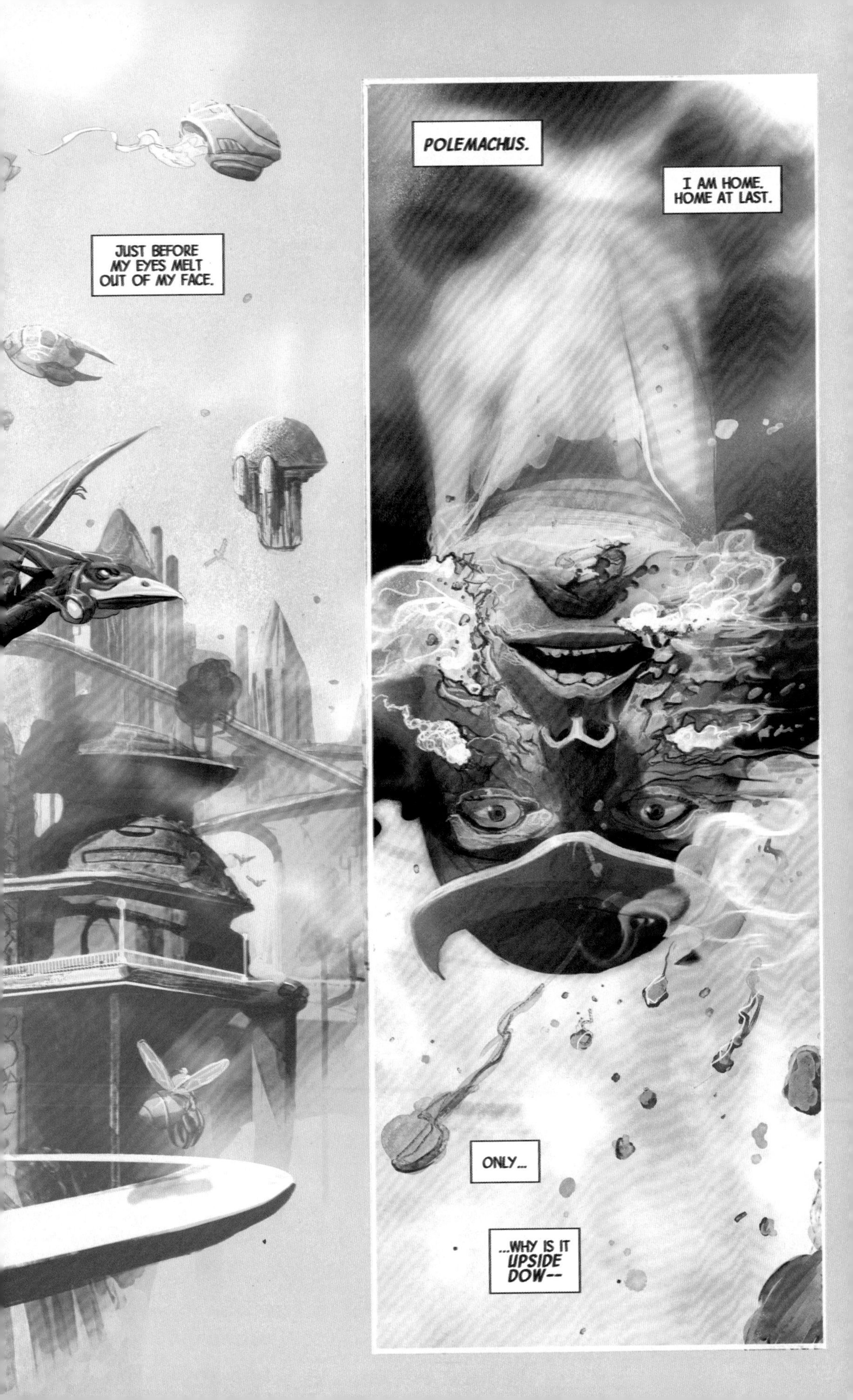
JUST BEFORE MY EYES MELT OUT OF MY FACE.
POLEMACHUS.
I AM HOME. HOME AT LAST.
ONLY...
...WHY IS IT UPSIDE DOW--

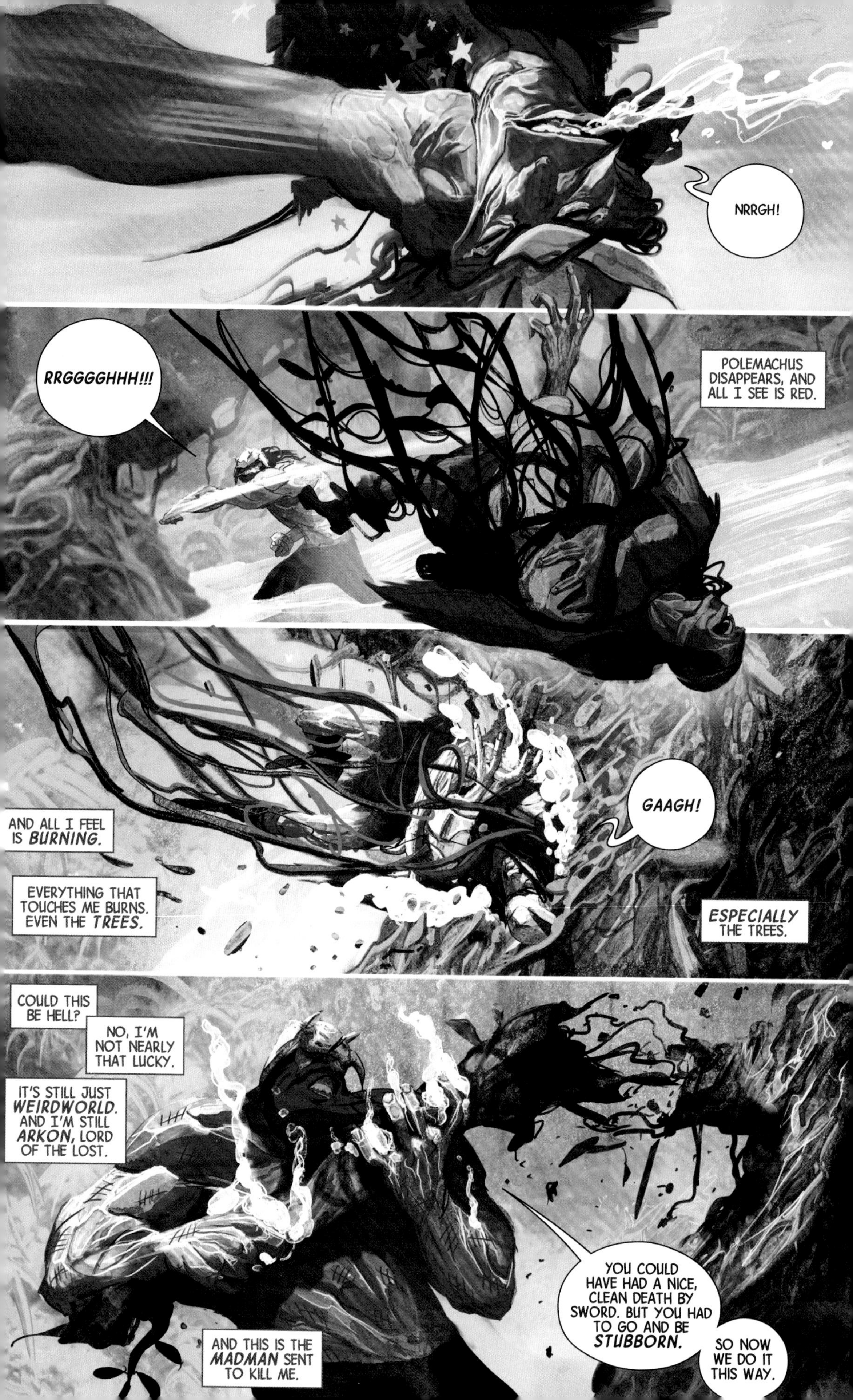

NRRGH!
RRGGGGHHH!!!
POLEMACHUS DISAPPEARS, AND ALL I SEE IS RED.
AND ALL I FEEL IS BURNING.
EVERYTHING THAT TOUCHES ME BURNS. EVEN THE TREES.
GAAGH!
ESPECIALLY THE TREES.
COULD THIS BE HELL?
NO, I'M NOT NEARLY THAT LUCKY.
IT'S STILL JUST WEIRDWORLD. AND I'M STILL ARKON, LORD OF THE LOST.
AND THIS IS THE MADMAN SENT TO KILL ME.
YOU COULD HAVE HAD A NICE, CLEAN DEATH BY SWORD. BUT YOU HAD TO GO AND BE STUBBORN.
SO NOW WE DO IT THIS WAY.

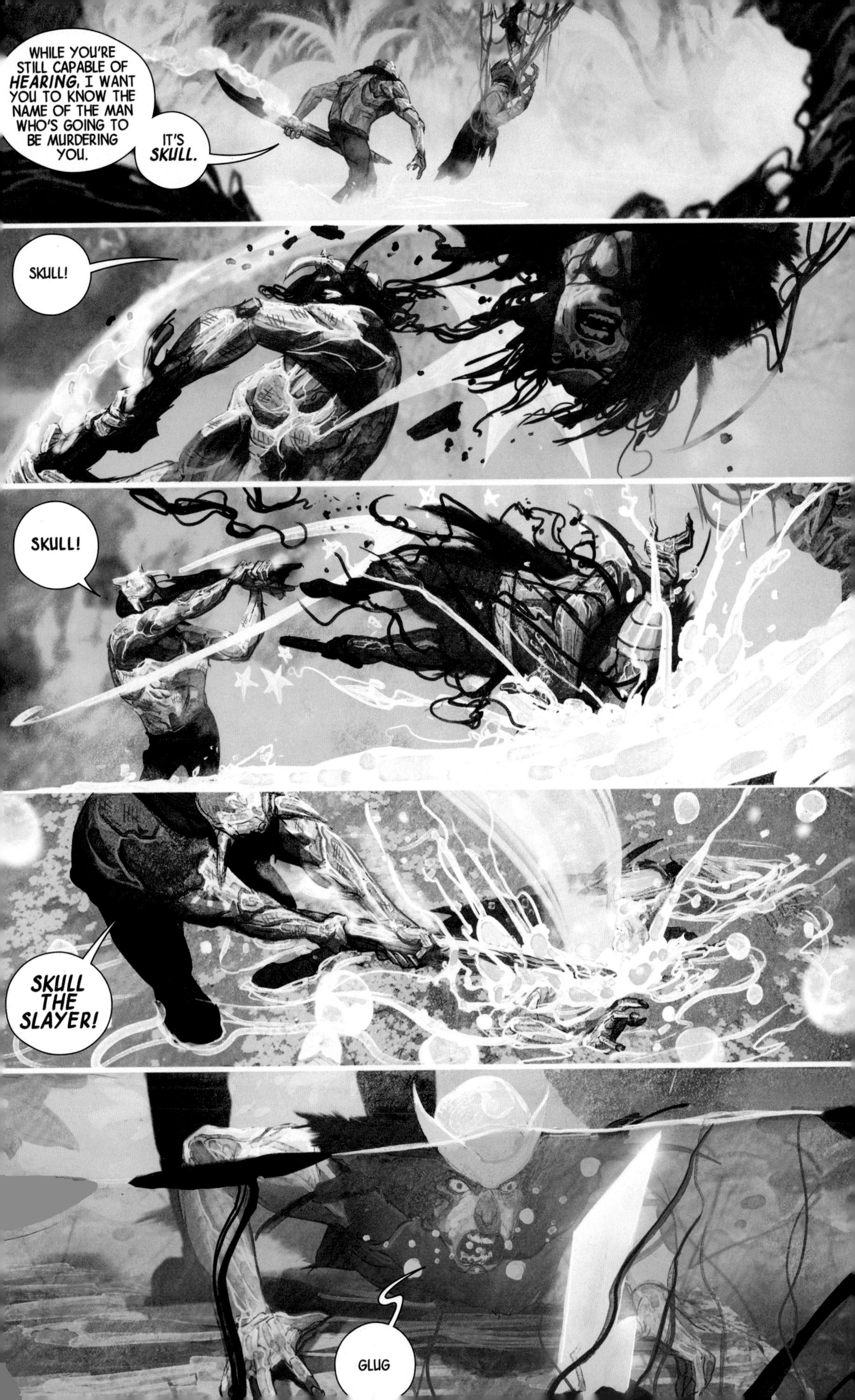
WHILE YOU'RE STILL CAPABLE OF HEARING, I WANT YOU TO KNOW THE NAME OF THE MAN WHO'S GOING TO BE MURDERING YOU.
IT'S SKULL.
SKULL!
SKULL!
SKULL THE SLAYER!
GLUG

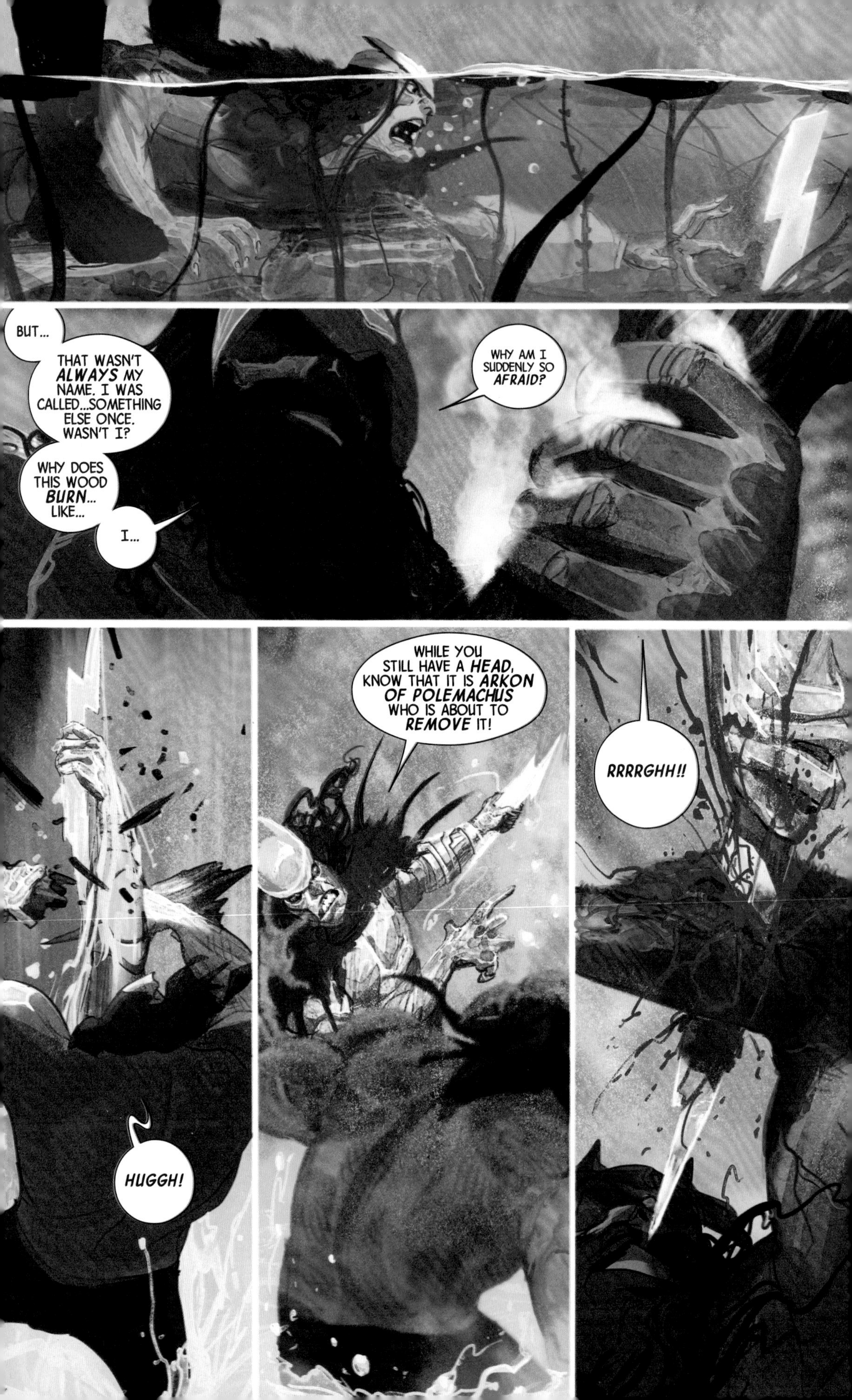
BUT...
THAT WASN'T ALWAYS MY NAME. I WAS CALLED...SOMETHING ELSE ONCE. WASN'T I?
WHY DOES THIS WOOD BURN... LIKE...
I...
WHY AM I SUDDENLY SO AFRAID?
HUGGH!
WHILE YOU STILL HAVE A HEAD, KNOW THAT IT IS ARKON OF POLEMACHUS WHO IS ABOUT TO REMOVE IT!
RRRRGHH!!

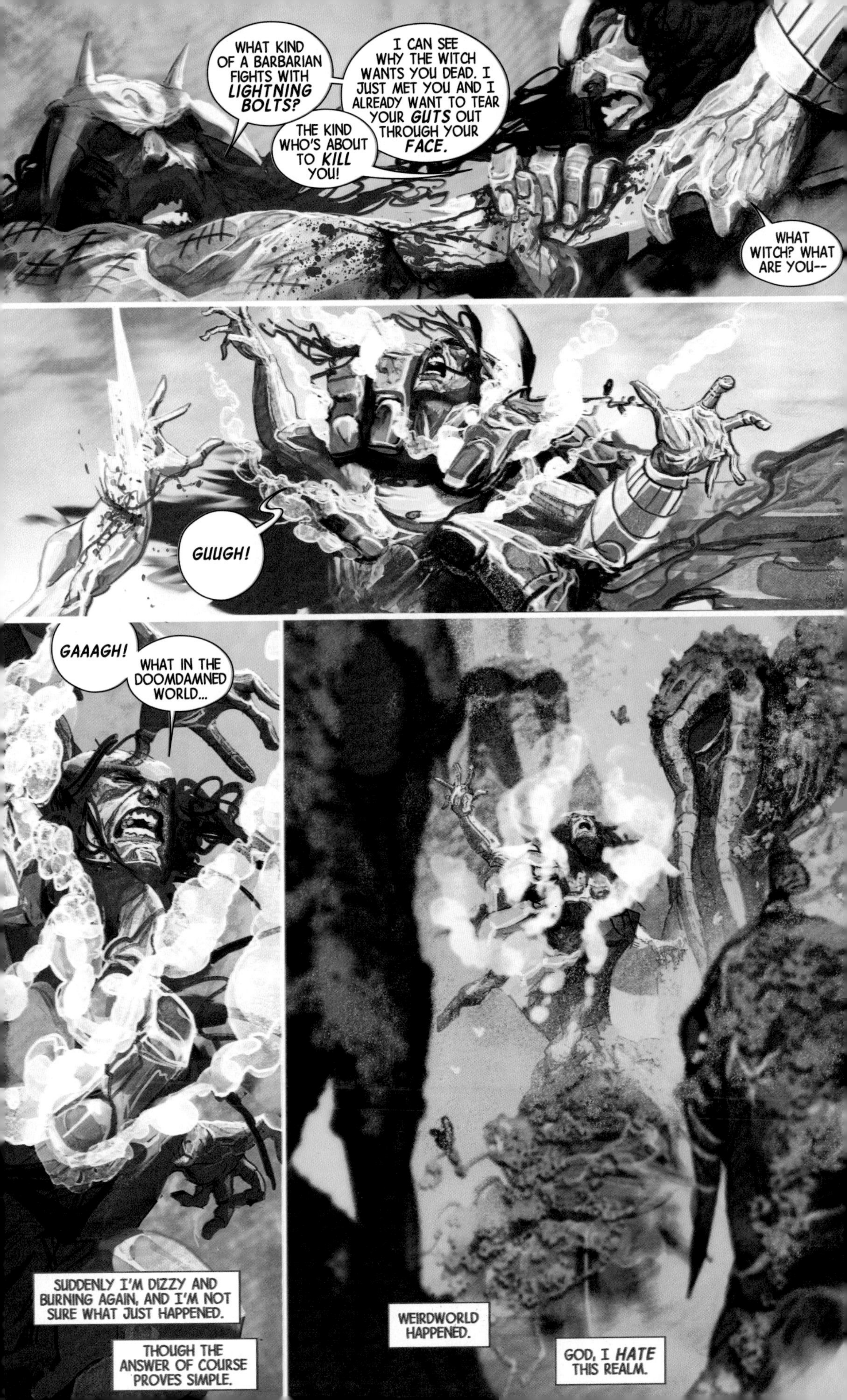
WHAT KIND OF A BARBARIAN FIGHTS WITH LIGHTNING BOLTS?
I CAN SEE WHY THE WITCH WANTS YOU DEAD. I JUST MET YOU AND I ALREADY WANT TO TEAR YOUR GUTS OUT THROUGH YOUR FACE.
THE KIND WHO'S ABOUT TO KILL YOU!
WHAT WITCH? WHAT ARE YOU--
GUUGH!
GAAAGH!
WHAT IN THE DOOMDAMNED WORLD...
SUDDENLY I'M DIZZY AND BURNING AGAIN, AND I'M NOT SURE WHAT JUST HAPPENED.
THOUGH THE ANSWER OF COURSE PROVES SIMPLE.
WEIRDWORLD HAPPENED.
GOD, I HATE THIS REALM.

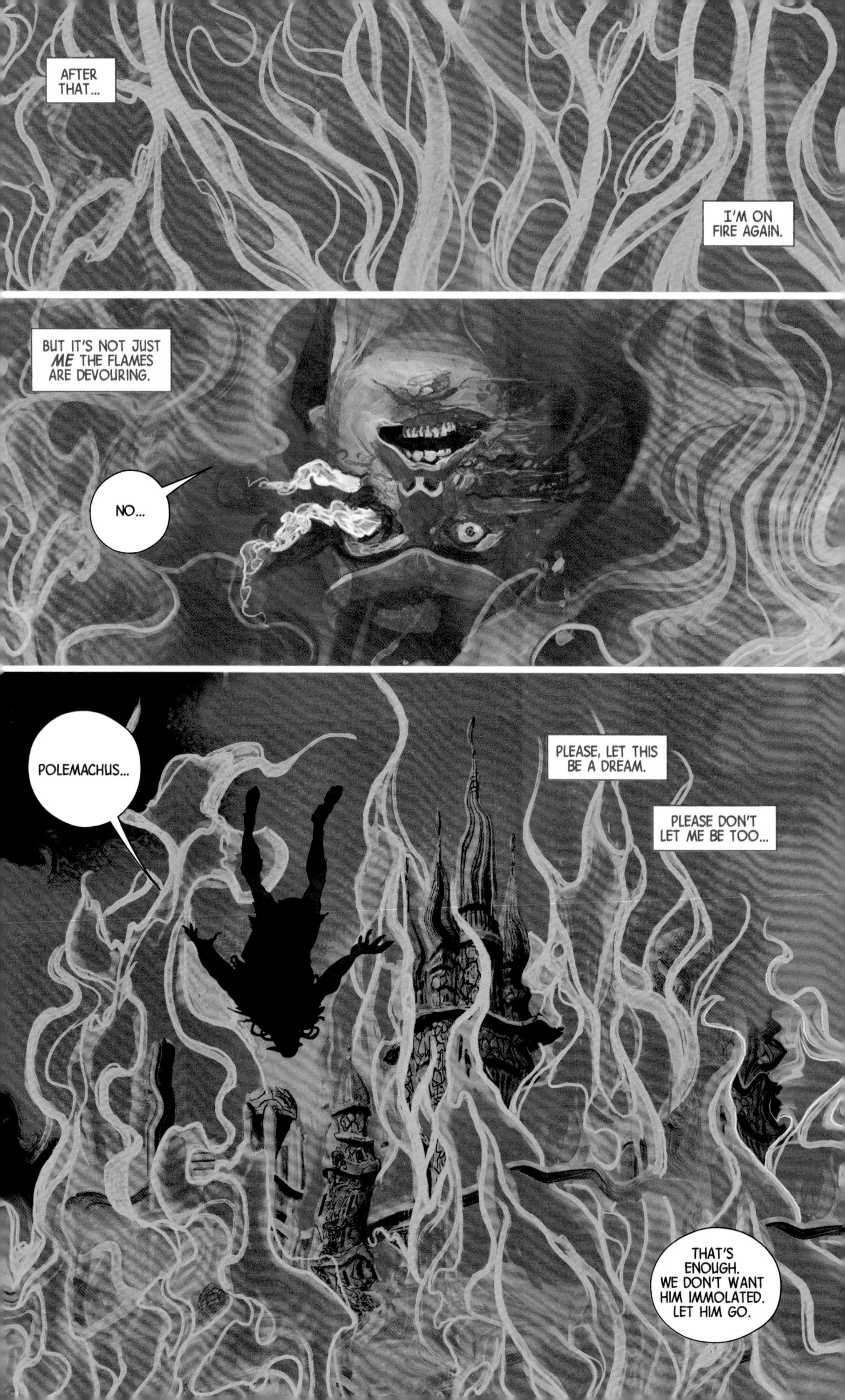
AFTER THAT...
I'M ON FIRE AGAIN.
BUT IT'S NOT JUST *ME* THE FLAMES ARE DEVOURING.
NO...
POLEMACHUS...
PLEASE, LET THIS BE A DREAM.
PLEASE DON'T LET ME BE TOO...
THAT'S ENOUGH. WE DON'T WANT HIM IMMOLATED. LET HIM GO.

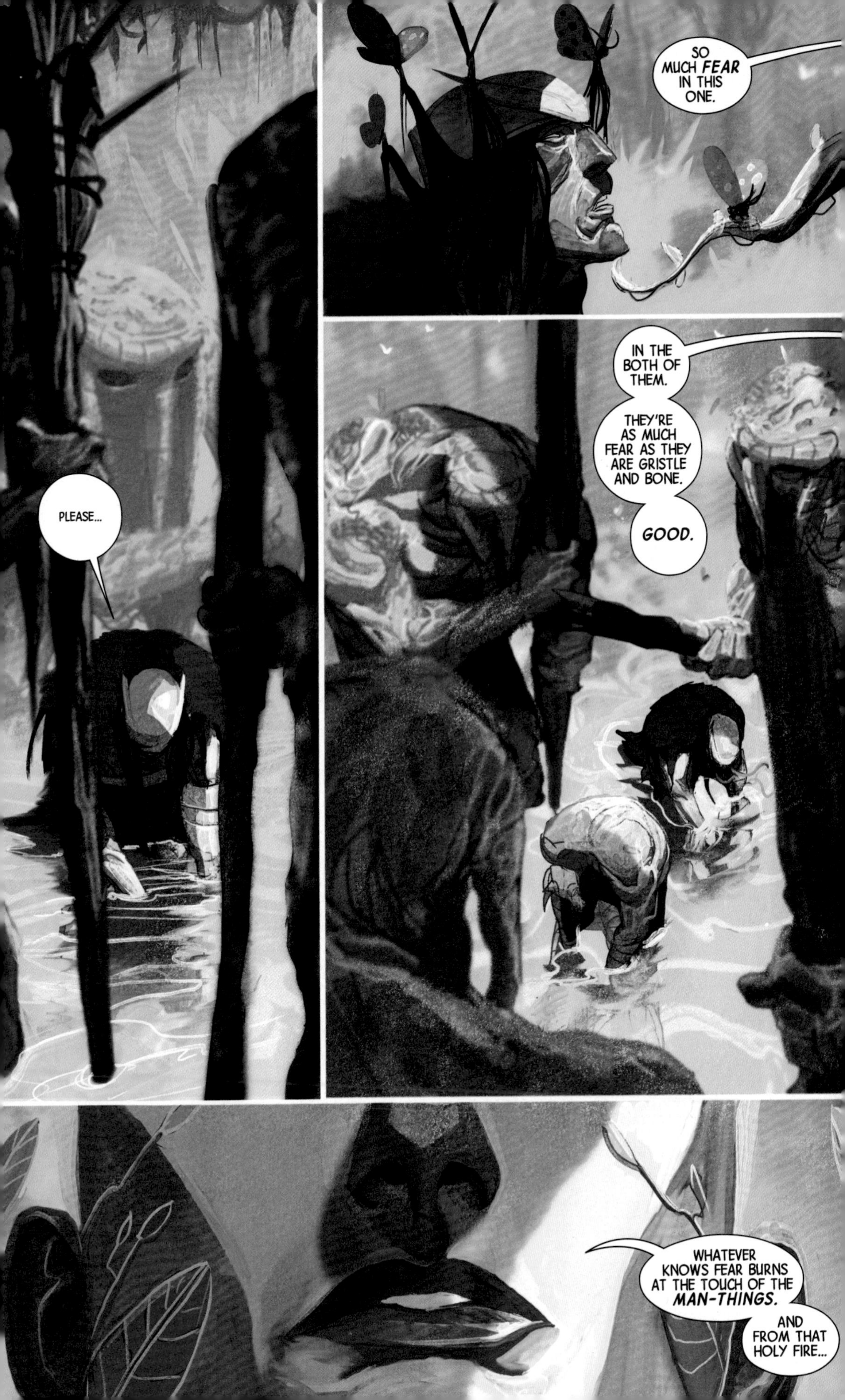
SO MUCH FEAR IN THIS ONE.
PLEASE...
IN THE BOTH OF THEM.
THEY'RE AS MUCH FEAR AS THEY ARE GRISTLE AND BONE.
GOOD.
WHATEVER KNOWS FEAR BURNS AT THE TOUCH OF THE MAN-THINGS.
AND FROM THAT HOLY FIRE...

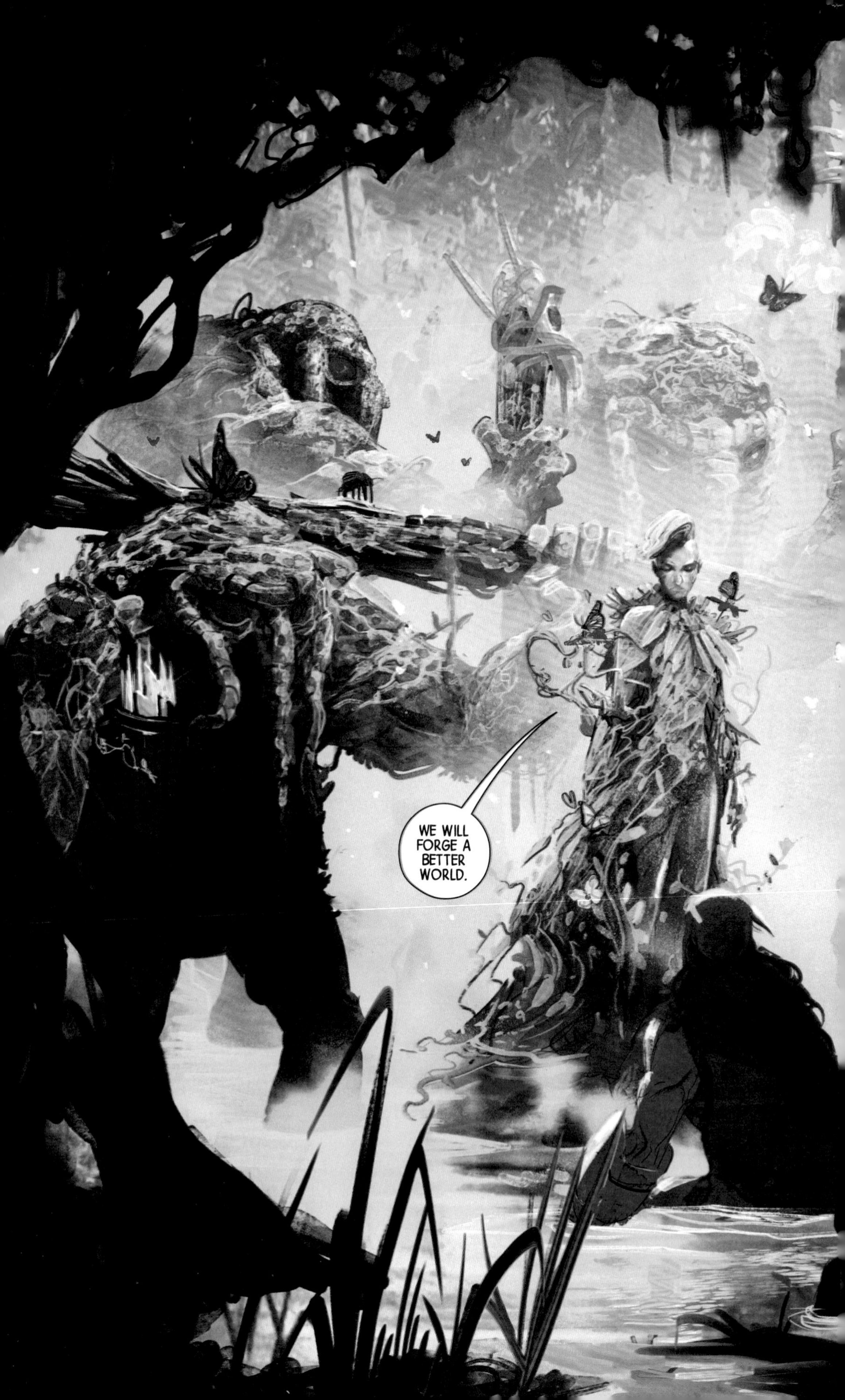
WE WILL FORGE A BETTER WORLD.

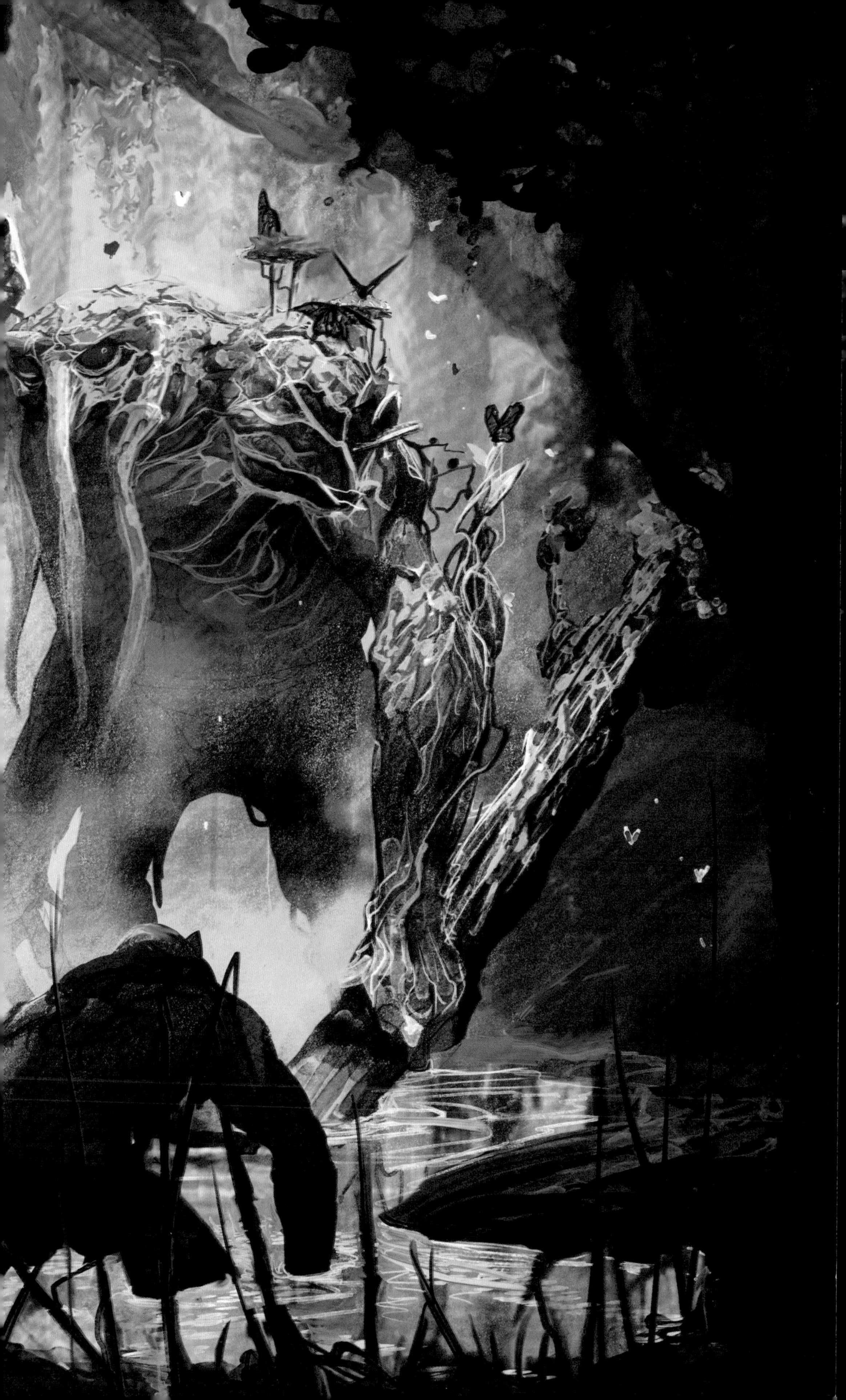

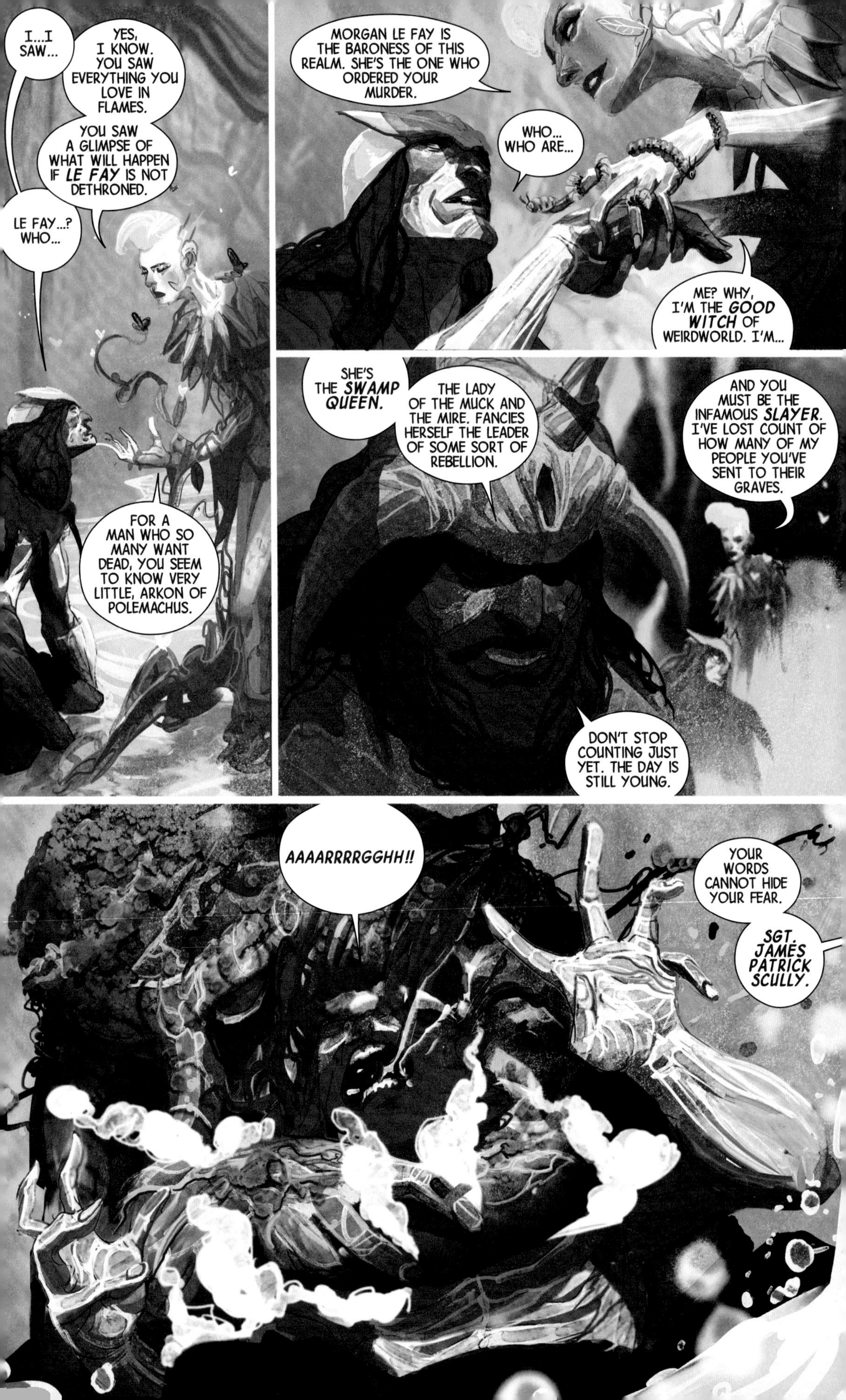
I...I SAW...
YES, I KNOW. YOU SAW EVERYTHING YOU LOVE IN FLAMES.
YOU SAW A GLIMPSE OF WHAT WILL HAPPEN IF LE FAY IS NOT DETHRONED.
LE FAY...? WHO...
FOR A MAN WHO SO MANY WANT DEAD, YOU SEEM TO KNOW VERY LITTLE, ARKON OF POLEMACHUS.
MORGAN LE FAY IS THE BARONESS OF THIS REALM. SHE'S THE ONE WHO ORDERED YOUR MURDER.
WHO... WHO ARE...
ME? WHY, I'M THE GOOD WITCH OF WEIRDWORLD. I'M...
SHE'S THE SWAMP QUEEN.
THE LADY OF THE MUCK AND THE MIRE. FANCIES HERSELF THE LEADER OF SOME SORT OF REBELLION.
AND YOU MUST BE THE INFAMOUS SLAYER. I'VE LOST COUNT OF HOW MANY OF MY PEOPLE YOU'VE SENT TO THEIR GRAVES.
DON'T STOP COUNTING JUST YET. THE DAY IS STILL YOUNG.
AAAARRRRGGHH!!
YOUR WORDS CANNOT HIDE YOUR FEAR.
SGT. JAMES PATRICK SCULLY.

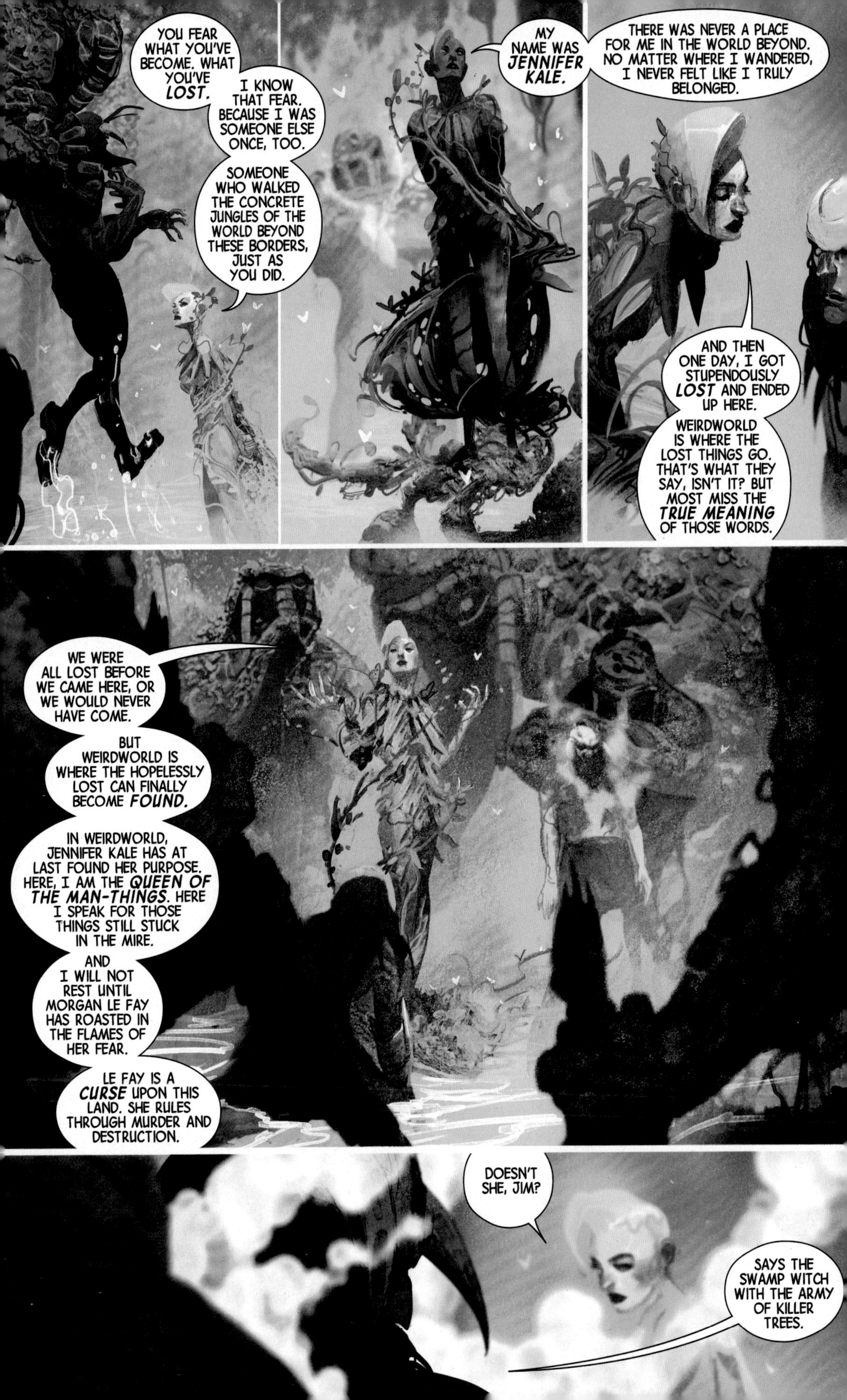
YOU FEAR WHAT YOU'VE BECOME. WHAT YOU'VE LOST.
I KNOW THAT FEAR. BECAUSE I WAS SOMEONE ELSE ONCE, TOO.
SOMEONE WHO WALKED THE CONCRETE JUNGLES OF THE WORLD BEYOND THESE BORDERS, JUST AS YOU DID.
MY NAME WAS JENNIFER KALE.
THERE WAS NEVER A PLACE FOR ME IN THE WORLD BEYOND. NO MATTER WHERE I WANDERED, I NEVER FELT LIKE I TRULY BELONGED.
AND THEN ONE DAY, I GOT STUPENDOUSLY LOST AND ENDED UP HERE.
WEIRDWORLD IS WHERE THE LOST THINGS GO. THAT'S WHAT THEY SAY, ISN'T IT? BUT MOST MISS THE TRUE MEANING OF THOSE WORDS.
WE WERE ALL LOST BEFORE WE CAME HERE, OR WE WOULD NEVER HAVE COME.
BUT WEIRDWORLD IS WHERE THE HOPELESSLY LOST CAN FINALLY BECOME FOUND.
IN WEIRDWORLD, JENNIFER KALE HAS AT LAST FOUND HER PURPOSE. HERE, I AM THE QUEEN OF THE MAN-THINGS. HERE I SPEAK FOR THOSE THINGS STILL STUCK IN THE MIRE.
AND I WILL NOT REST UNTIL MORGAN LE FAY HAS ROASTED IN THE FLAMES OF HER FEAR.
LE FAY IS A CURSE UPON THIS LAND. SHE RULES THROUGH MURDER AND DESTRUCTION.
DOESN'T SHE, JIM?
SAYS THE SWAMP WITCH WITH THE ARMY OF KILLER TREES.

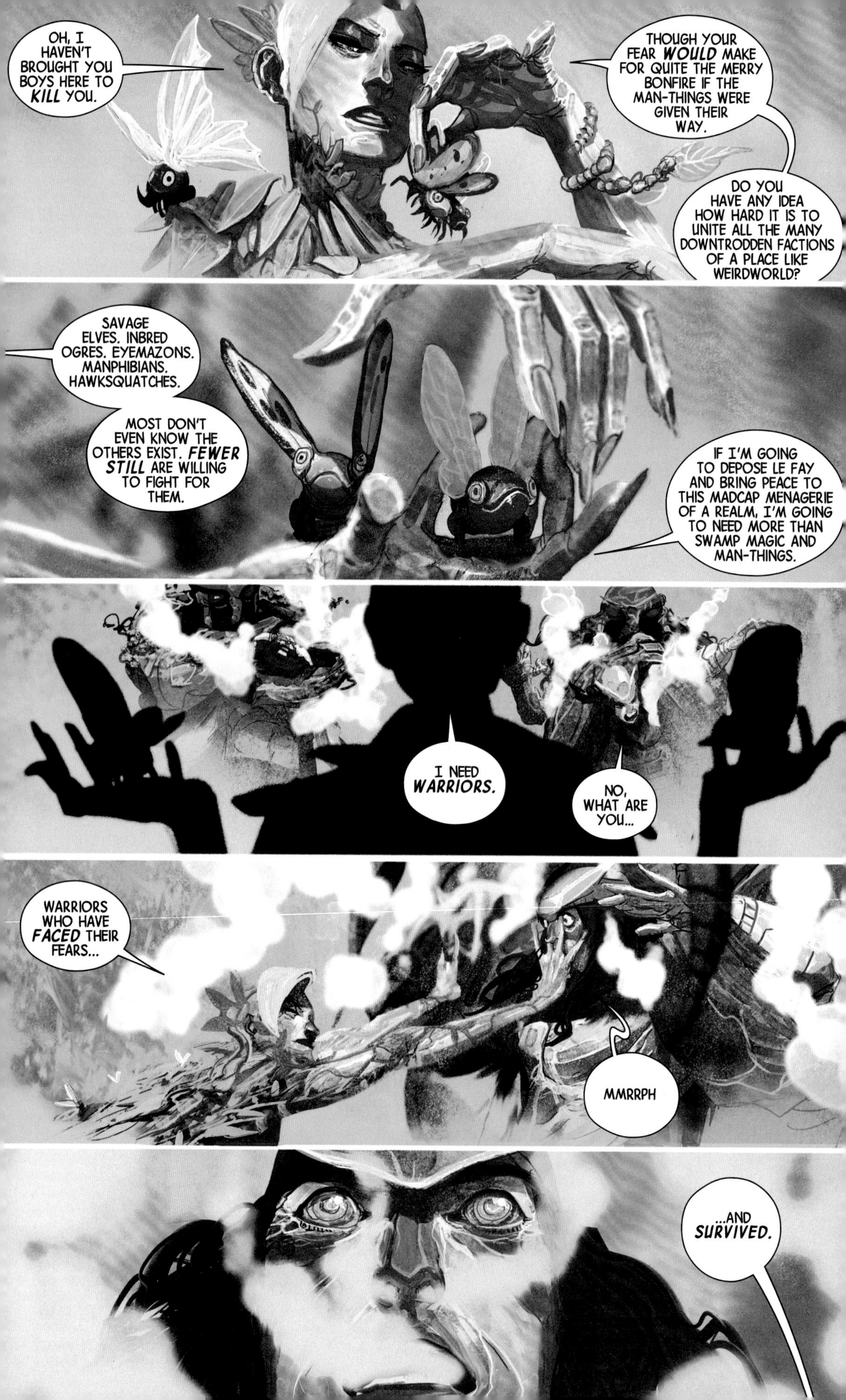
OH, I HAVEN'T BROUGHT YOU BOYS HERE TO KILL YOU.
THOUGH YOUR FEAR WOULD MAKE FOR QUITE THE MERRY BONFIRE IF THE MAN-THINGS WERE GIVEN THEIR WAY.
DO YOU HAVE ANY IDEA HOW HARD IT IS TO UNITE ALL THE MANY DOWNTRODDEN FACTIONS OF A PLACE LIKE WEIRDWORLD?
SAVAGE ELVES. INBRED OGRES. EYEMAZONS. MANPHIBIANS. HAWKSQUATCHES.
MOST DON'T EVEN KNOW THE OTHERS EXIST. FEWER STILL ARE WILLING TO FIGHT FOR THEM.
IF I'M GOING TO DEPOSE LE FAY AND BRING PEACE TO THIS MADCAP MENAGERIE OF A REALM, I'M GOING TO NEED MORE THAN SWAMP MAGIC AND MAN-THINGS.
I NEED WARRIORS.
NO, WHAT ARE YOU...
WARRIORS WHO HAVE FACED THEIR FEARS...
MMRRPH
...AND SURVIVED.

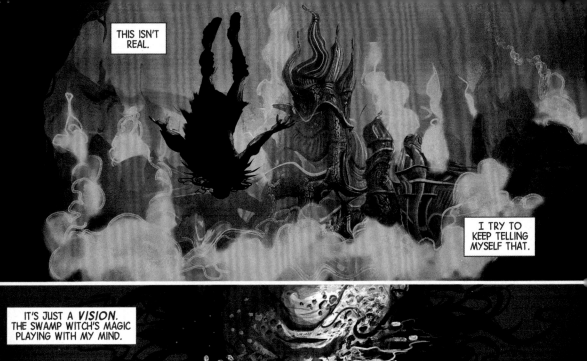

THIS ISN'T REAL.

I TRY TO KEEP TELLING MYSELF THAT.

IT'S JUST A *VISION*. THE SWAMP WITCH'S MAGIC PLAYING WITH MY MIND.

THIS IS MY FEAR MADE REAL. MY FEAR OF LOSING POLEMACHUS, OF MY WORLD BEING TURNED UPSIDE DOWN.

AND YET...

I RECOGNIZE THE VOICES BEHIND EVERY SCREAM. I CAN PUT A NAME TO EVERY DEAD FACE.

I KNOW THESE ROCKS, THESE TREES. EVEN UPSIDE DOWN, I KNOW THIS...

I *KNOW*... THIS PLACE. I...

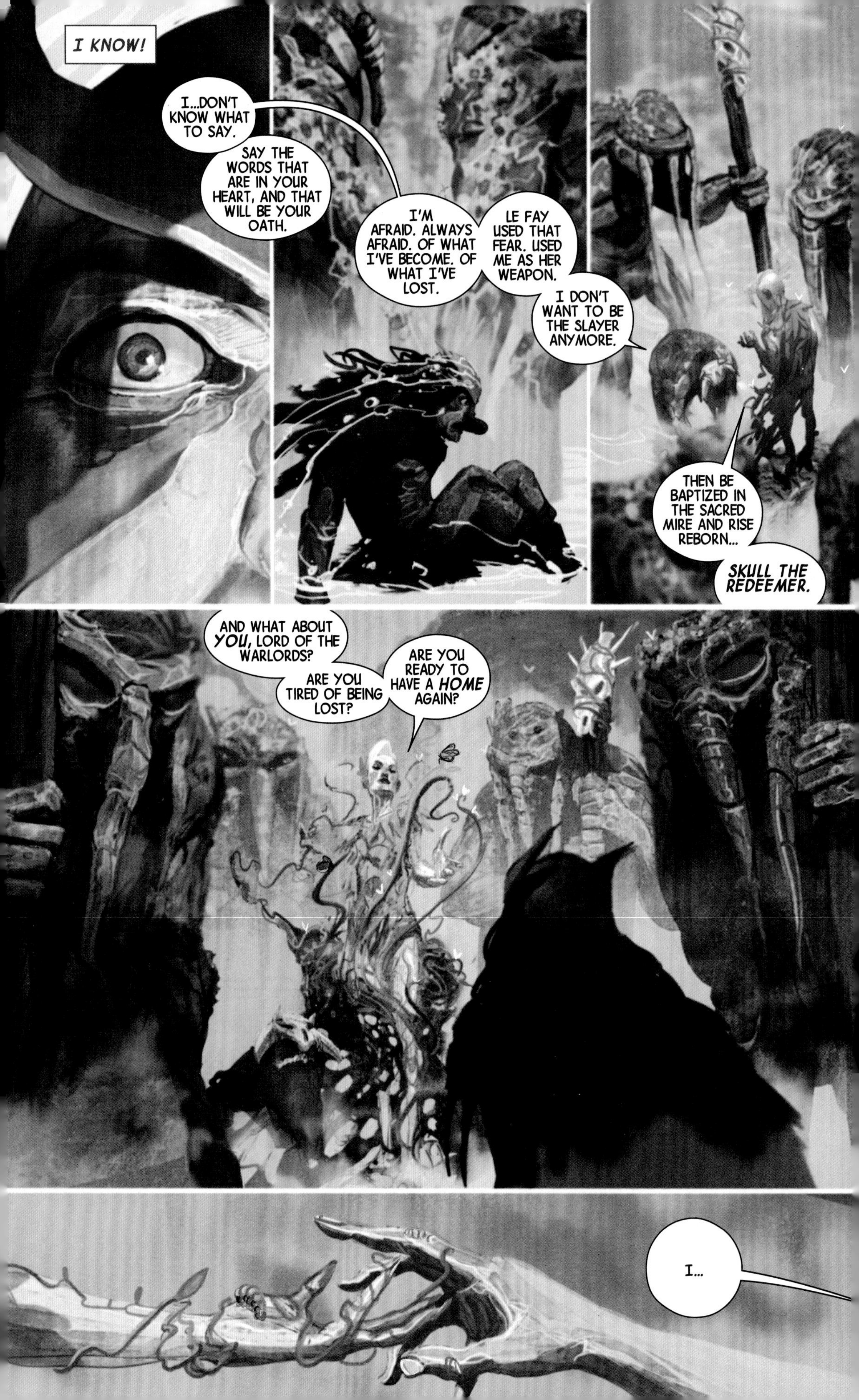
I KNOW!
I...DON'T KNOW WHAT TO SAY.
SAY THE WORDS THAT ARE IN YOUR HEART, AND THAT WILL BE YOUR OATH.
I'M AFRAID. ALWAYS AFRAID. OF WHAT I'VE BECOME. OF WHAT I'VE LOST.
LE FAY USED THAT FEAR. USED ME AS HER WEAPON.
I DON'T WANT TO BE THE SLAYER ANYMORE.
THEN BE BAPTIZED IN THE SACRED MIRE AND RISE REBORN...
SKULL THE REDEEMER.
AND WHAT ABOUT YOU, LORD OF THE WARLORDS?
ARE YOU TIRED OF BEING LOST?
ARE YOU READY TO HAVE A HOME AGAIN?
I...

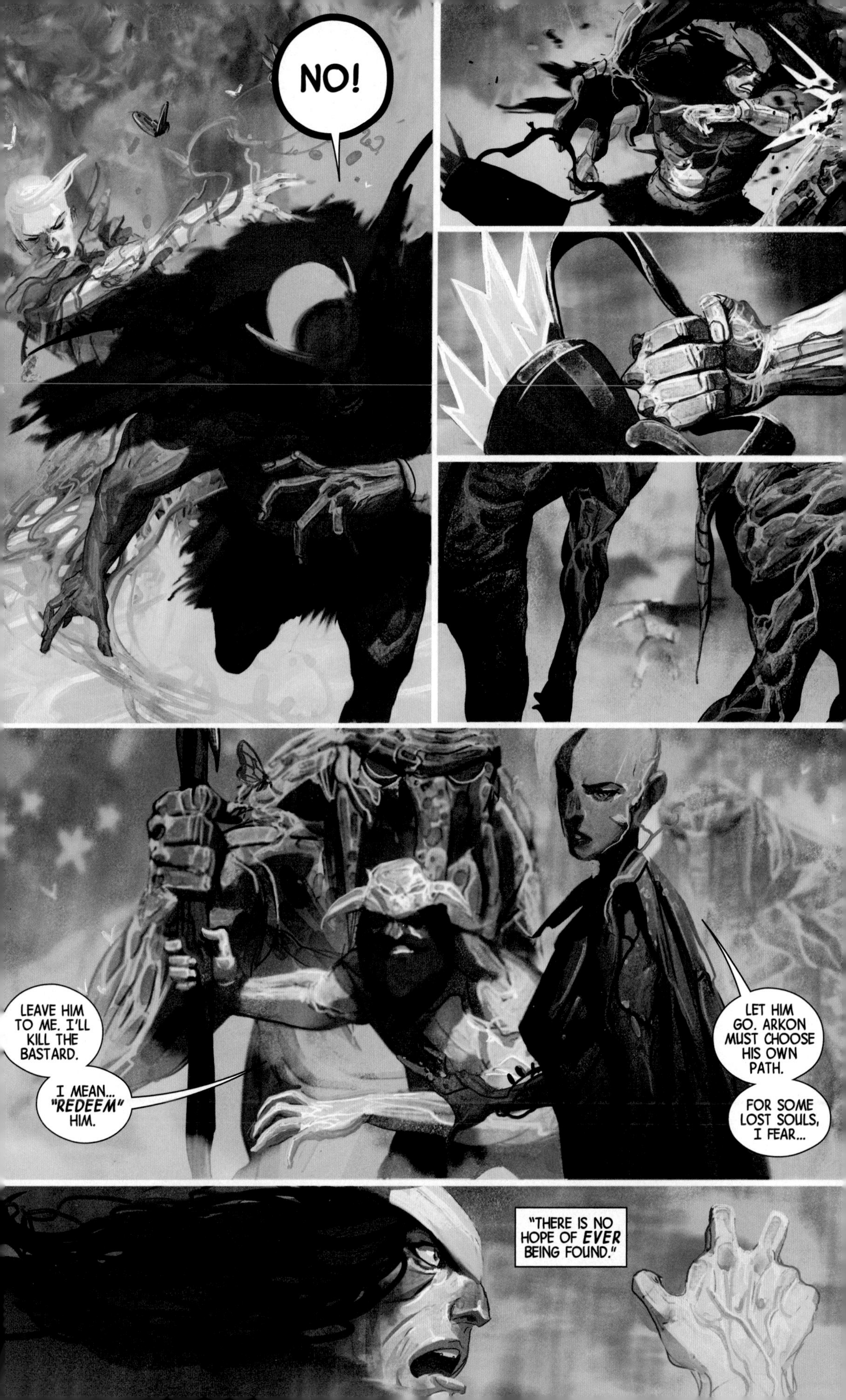
NO!
LEAVE HIM TO ME. I'LL KILL THE BASTARD.
I MEAN... "REDEEM" HIM.
LET HIM GO. ARKON MUST CHOOSE HIS OWN PATH.
FOR SOME LOST SOULS, I FEAR...
"THERE IS NO HOPE OF EVER BEING FOUND."

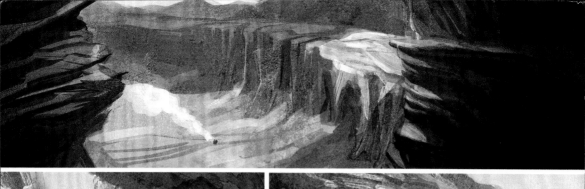

I KNOW.

I FINALLY REMEMBER.

THAT ROCK! I REMEMBER THAT ROCK!

THIS IS *IT.* POLEMACHUS, MY HOME, IS RIGHT PAST THIS...

ROCK...

I DON'T UNDERSTAND...

IT SHOULD BE... RIGHT HERE.

MY HOME. IT'S...

IT'S GONE.

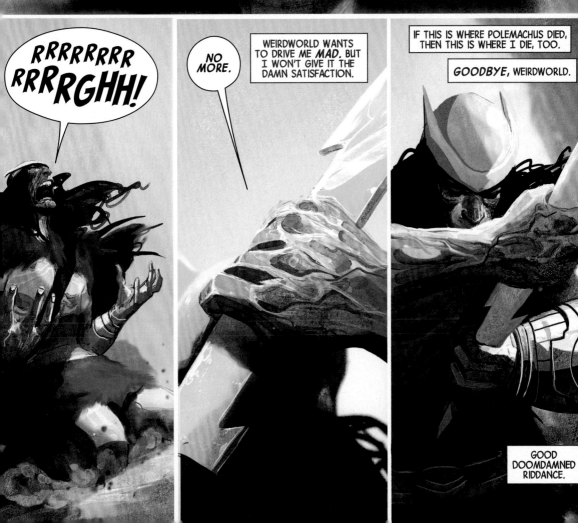

RRRRRRRR RRRRGHH!

NO MORE.

WEIRDWORLD WANTS TO DRIVE ME MAD, BUT I WON'T GIVE IT THE DAMN SATISFACTION.

IF THIS IS WHERE POLEMACHUS DIED, THEN THIS IS WHERE I DIE, TOO.

GOODBYE, WEIRDWORLD.

GOOD DOOMDAMNED RIDDANCE.

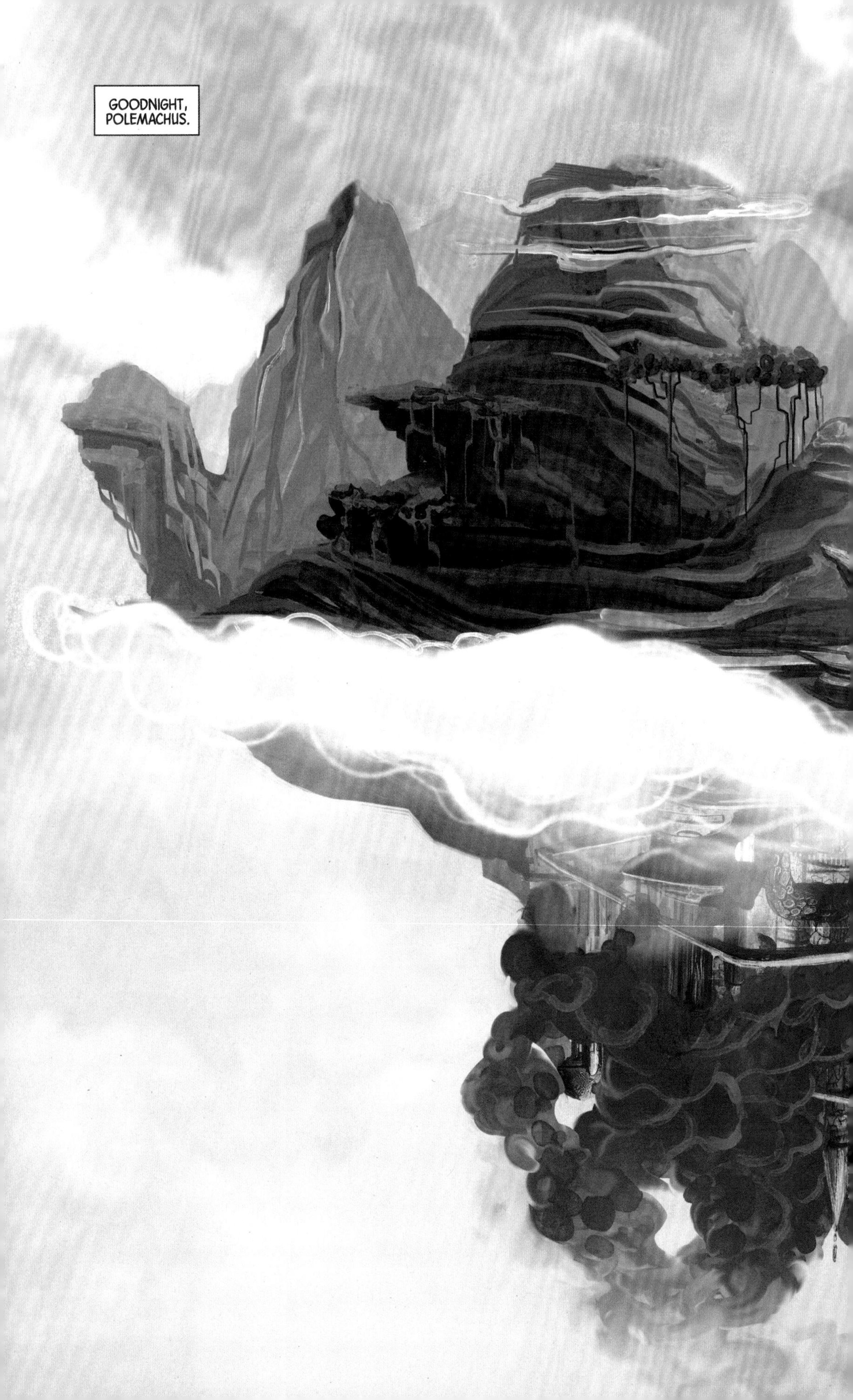
GOODNIGHT, POLEMACHUS.

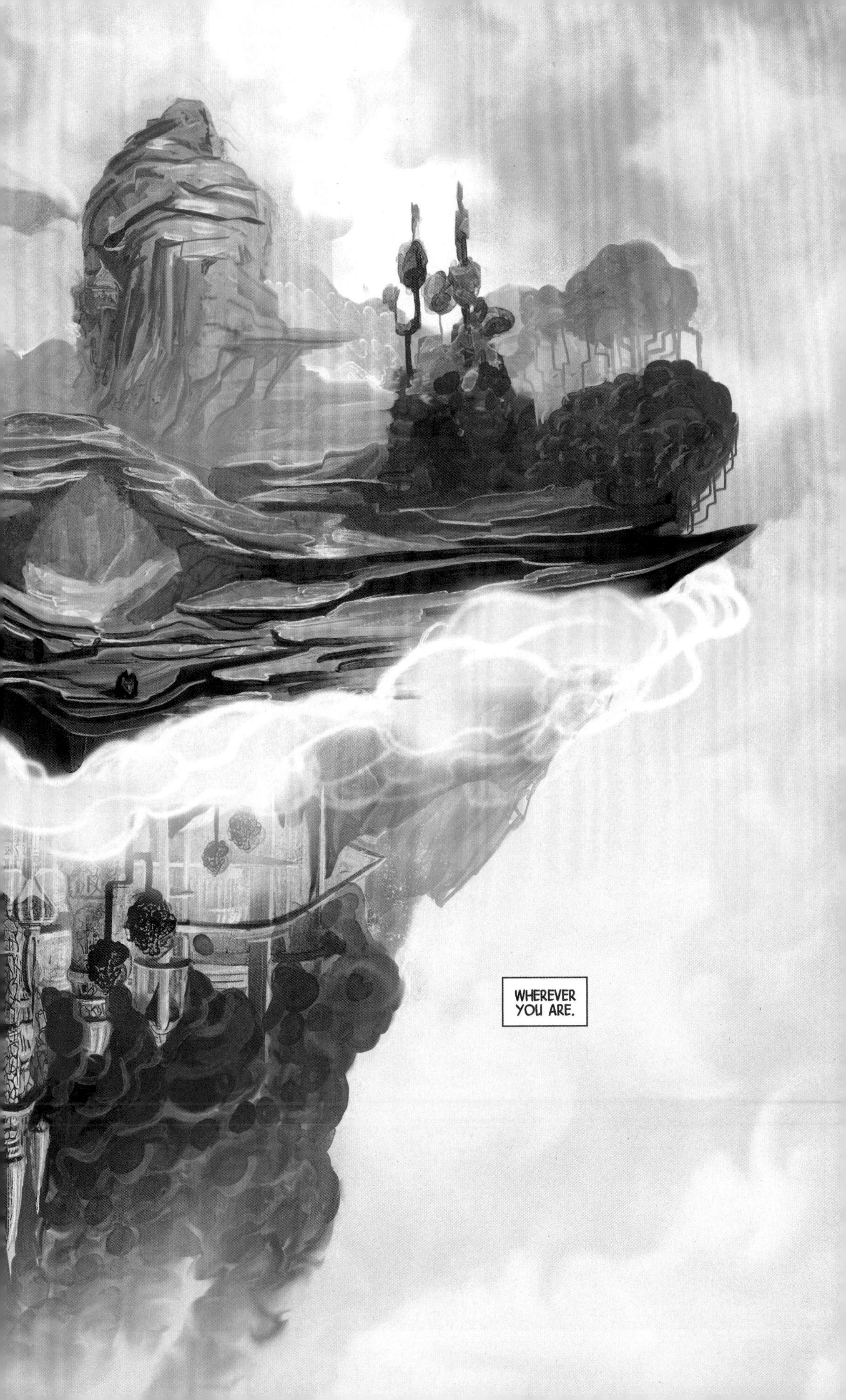
WHEREVER YOU ARE.

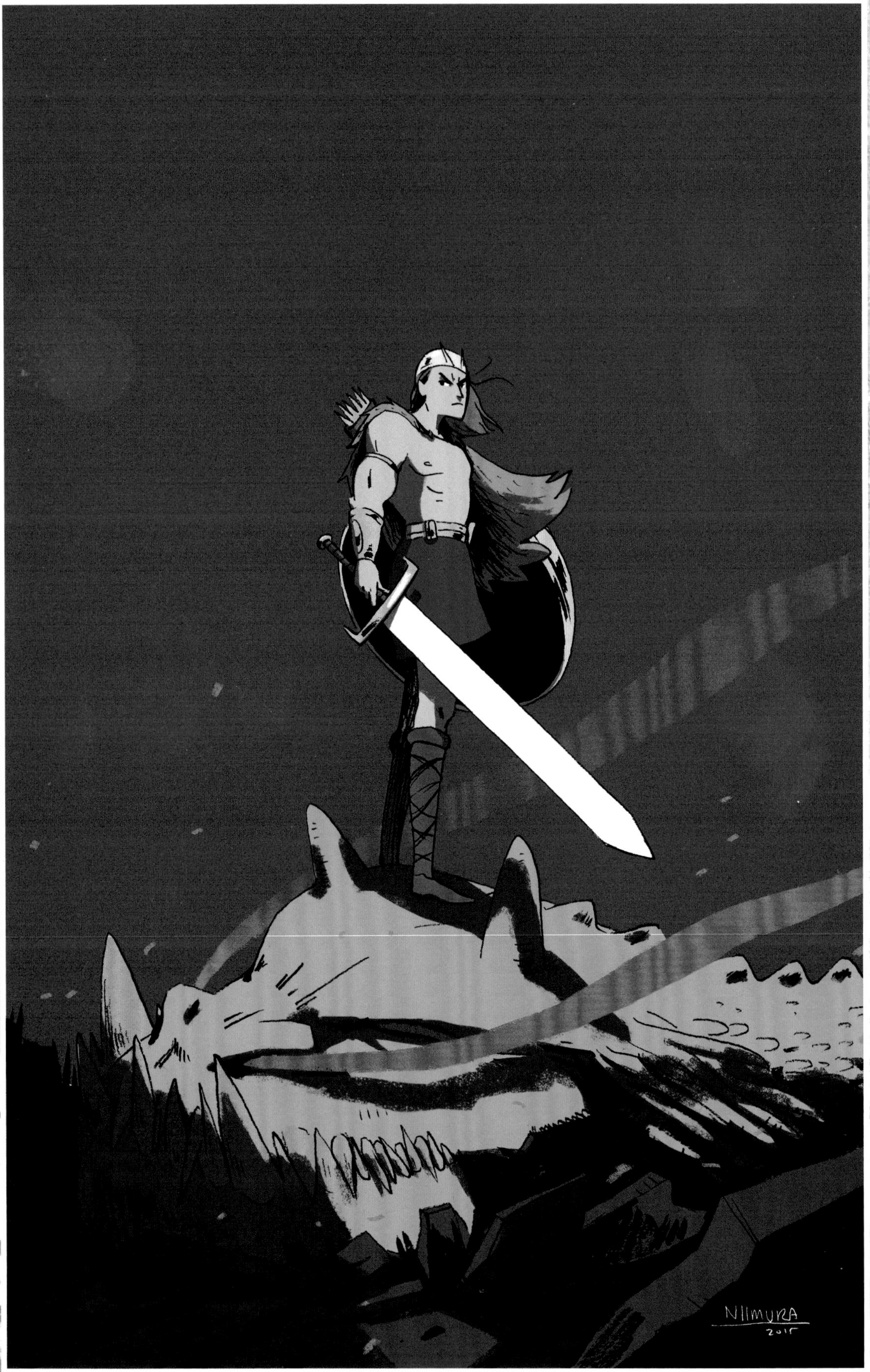
NIIMURA
2015

#4 VARIANT BY KEN NIIMURA

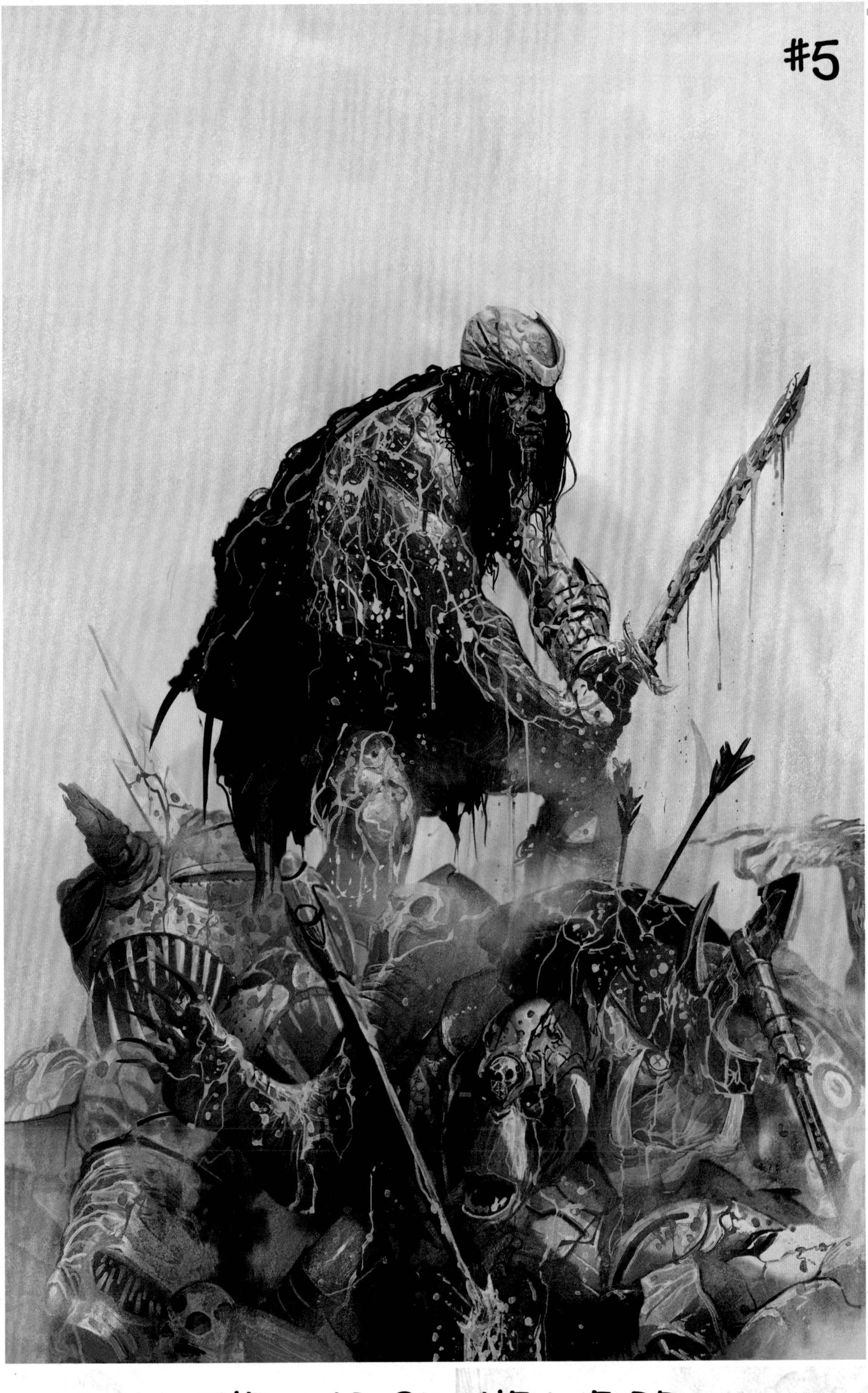
#5

• THE WAR OF THE WEIRD •

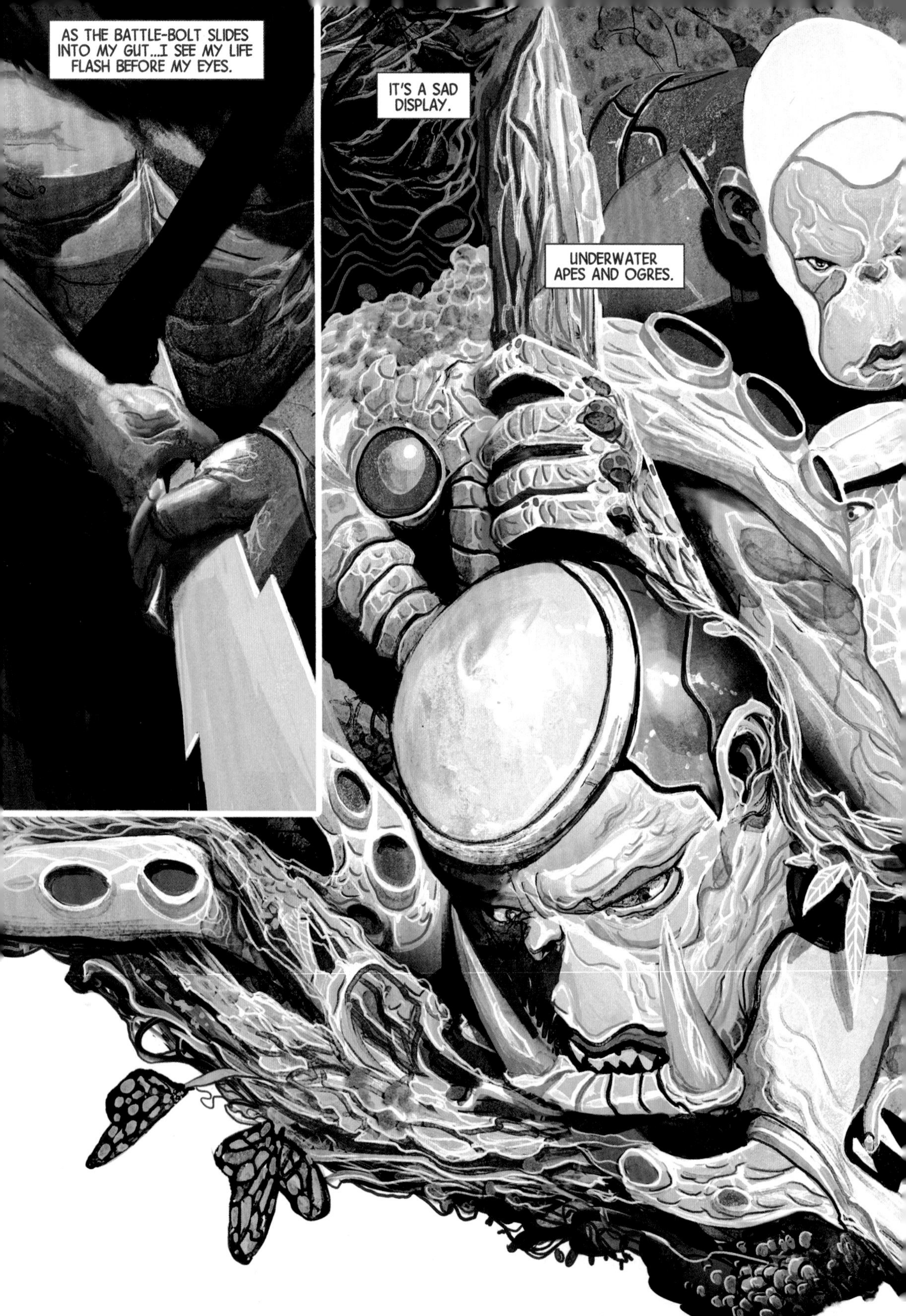
AS THE BATTLE-BOLT SLIDES INTO MY GUT...I SEE MY LIFE FLASH BEFORE MY EYES.
IT'S A SAD DISPLAY.
UNDERWATER APES AND OGRES.

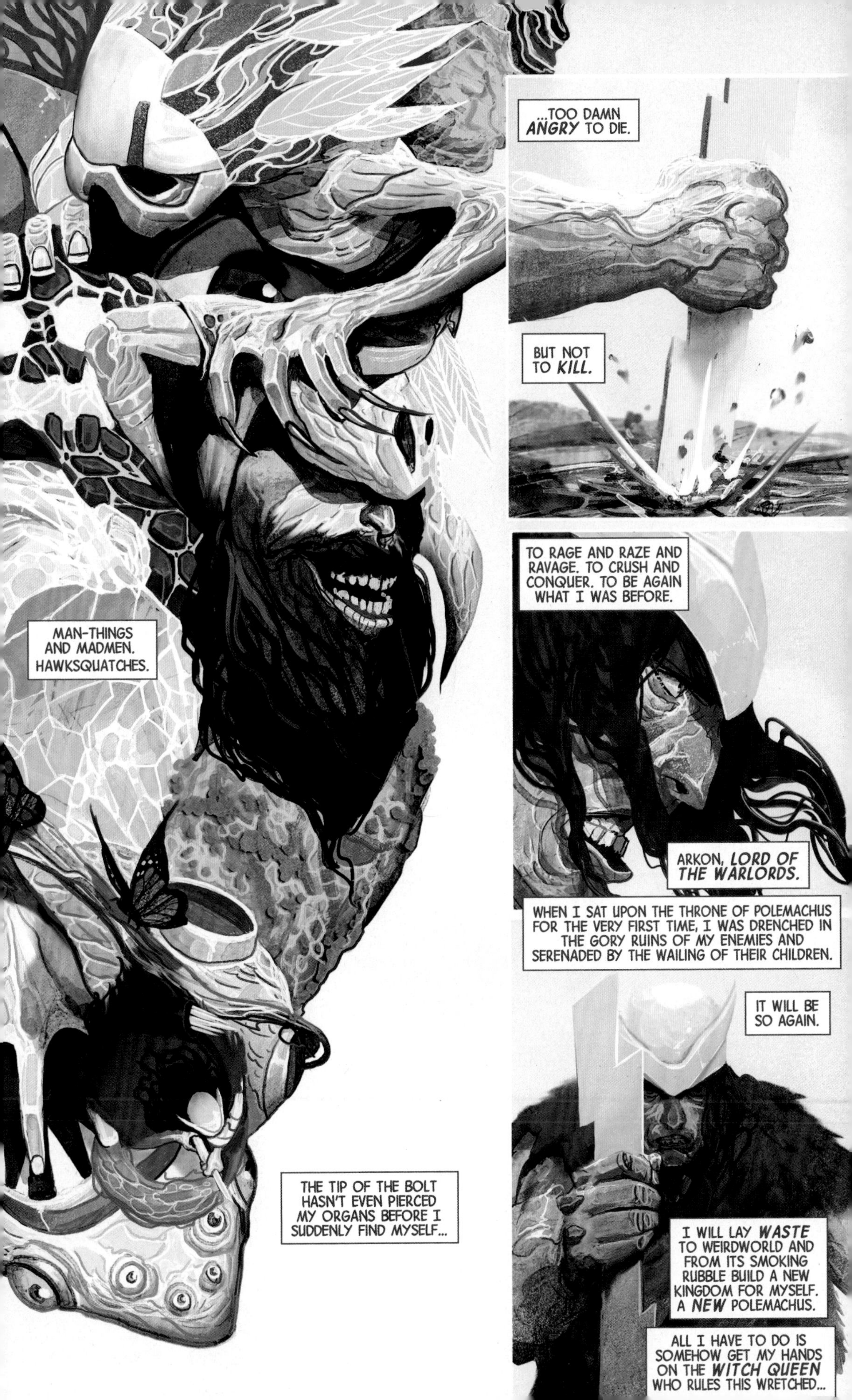
MAN-THINGS AND MADMEN. HAWKSQUATCHES.
THE TIP OF THE BOLT HASN'T EVEN PIERCED MY ORGANS BEFORE I SUDDENLY FIND MYSELF...
...TOO DAMN ANGRY TO DIE.
BUT NOT TO KILL.
TO RAGE AND RAZE AND RAVAGE. TO CRUSH AND CONQUER. TO BE AGAIN WHAT I WAS BEFORE.
ARKON, LORD OF THE WARLORDS.
WHEN I SAT UPON THE THRONE OF POLEMACHUS FOR THE VERY FIRST TIME, I WAS DRENCHED IN THE GORY RUINS OF MY ENEMIES AND SERENADED BY THE WAILING OF THEIR CHILDREN.
IT WILL BE SO AGAIN.
I WILL LAY WASTE TO WEIRDWORLD AND FROM ITS SMOKING RUBBLE BUILD A NEW KINGDOM FOR MYSELF. A NEW POLEMACHUS.
ALL I HAVE TO DO IS SOMEHOW GET MY HANDS ON THE WITCH QUEEN WHO RULES THIS WRETCHED...

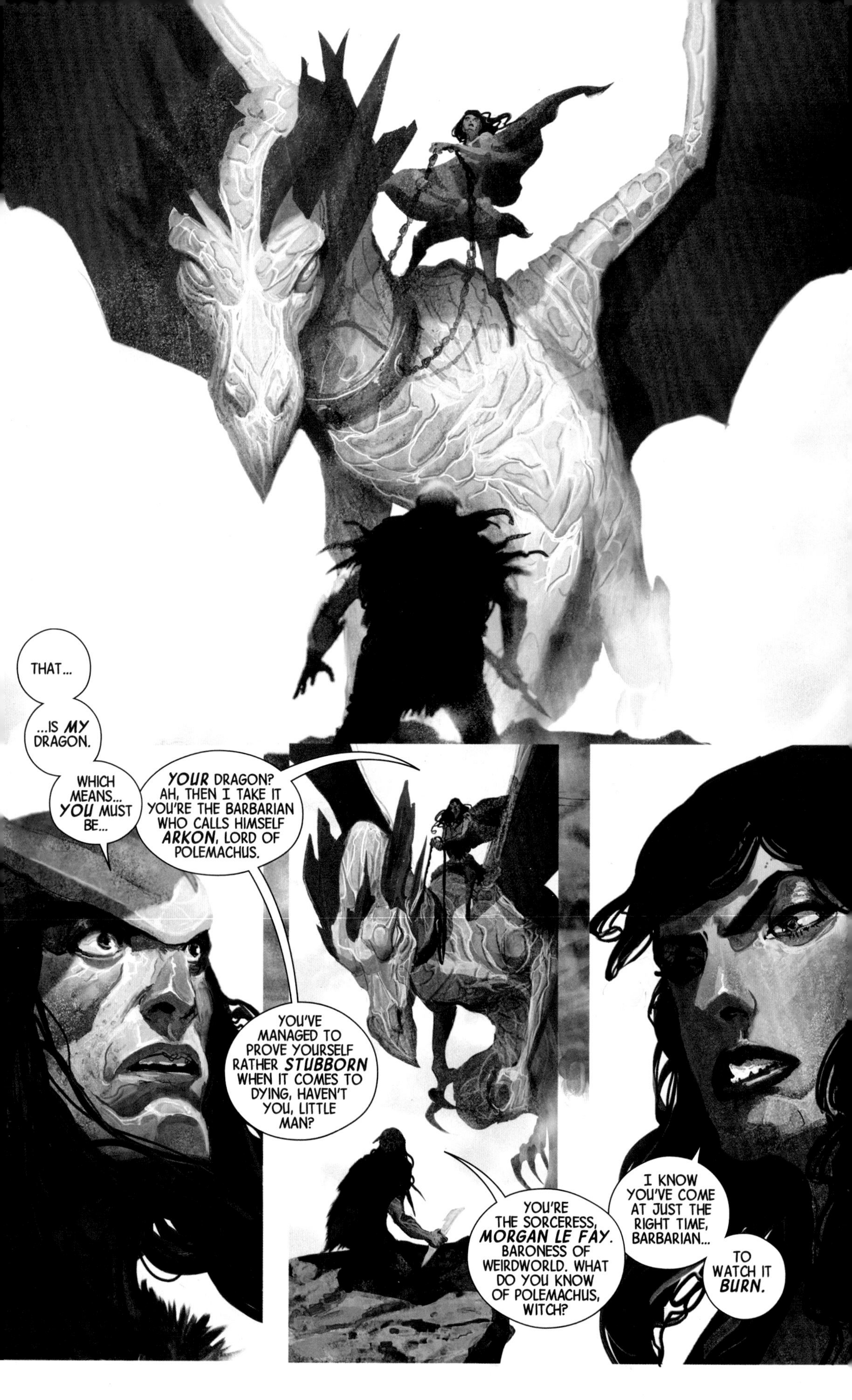
THAT...
...IS MY DRAGON.
WHICH MEANS... YOU MUST BE...
YOUR DRAGON? AH, THEN I TAKE IT YOU'RE THE BARBARIAN WHO CALLS HIMSELF ARKON, LORD OF POLEMACHUS.
YOU'VE MANAGED TO PROVE YOURSELF RATHER STUBBORN WHEN IT COMES TO DYING, HAVEN'T YOU, LITTLE MAN?
YOU'RE THE SORCERESS, MORGAN LE FAY. BARONESS OF WEIRDWORLD. WHAT DO YOU KNOW OF POLEMACHUS, WITCH?
I KNOW YOU'VE COME AT JUST THE RIGHT TIME, BARBARIAN...
TO WATCH IT BURN.

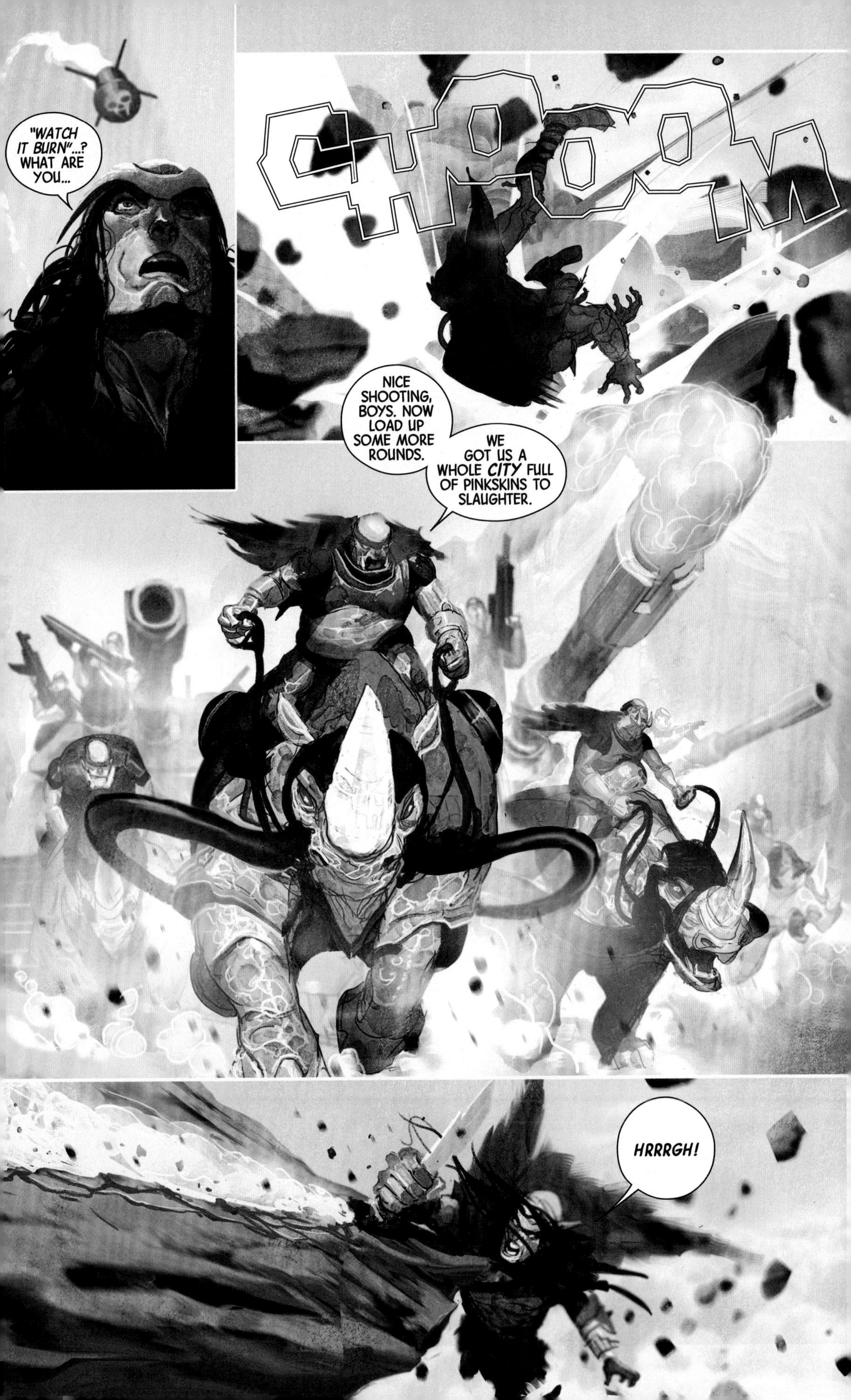
"WATCH IT BURN"...? WHAT ARE YOU...
CHOOOOM
NICE SHOOTING, BOYS. NOW LOAD UP SOME MORE ROUNDS.
WE GOT US A WHOLE *CITY* FULL OF PINKSKINS TO SLAUGHTER.
HRRRGH!

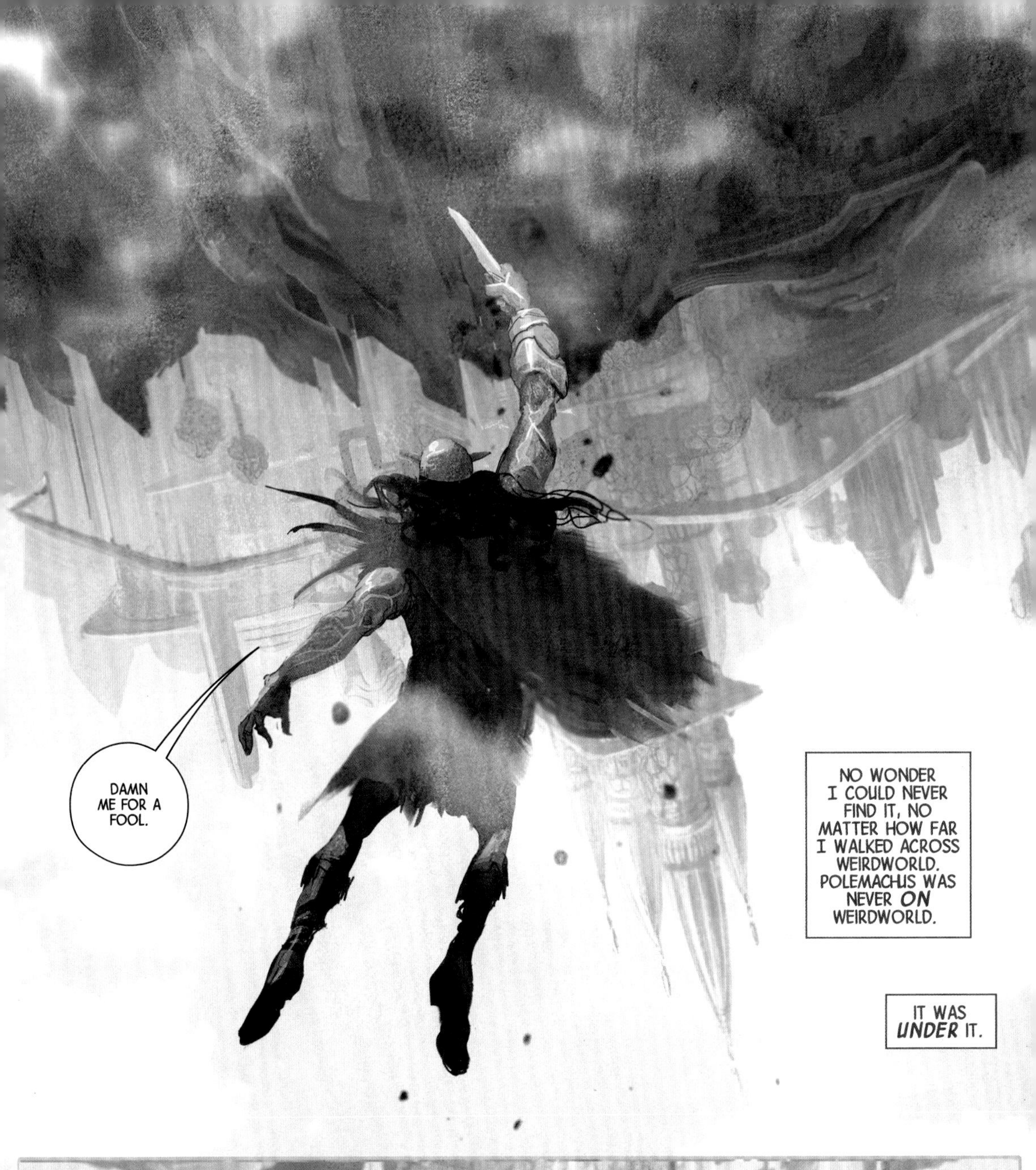
DAMN ME FOR A FOOL.
NO WONDER I COULD NEVER FIND IT, NO MATTER HOW FAR I WALKED ACROSS WEIRDWORLD. POLEMACHUS WAS NEVER ON WEIRDWORLD.
IT WAS UNDER IT.

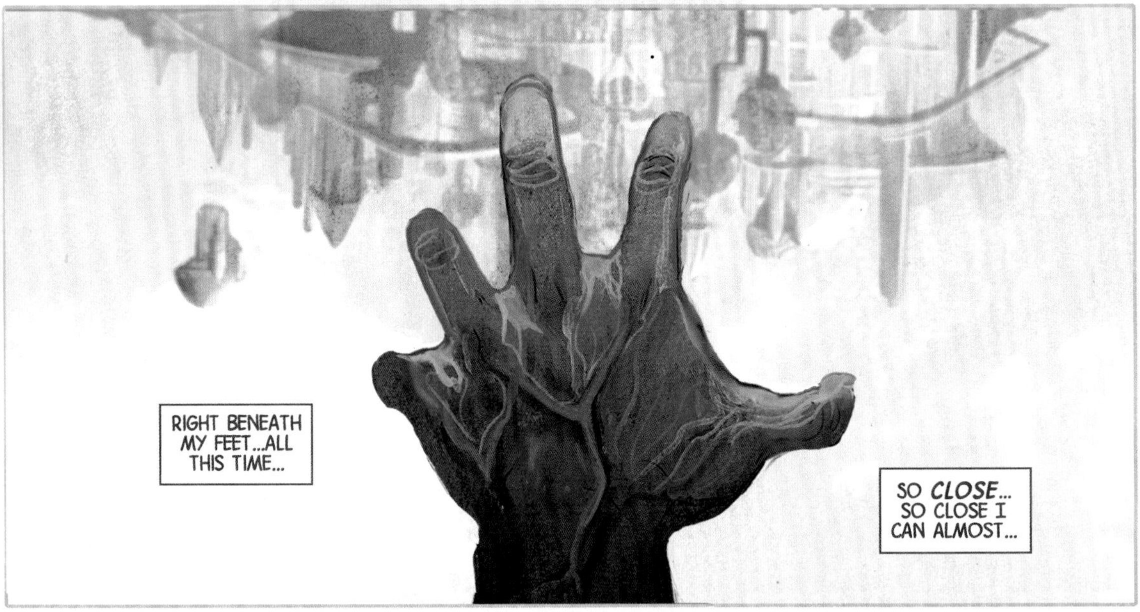
RIGHT BENEATH MY FEET...ALL THIS TIME...
SO CLOSE... SO CLOSE I CAN ALMOST...

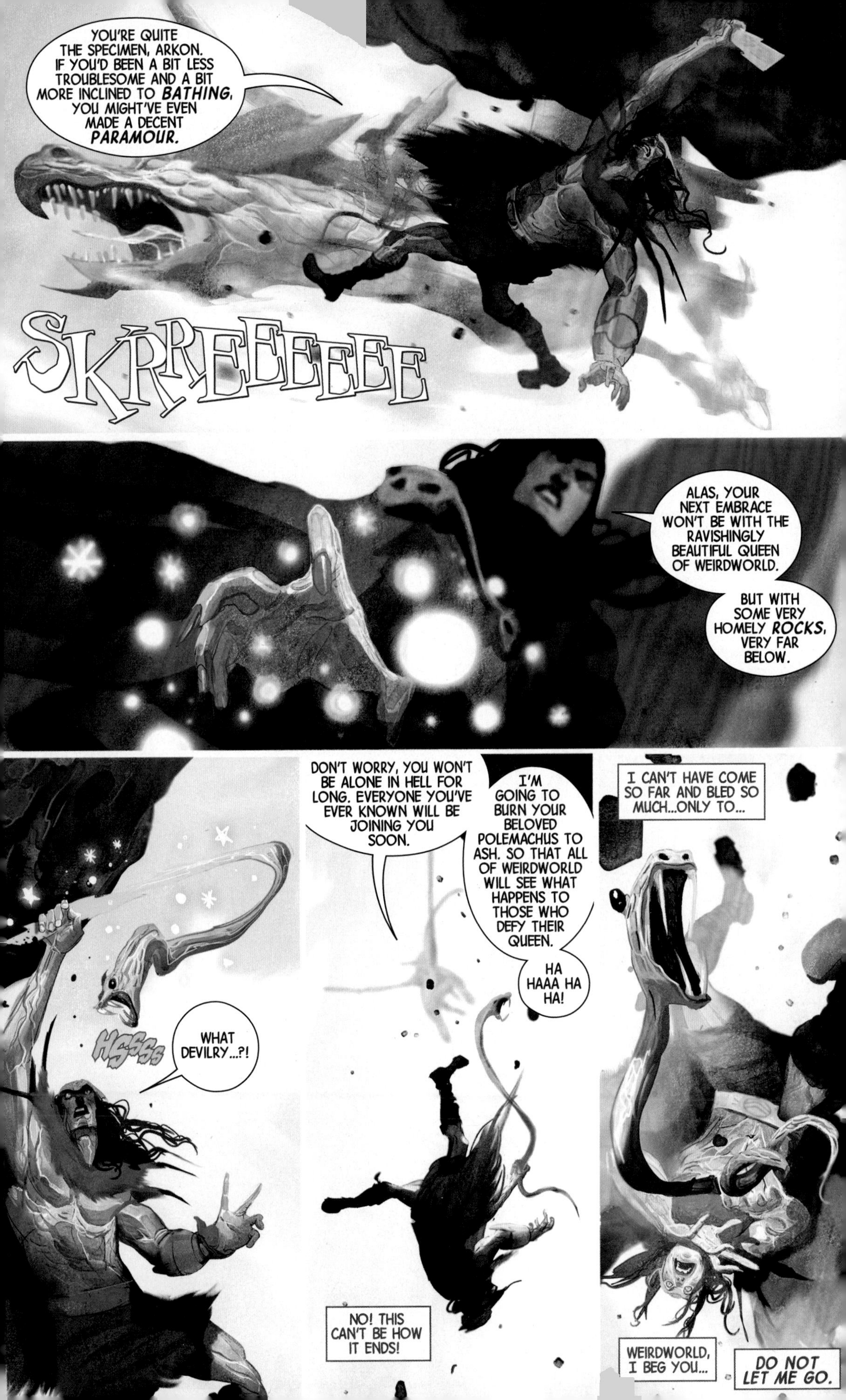

YOU'RE QUITE THE SPECIMEN, ARKON. IF YOU'D BEEN A BIT LESS TROUBLESOME AND A BIT MORE INCLINED TO BATHING, YOU MIGHT'VE EVEN MADE A DECENT PARAMOUR.
SKRREEEEEEE
ALAS, YOUR NEXT EMBRACE WON'T BE WITH THE RAVISHINGLY BEAUTIFUL QUEEN OF WEIRDWORLD.
BUT WITH SOME VERY HOMELY ROCKS, VERY FAR BELOW.
HSSSS
WHAT DEVILRY...?!
DON'T WORRY, YOU WON'T BE ALONE IN HELL FOR LONG. EVERYONE YOU'VE EVER KNOWN WILL BE JOINING YOU SOON.
I'M GOING TO BURN YOUR BELOVED POLEMACHUS TO ASH. SO THAT ALL OF WEIRDWORLD WILL SEE WHAT HAPPENS TO THOSE WHO DEFY THEIR QUEEN.
HA HAAA HA HA!
NO! THIS CAN'T BE HOW IT ENDS!
I CAN'T HAVE COME SO FAR AND BLED SO MUCH...ONLY TO...
WEIRDWORLD, I BEG YOU...
DO NOT LET ME GO.

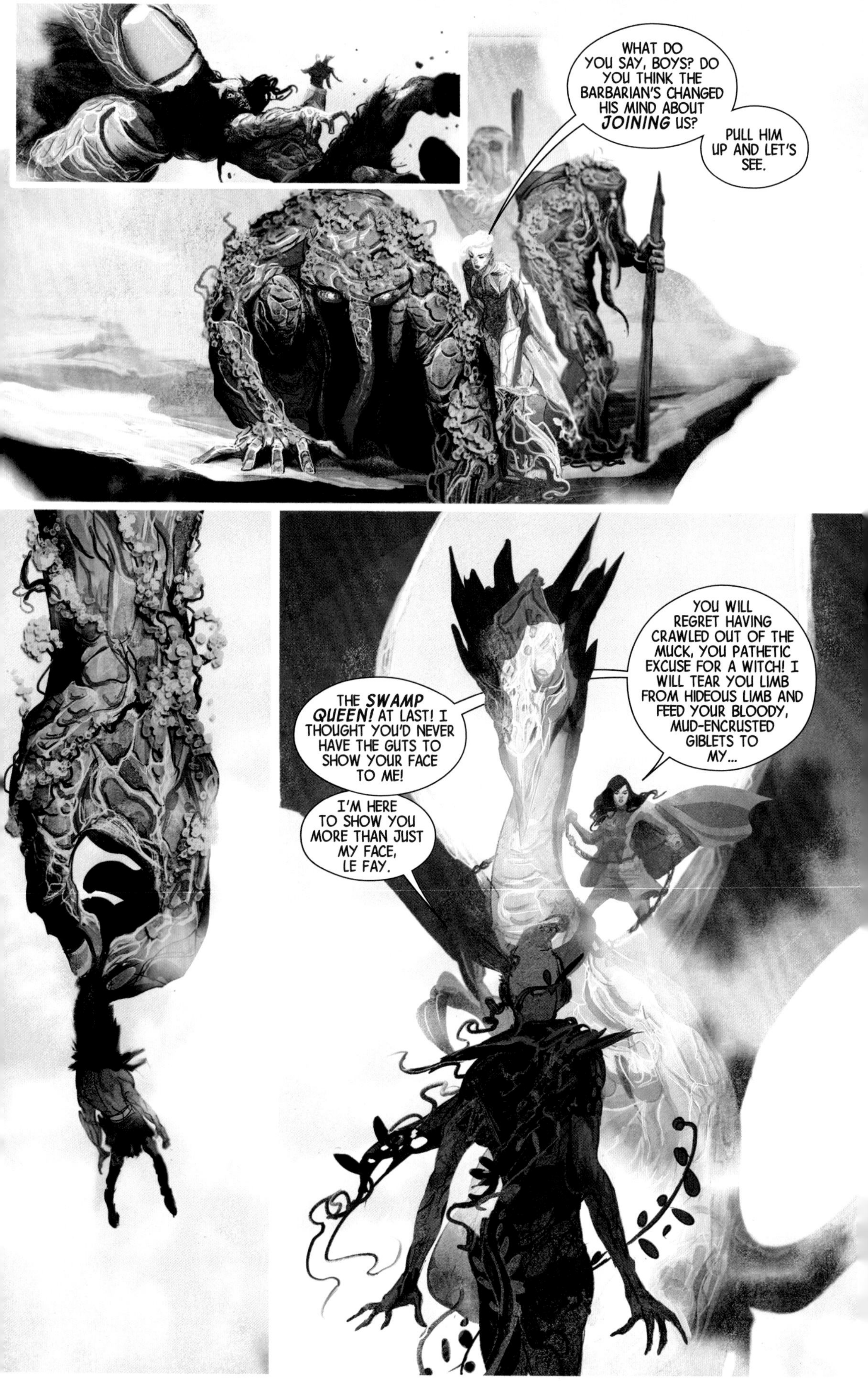
WHAT DO YOU SAY, BOYS? DO YOU THINK THE BARBARIAN'S CHANGED HIS MIND ABOUT JOINING US?
PULL HIM UP AND LET'S SEE.
THE SWAMP QUEEN! AT LAST! I THOUGHT YOU'D NEVER HAVE THE GUTS TO SHOW YOUR FACE TO ME!
I'M HERE TO SHOW YOU MORE THAN JUST MY FACE, LE FAY.
YOU WILL REGRET HAVING CRAWLED OUT OF THE MUCK, YOU PATHETIC EXCUSE FOR A WITCH! I WILL TEAR YOU LIMB FROM HIDEOUS LIMB AND FEED YOUR BLOODY, MUD-ENCRUSTED GIBLETS TO MY...

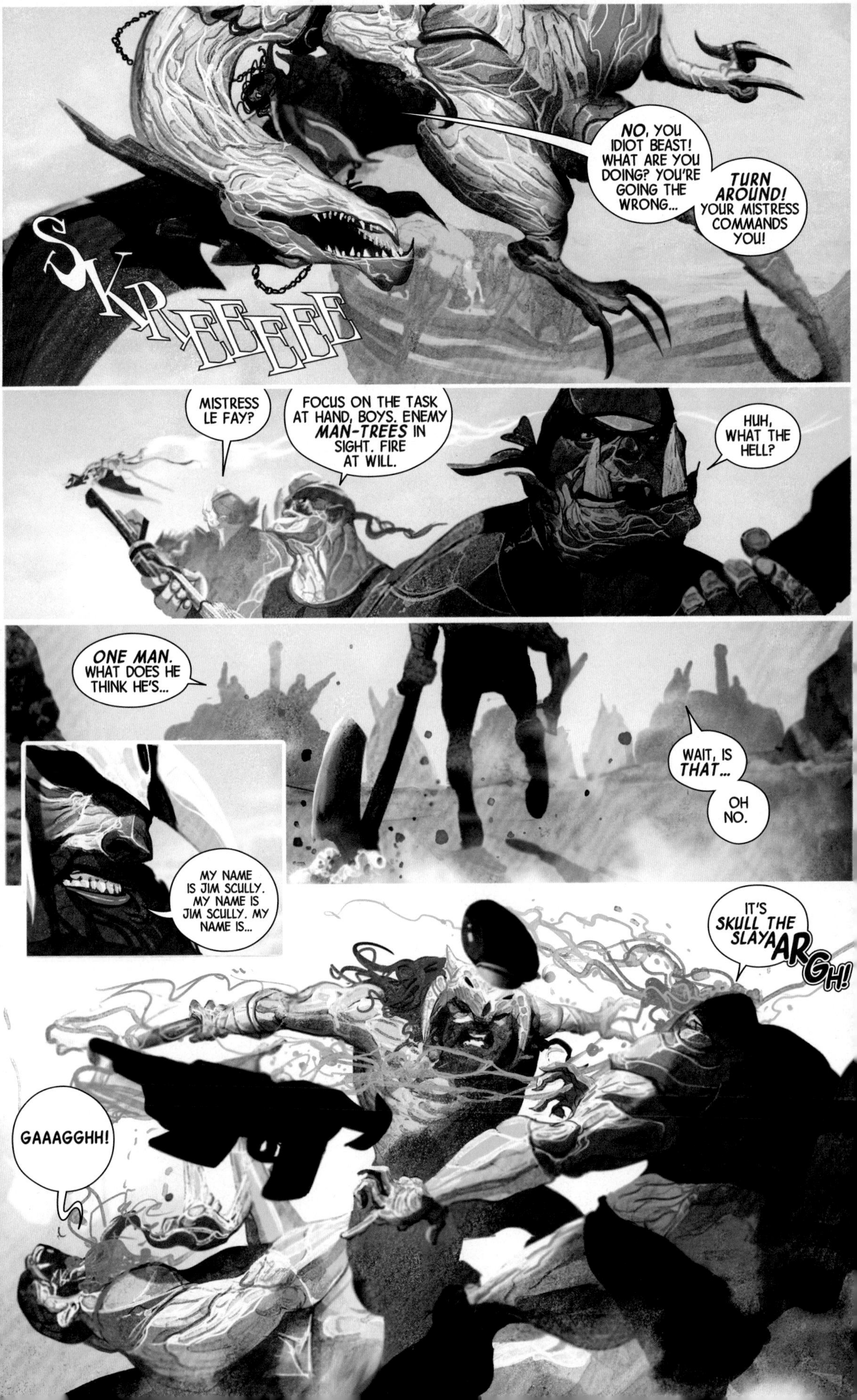
NO, YOU IDIOT BEAST! WHAT ARE YOU DOING? YOU'RE GOING THE WRONG...
TURN AROUND! YOUR MISTRESS COMMANDS YOU!
SKREEEEEE
MISTRESS LE FAY?
FOCUS ON THE TASK AT HAND, BOYS. ENEMY MAN-TREES IN SIGHT. FIRE AT WILL.
HUH, WHAT THE HELL?
ONE MAN. WHAT DOES HE THINK HE'S...
WAIT, IS THAT...
OH NO.
MY NAME IS JIM SCULLY. MY NAME IS JIM SCULLY. MY NAME IS...
IT'S SKULL THE SLAYAARGH!
GAAAGGHH!

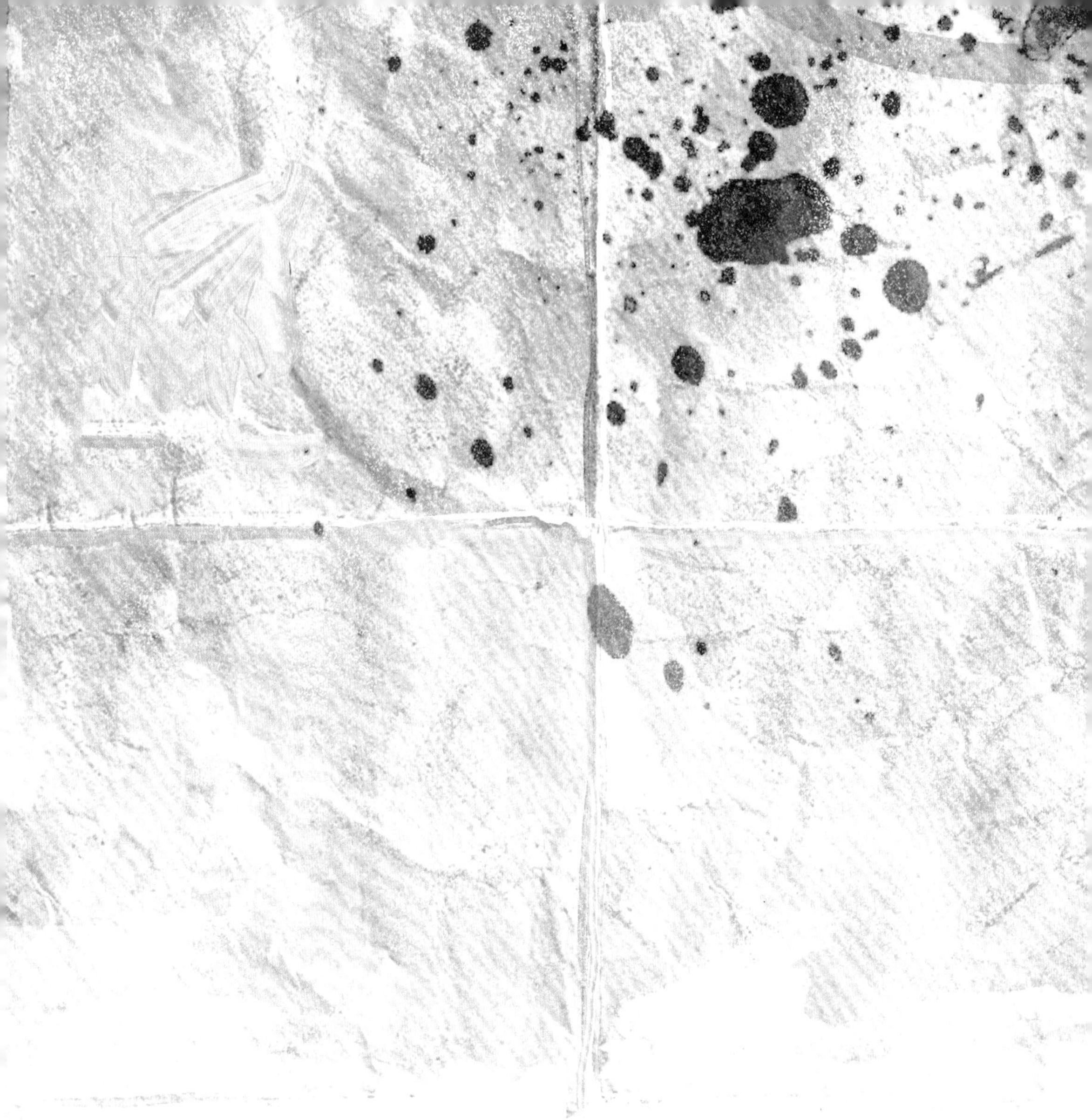

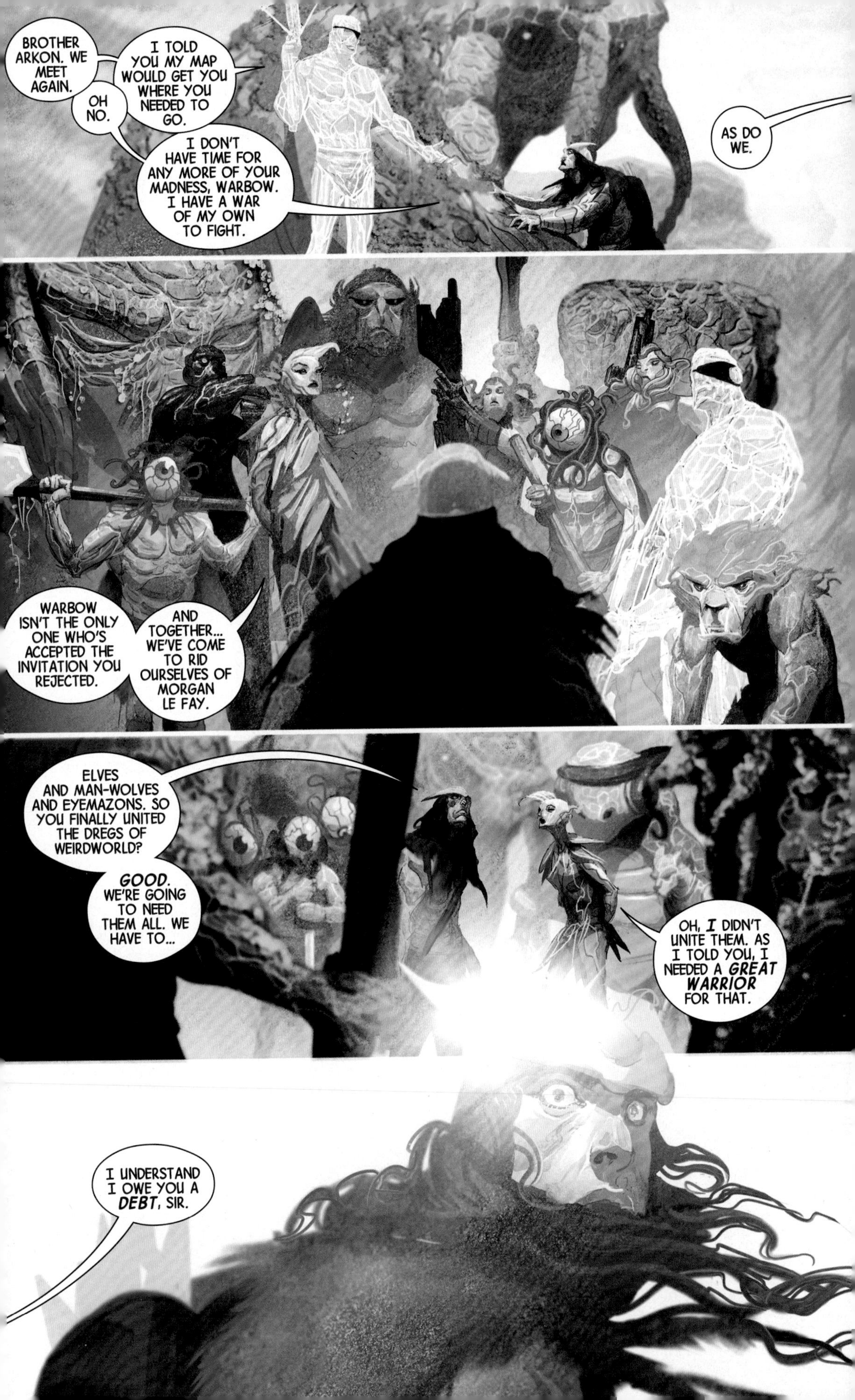
BROTHER ARKON. WE MEET AGAIN.
I TOLD YOU MY MAP WOULD GET YOU WHERE YOU NEEDED TO GO.
OH NO.
I DON'T HAVE TIME FOR ANY MORE OF YOUR MADNESS, WARBOW. I HAVE A WAR OF MY OWN TO FIGHT.
AS DO WE.
WARBOW ISN'T THE ONLY ONE WHO'S ACCEPTED THE INVITATION YOU REJECTED.
AND TOGETHER... WE'VE COME TO RID OURSELVES OF MORGAN LE FAY.
ELVES AND MAN-WOLVES AND EYEMAZONS. SO YOU FINALLY UNITED THE DREGS OF WEIRDWORLD?
GOOD. WE'RE GOING TO NEED THEM ALL. WE HAVE TO...
OH, I DIDN'T UNITE THEM. AS I TOLD YOU, I NEEDED A GREAT WARRIOR FOR THAT.
I UNDERSTAND I OWE YOU A DEBT, SIR.

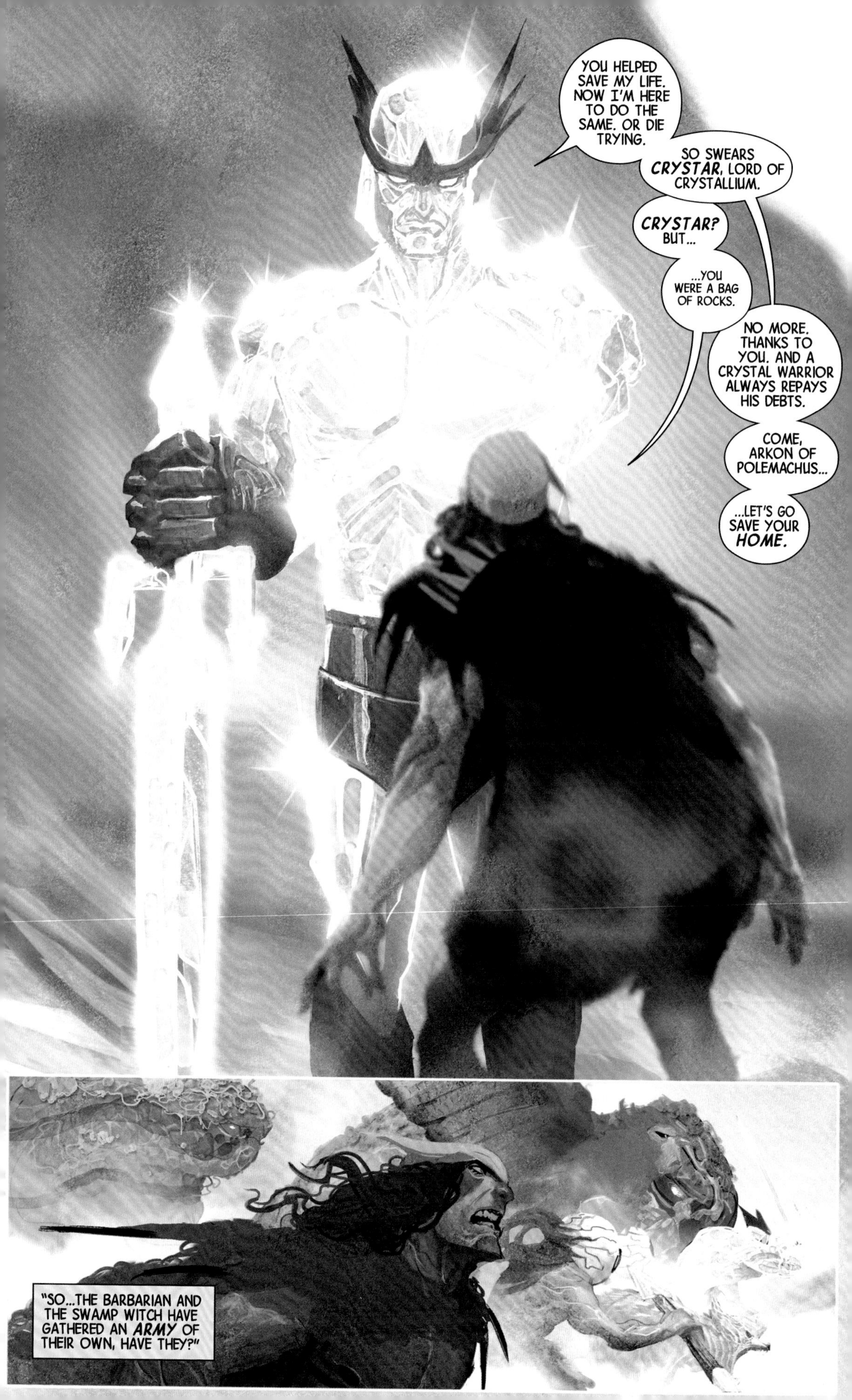
YOU HELPED SAVE MY LIFE. NOW I'M HERE TO DO THE SAME. OR DIE TRYING.
SO SWEARS CRYSTAR, LORD OF CRYSTALLIUM.
CRYSTAR? BUT...
...YOU WERE A BAG OF ROCKS.
NO MORE. THANKS TO YOU. AND A CRYSTAL WARRIOR ALWAYS REPAYS HIS DEBTS.
COME, ARKON OF POLEMACHUS...
...LET'S GO SAVE YOUR HOME.
"SO...THE BARBARIAN AND THE SWAMP WITCH HAVE GATHERED AN ARMY OF THEIR OWN, HAVE THEY?"

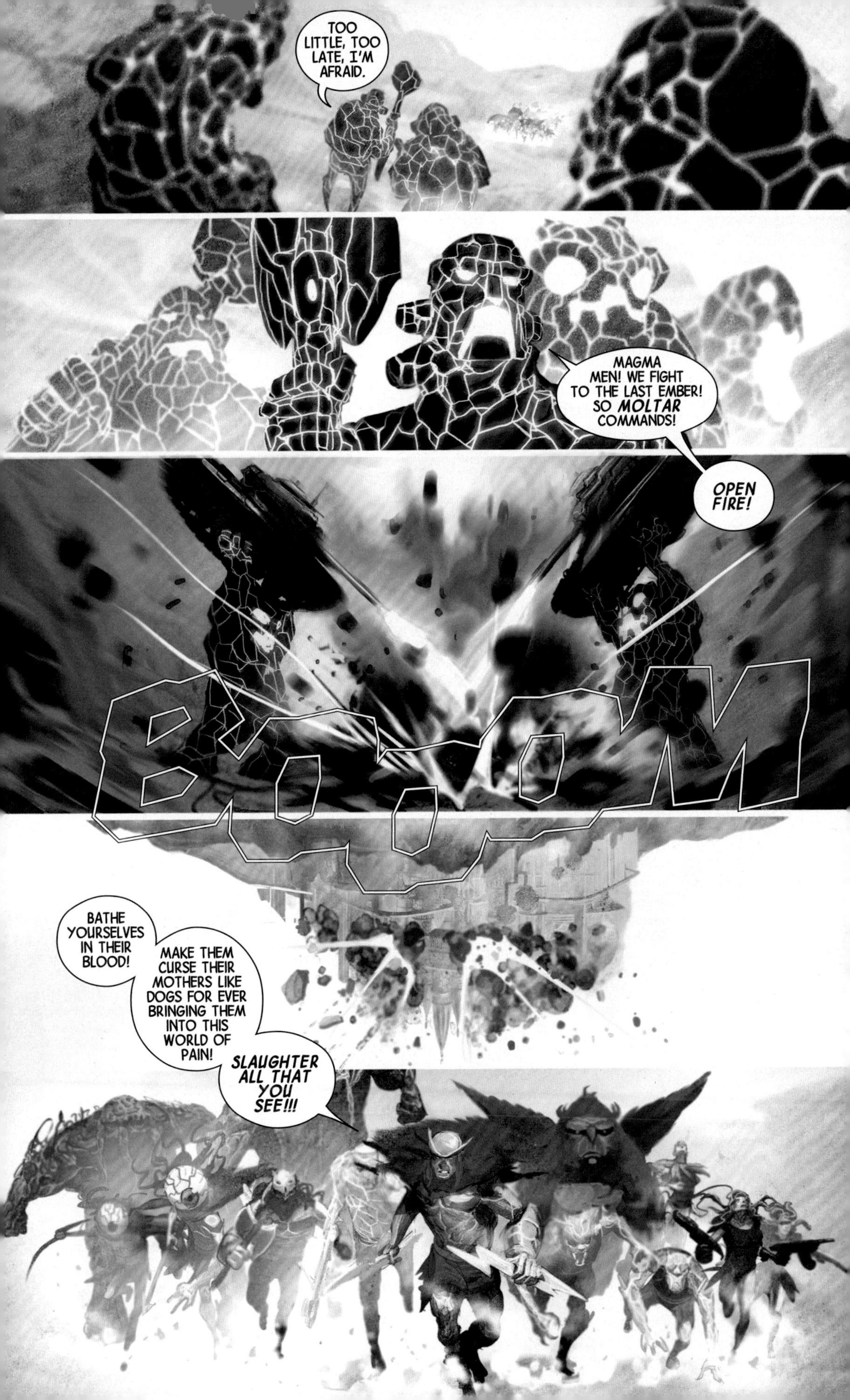
TOO LITTLE, TOO LATE, I'M AFRAID.
MAGMA MEN! WE FIGHT TO THE LAST EMBER! SO MOLTAR COMMANDS!
OPEN FIRE!
BOOOOM
BATHE YOURSELVES IN THEIR BLOOD!
MAKE THEM CURSE THEIR MOTHERS LIKE DOGS FOR EVER BRINGING THEM INTO THIS WORLD OF PAIN!
SLAUGHTER ALL THAT YOU SEE!!!

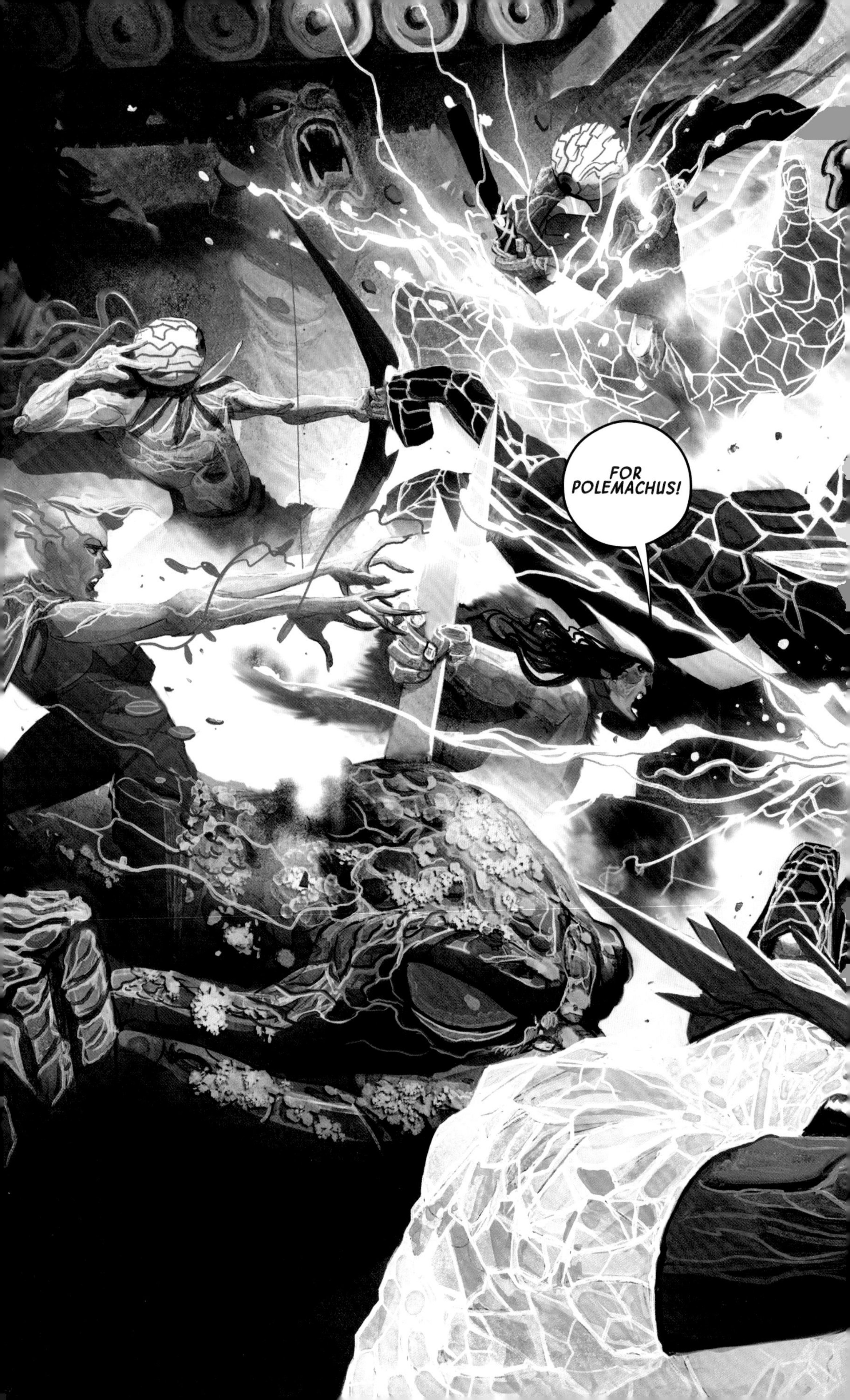
FOR POLEMACHUS!

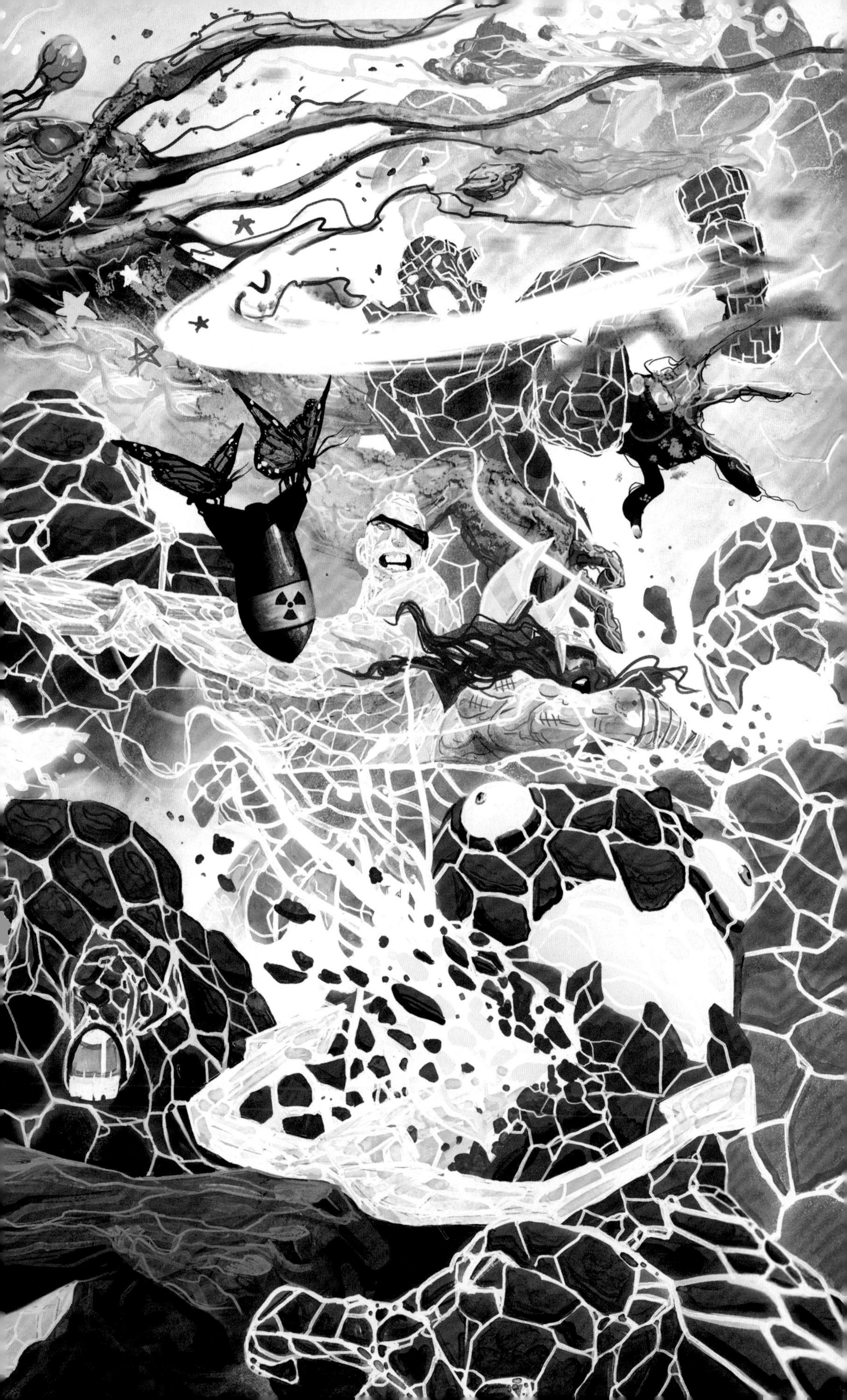

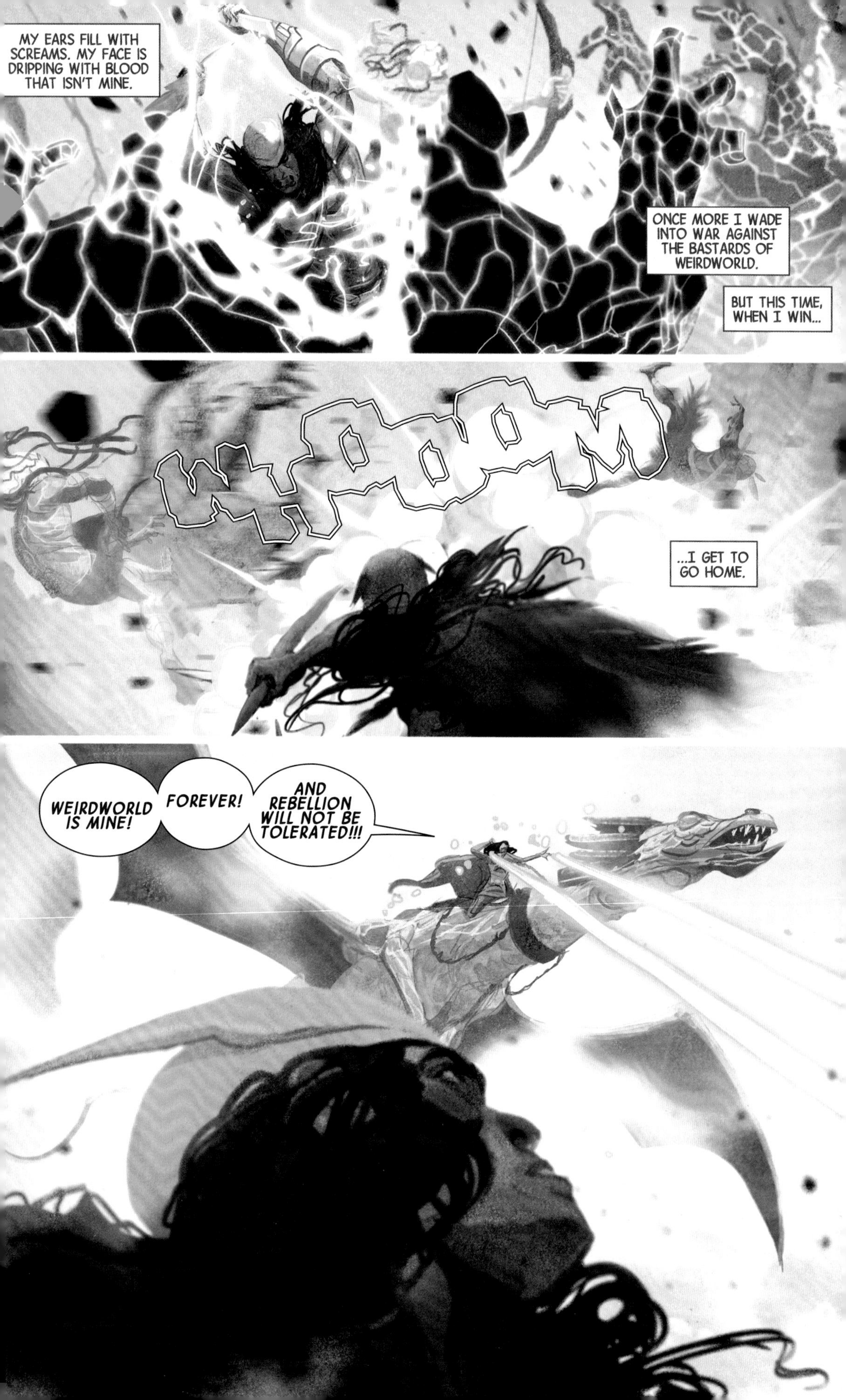
MY EARS FILL WITH SCREAMS. MY FACE IS DRIPPING WITH BLOOD THAT ISN'T MINE.
ONCE MORE I WADE INTO WAR AGAINST THE BASTARDS OF WEIRDWORLD.
BUT THIS TIME, WHEN I WIN...
KRAAAM
...I GET TO GO HOME.
WEIRDWORLD IS MINE!
FOREVER!
AND REBELLION WILL NOT BE TOLERATED!!!

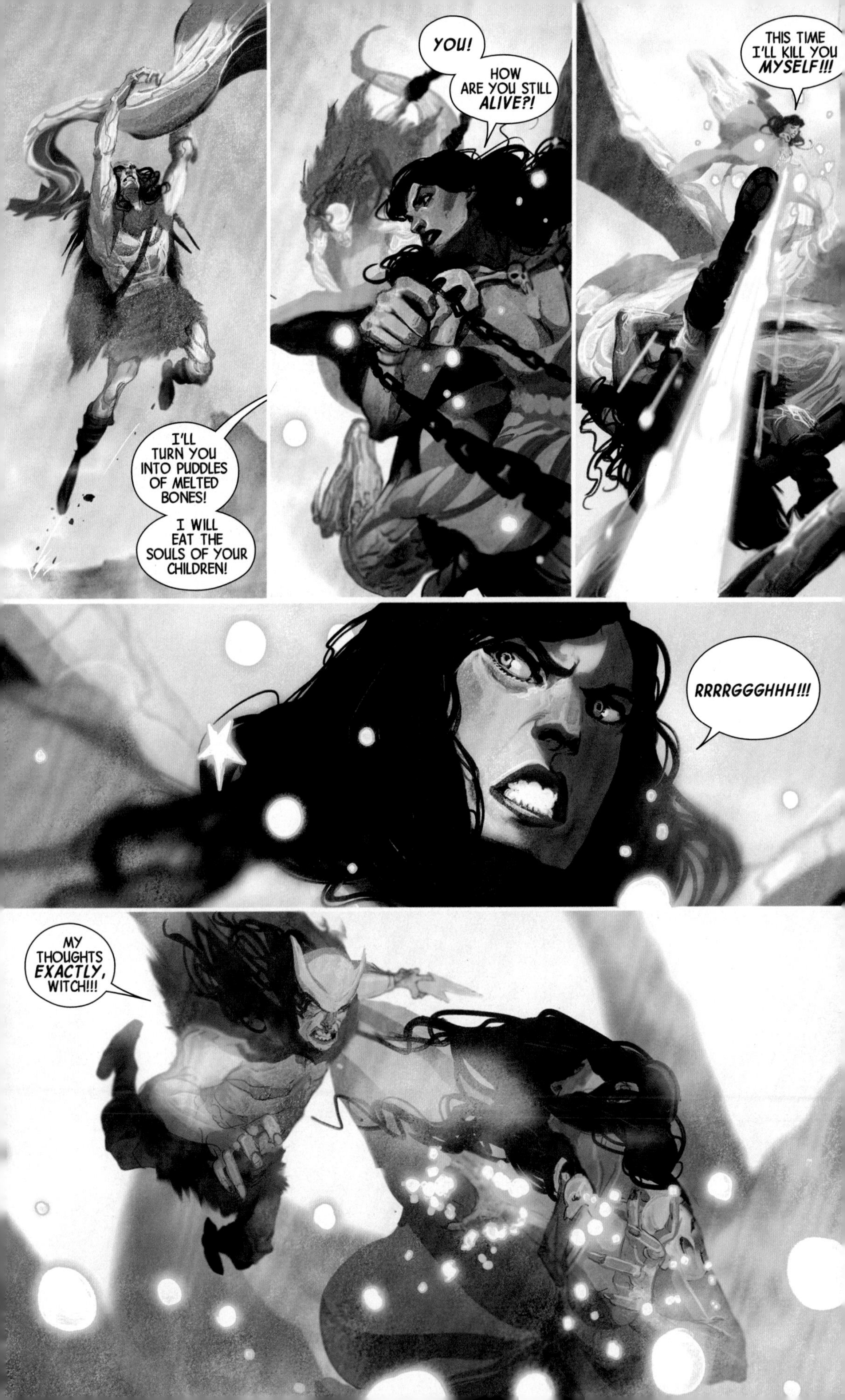

I'LL TURN YOU INTO PUDDLES OF MELTED BONES!
I WILL EAT THE SOULS OF YOUR CHILDREN!
YOU!
HOW ARE YOU STILL ALIVE?!
THIS TIME I'LL KILL YOU MYSELF!!!
RRRRGGGHHH!!!
MY THOUGHTS EXACTLY, WITCH!!!

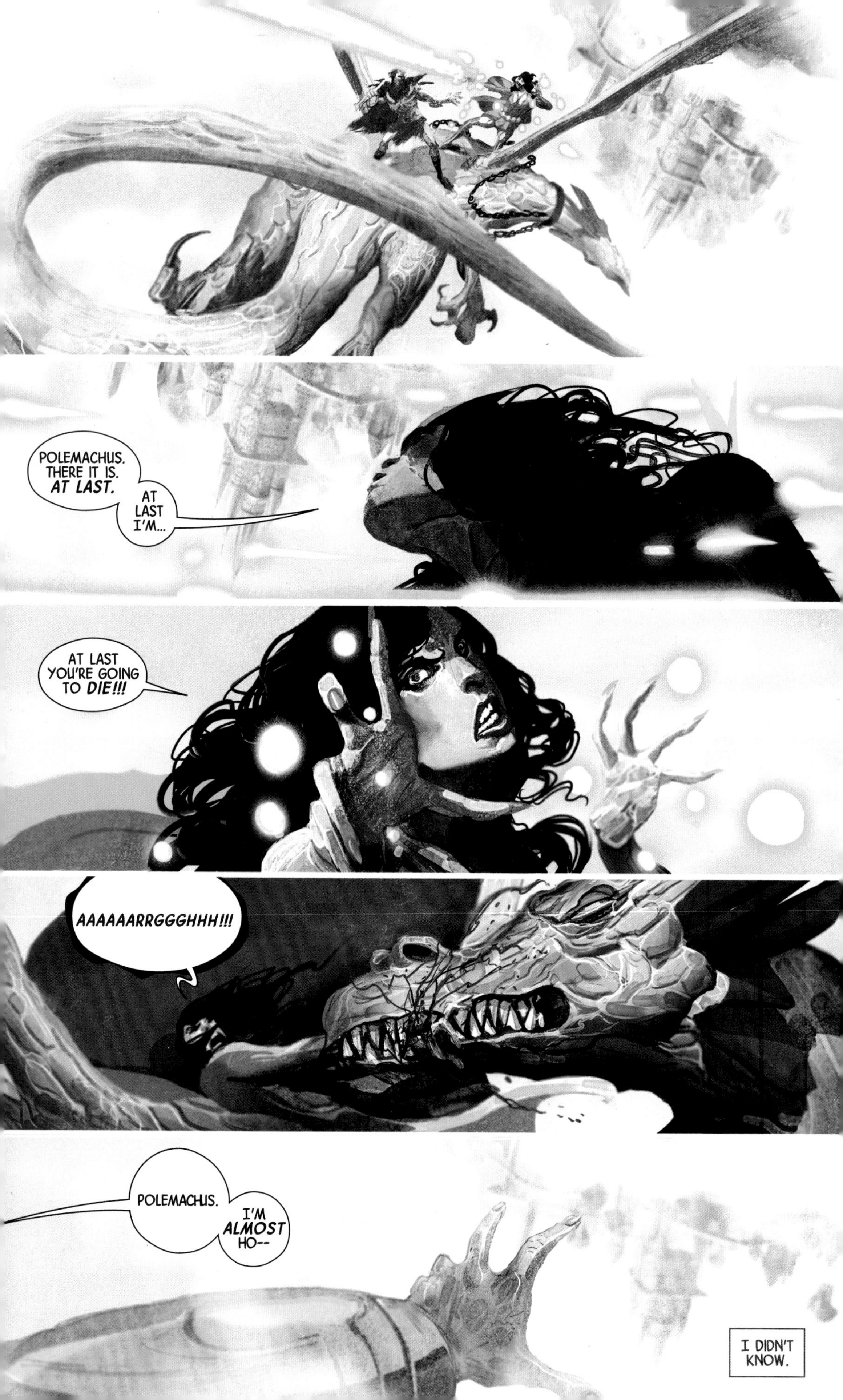
POLEMACHUS. THERE IT IS. AT LAST.
AT LAST I'M...
AT LAST YOU'RE GOING TO DIE!!!
AAAAAARRGGGHHH!!!
POLEMACHUS.
I'M ALMOST HO--
I DIDN'T KNOW.

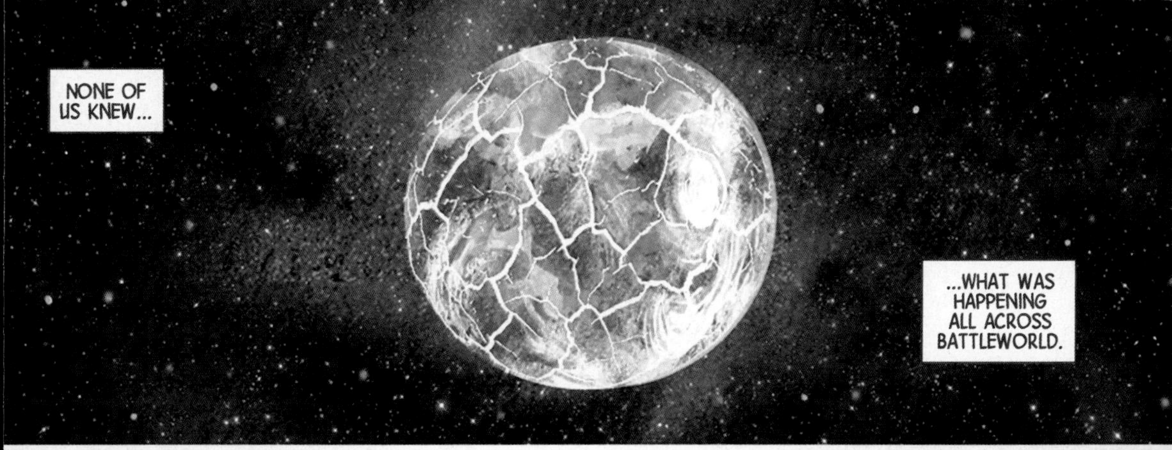
NONE OF US KNEW...
...WHAT WAS HAPPENING ALL ACROSS BATTLEWORLD.

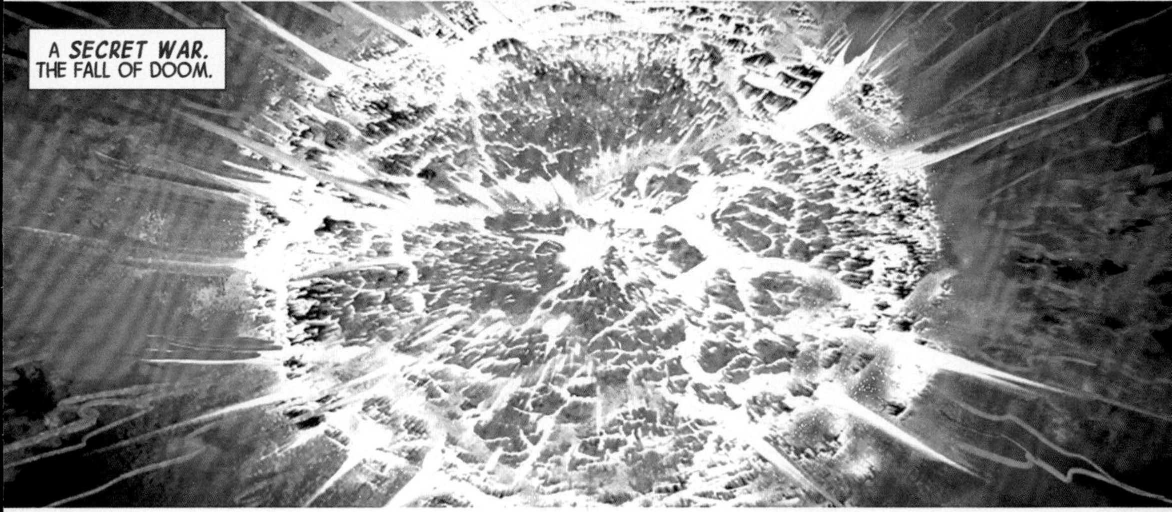
A *SECRET WAR.* THE FALL OF DOOM.

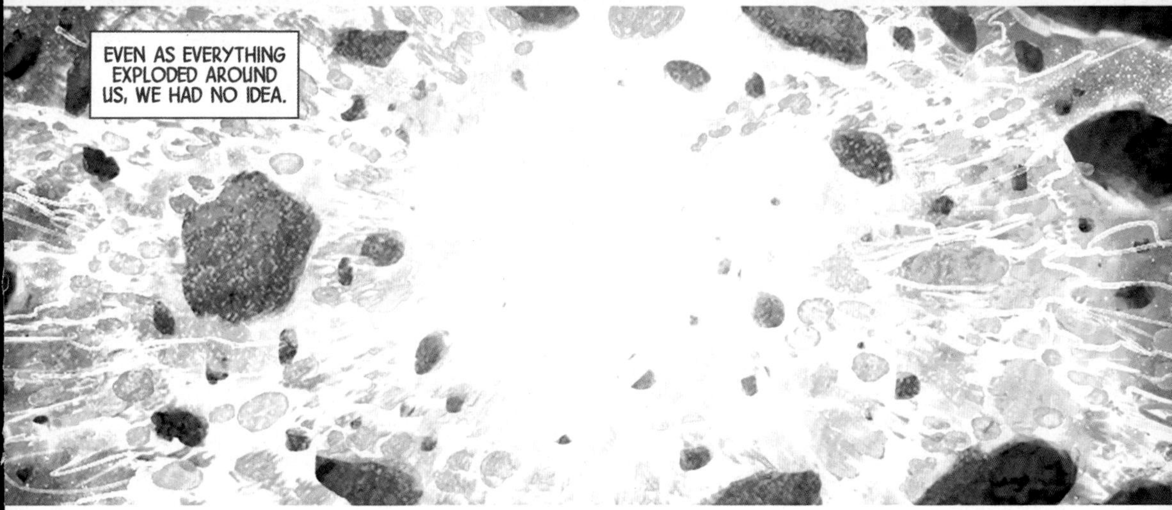
EVEN AS EVERYTHING EXPLODED AROUND US, WE HAD NO IDEA.

AND WE NEVER WOULD.

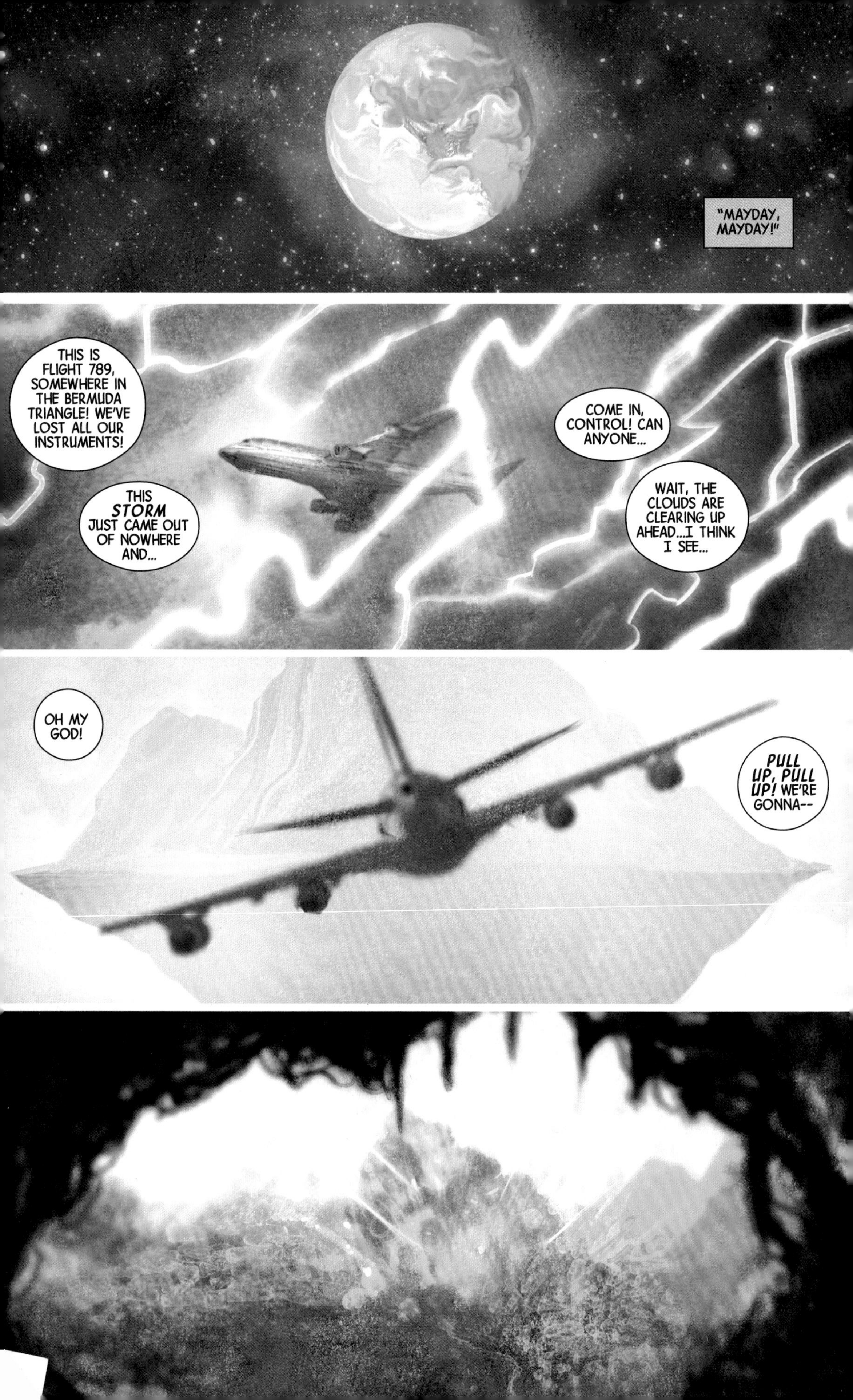
"MAYDAY, MAYDAY!"
THIS IS FLIGHT 789, SOMEWHERE IN THE BERMUDA TRIANGLE! WE'VE LOST ALL OUR INSTRUMENTS!
THIS STORM JUST CAME OUT OF NOWHERE AND...
COME IN, CONTROL! CAN ANYONE...
WAIT, THE CLOUDS ARE CLEARING UP AHEAD...I THINK I SEE...
OH MY GOD!
PULL UP, PULL UP! WE'RE GONNA--

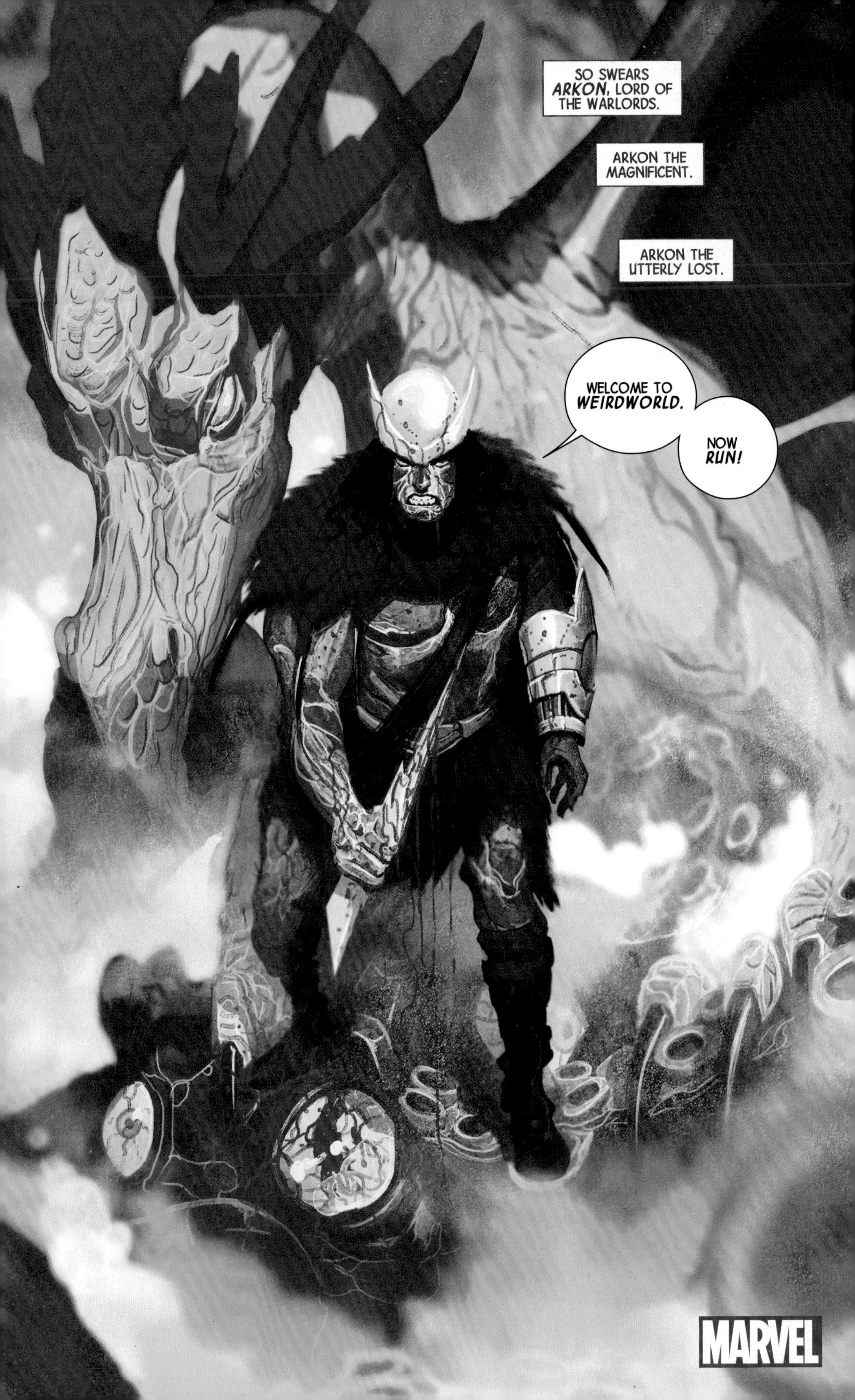
SO SWEARS ARKON, LORD OF THE WARLORDS.
ARKON THE MAGNIFICENT.
ARKON THE UTTERLY LOST.
WELCOME TO WEIRDWORLD.
NOW RUN!
MARVEL

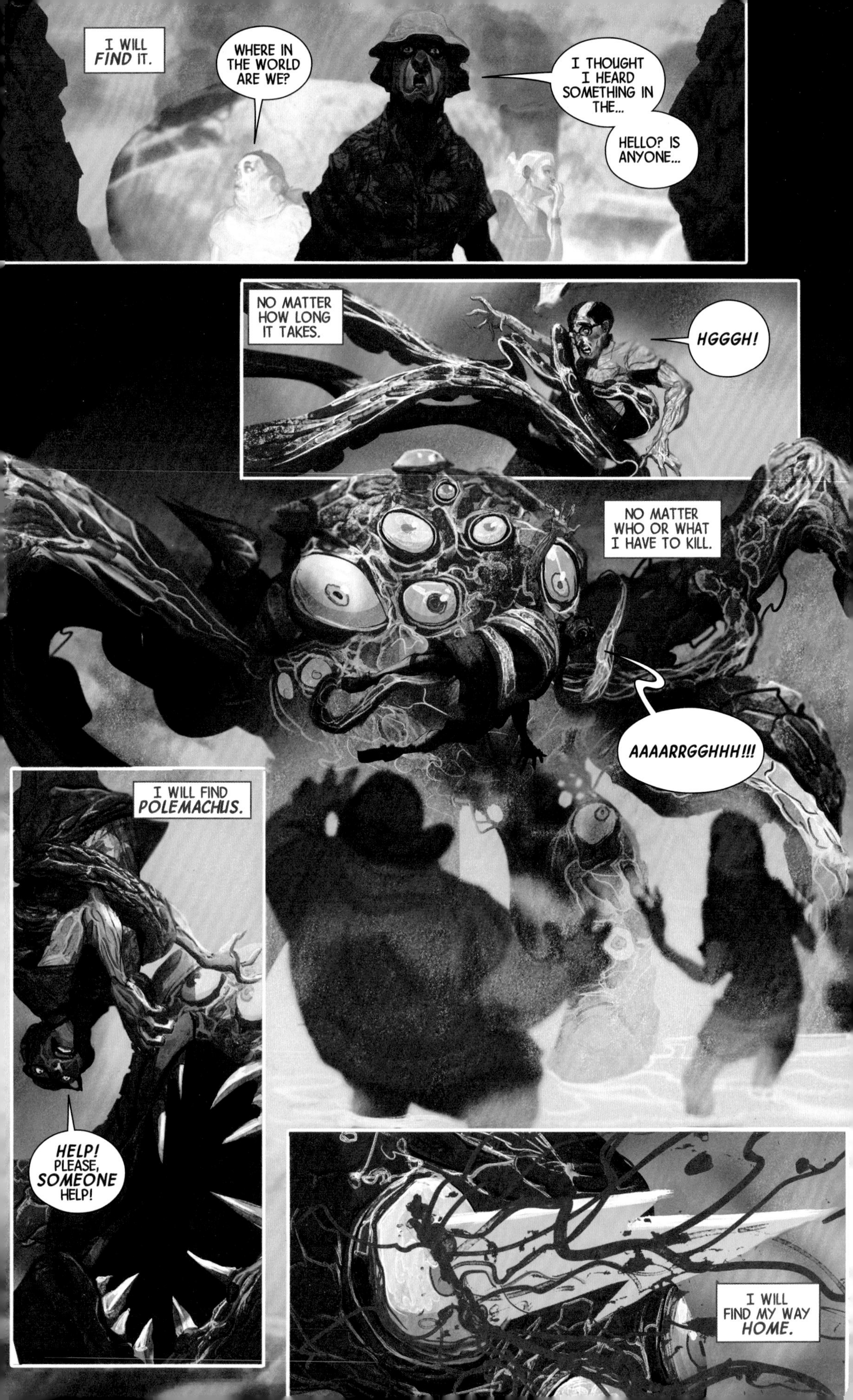
I WILL *FIND* IT.
WHERE IN THE WORLD ARE WE?
I THOUGHT I HEARD SOMETHING IN THE...
HELLO? IS ANYONE...
NO MATTER HOW LONG IT TAKES.
HGGGH!
NO MATTER WHO OR WHAT I HAVE TO KILL.
AAAARRGGHHH!!!
I WILL FIND *POLEMACHUS.*
HELP! PLEASE, *SOMEONE* HELP!
I WILL FIND MY WAY *HOME.*